COCKTAILS

180 RECIPES WITH **DELICIOUS** FOOD **PAIRINGS**

WHITE STAR PUBLISHERS

RECIPES BY

GIANFRANCO DI NISO
DAVIDE MANZONI

PHOTOGRAPHY BY

FABIO PETRONI

GRAPHIC DESIGN
MARINELLA DEBERNARDI

GRAPHIC LAYOUT
GIOVANNI BERTOZZI

EDITORIAL STAFF
LAURA ACCOMAZZO
GIORGIO FERRERO
FEDERICA ROMAGNOLI

CONTENTS

Measurements given in the preparation of cocktails are per 1 person.

PREFACE

This book comes after a long and happy career working as a bartender in cafés, bars, restaurants and discos. During these years behind the counter, serving different types of drinkers – and often acting as a confidante – I noticed a growing interest in cocktails.

"What is this drink?"

"This drink is great. . . What's in it?"

"Is it hard to make this at home?"

These are questions I often heard, and usually, people were looking to enliven upcoming events, meetings and parties with a special drink (or drinks).

On one occasion, a clearly stressed-out girl came into the bar where I was working. She had a problem that needed a solution. "Franco, I'm desperate!" she said. "Tonight I have to serve an aperitif to a dozen colleagues and I want to make a good impression. You absolutely have to help me find something simple and fast. Could you give me the recipe for one of those fancy drinks you know how to make?". I wrote the recipe of a recent creation on a napkin and watched her happily leave the bar.

Over time, this scenario repeated itself many times over, with other customers asking me for the recipes to their favorite drinks. It seemed clear, then, that this sort of collection would appeal to people. Still, I felt as if something was missing. Then, one day, while writing the recipe of a famous Cuban cocktail for a patron, the idea of adding notes about the drink's origins came to me. This, I thought, would allow readers to entertain their guests with legends and oddities related to the drink they were enjoying.

With this idea, the goal of the book was clear: to create a simple to follow collection that was modern and comprehensive, providing the general public with a convenient manual on a range of cocktails, long drinks and digestives. It would also be an innovative recipe book for professionals, offering unusual recipes, including the numerous iterations of the Mojito and ice cream-based drinks.

Right away, though, I realized that drink recipes and history would not be enough. A food accompaniment, I thought, often brings out the best in a cocktail. Why not offer a suggested food pairing with every cocktail? It was time to get a culinary expert involved in the project.

With Davide on board, we started researching the correlation between drinking and food to provide gastronomic suggestions (appetizers, entrees and desserts) that we believe can be happily married with aperitifs (made from herbs, spices and bitter liqueurs, they open up the appetite), long drinks (which can be enjoyed at all hours of the day – the suggested food pairings reflect this versatility) and digestifs (consisting of sweet liqueurs, creams, or herbs and spices that aid digestion). All this without completely betraying the main reason behind this book: to give the tools and knowledge to produce drinks, snacks and meals with the skill and confidence of seasoned bartenders and chefs. The book

also makes a point to emphasize easy to find equipment and ingredients (the graduated cylinder, which the reader will discover is involved in all the cocktails in this book, is readily available and incredibly useful: it provides consistency, allowing you to replicate the same delicious drinks every single time).

This cookbook, therefore, includes 180 full gourmet cocktails with suggested food pairings. Drinks are divided into 12 chapters preceded by a brief introduction. The collection starts with the most famous cocktails in the world (Negroni, Mojito, Cosmopolitan, etc.) and then proceeds with 7 chapters dedicated to cocktails prepared with the major spirits: gin, vodka, rum, cognac, brandy, whisky, tequila, grappa and pisco. The final four chapters are devoted to drinks made with a blender, the mojito, ice-cream based drinks and other classic and modern cocktails.

Each chapter has 15 drinks, from the most famous to the most recent, eye-catching or unique in a particular geographic area (batida, colada, caipirinha. . .). There is therefore a wide choice at hand, ensuring that the readers have every opportunity to transform their home into a veritable top-class bar and kitchen, preparing and serving elegant, colorful and refreshing drinks with attractive accompanying appetizers, main courses, traditional side dishes and delicious desserts.

Every chapter presents the reader with a simple to read explanation of the cocktail, including a photograph of the completed drink. Entries are divided into the following items:

Ingredients
Origins and Odddities
Preparation
Suggested Use

Entries are then completed with a suggested gourmet food pairing (serving 4 to 8 people), which includes ingredients, level of difficulty, cooking time, and a step-by-step preparation of the dish.

Davide and I want to stress the fact that our intention is not to teach anything when it comes to mixing drinks and cooking. We are simply trying to help those captivated by the world of cocktails, offering them simple but practical tips and solutions that can enliven drinks, get-togethers and events. Above all, we hope that this collection encourages our readers to have fun in the company of loved ones, acting as defacto bartenders and chefs in their own homes, all while honoring the skills, knowledge and talent put forth by those in the service trades.

Gianfranco and Davide

INTRODUCTION

If we're unsure about the origin of the term "cocktail", we're even less sure about who invented this type of drink. The first who might be able to claim authorship may be Hippocrates, the father of greek medicine, who it has been said, used wormwood to flavor wine. The practice of flavoring wine with herbs, berries and honey, after all, was common among ancient people.

A few centuries later, another historical figure helped develop the cocktail: Catherine de' Medici.

The Florentine noblewoman emigrated to France to marry the Duke of Orleans (the future king), bringing with her the idea of mixing drinks to get new ones. This certainly helped make the idea commonplace, however, when searching for the etymology of the word "cocktail", there are a number of other legends that may or may not be true.

One such legend takes us to the area of Campeche on the Gulf of Mexico, where a young Mayan wanted to woo the daughter of a powerful local dignitary. After failing initially, he eventually had a priest prepare him a friendship beverage, which he brought to the girl's parents. Once they had drank the concoction, they changed their impression of him and enthusiastically granted him their daughter's hand. The girl in question was named Cochtil, from which the word cocktail is derived.

Like any legend, this one seems to have a grain of truth: according to the journals of English sailors, the ancient Maya in Campeche propitiated the favor of the gods by offering a mix of alcoholic beverages, which were prepared with a long spoon, called "rooster tail" (cock tail in English).

An altogether different story can be found in New Amsterdam, the original name of New York City. About two centuries ago, cock fighting was one of the favorite pastimes of New World inhabitants. One particularly passionate tavern-keeper, as the story goes, lost his best cock and promised his daughter to the person who found it. A regular patron of the tavern, who was already in love with the girl (and disliked by the father), ended up finding the animal. To smooth things over between them, the girl prepared a mixture of spirits to help break the ice. While preparing this mix, one of the rooster's feathers fell into the glass, giving us the name "cocktail". Here too there is a grain of truth: the winners of cock fights were always toasted, with the tail of the defeated rooster handed out as a trophy.

There is, however, another New World tale regarding the word "cocktail", which attributes the origin to hens' eggs. As the story goes, a pharmacist in New Orleans used an egg cup (coquetier in French) to prepare toning mixtures. The term cocktail, therefore, is said to be a mispronunciation of the French term.

Either way, the term cocktail, reminding us of the bright plumes of a rooster's tail, has came to represent the assortment of ingredients that can be assimilated in the preparation of a cocktail.

Cocktails themselves, however, most likely arose as a natural consequence of the demands of the "market". Spirits of the past were very rough and sharp, and not well liked by drinkers. A few bartenders, therefore, tried to round out the taste of these drinks by adding small doses of sweet liqueur. In this way, various combinations were developed, and much more effort was put into improving the appearance and presentation of beverages.

This modern history of the cocktail can be traced back to the nineteenth century. An important figure is Jeremy Thomas, a well-known American barman of the era. Thomas distin-

guished himself for his ability to mix a variety of products, making colorful and tasteful cocktails. His pioneering work contributed significantly to the spread of the cocktail in the United States, and his outstanding creative talent helped shape the image of the professional and creative bartender.

Born on November 1, 1830 in Sacket Harbor (New York) near Lake Ontario, the young Thomas moved to New Haven (Connecticut) in 1840. He would begin his bartending career six years later. At 18, he embarked as a sailor on the ship "Ann Smith", where he changed the recipe of the "grog" (a drink made of rum, water, sugar and lime juice) served on board, much to the enjoyment of crew and passengers. At age 19, he arrived in San Francisco and fell into the "gold rush" that was captivating the American West, though he continued working in the thriving Saloon business.

In 1852, Thomas returned to the East Coast, opening his own bar, "the Exchange" in New York. The Exchange was highly successful, mostly because of the drinks on offer, including standouts the such as the Julep and the Brandy Punch. Thomas, however, would also work in Charleston, Chicago and St. Louis, until 1858, when he accepted a prestigious job offer to be the head bartender at the Metropolitan Hotel in New York. As the most fashionable bar in the city, this position established him as America's most famous bartender. Two years later he founded another bar, Jerry Thomas's, which immediately became very popular among that era's movers and shakers.

In 1862, Thomas collected his formulas and recipes, including preparation techniques, and had them published in a guide. Until then, bartenders jealously guarded their secrets, telling only their apprentices what went into certain cocktails. Thomas allowed a wider audience to know the recipes for well-known drinks, but he also included the formulas for the preparation of necessary syrups, bitters and cordials. *The Bar-Tender's Guide* or *How to Mix Drinks* is the first guide of its kind ever published, and in its pages, recipes for "cocktails" appaeread for the first time. These included the Martinez, considered the ancestor of the famous Martini, which was obtained by mixing three parts sweet red vermouth and one part gin, garnished with a cherry. The Martini would eventually emerge, at the beginning of the twentieth century, as the cocktail par excellence on both sides of the Atlantic.

During Prohibition (1919–1933), cocktails (and other alcohol) was consumed in speakeasies, underground bars hidden in the back room or cellar of other establishments, usually restaurants. Often the owners of these establishments assembled homemade gin, vermouth and whisky in large containers, such as tubs and makeshift bathtubs, creating so-called "bathtub gin". Cocktails, in particular, were therefore especially successful because they served to mask the bad taste of the illegally produced liqueurs and spirits. Many of the cocktail recipes still enjoyed today were developed in this time period.

In the second half of the twentieth century, cocktails gained more and more ground, and recipes have been enhanced with new variations, imaginative names, spirits and ingredients. Cinema and literature, meanwhile, have also helped make cocktails more and more popular and widespread.

In 2011 the official list of cocktails published by the IBA (the International Bartenders Association) included more than 60 cocktails divided into 3 categories (unforgettable, contemporary classics and new age drinks).

EQUIPMENT

THE GRADUATED CYLINDER

The graduated cylinder is an indispensable tool that will allow readers to consistently prepare cocktails the same way, respecting the measurements indicated in the recipe. Graduated cylinders can be plastic or glass, and you can find them in pharmacies, chemical laboratories, plastic producing factories, hardware stores and other stores that sell rubber products.

THE CONTINENTAL SHAKER (ALSO CALLED TRADITIONAL)

The symbolic bartending tool, the shaker is essential to blend the best ingredients. Shaker are divided into 3 parts:

- a lower part (steel, glass or plastic) that serves as a container for ice and various ingredients
- an upper part that consists of a perforated cap that acts as a filter, keeping out everything that does not end up in the glass (ice, fruit, spices, etc.);
- a second upper part that consists of the cap (or lid), which crucially keeps the ingredients in place during the act of shaking. The cap can also be used as a dispenser for liquid ingredients.

The three parts of the shaker must be perfectly joined together. Cocktails can be poured by simply opening the lid.

THE FRUIT KNIFE

It is advisable to have a variety of knives, in different sizes and shapes, with both smooth and serrated blades, in order to cut or engrave different fruits and vegetables.

THE MIXING GLASS

This is used in the preparation of drinks that do not need to be shaken. It can, however, be replaced with a Boston shaker, which is used by professional bartenders around the world. It is nevertheless required to make certain famous drinks like the Martini and the Manhattan.

The equipment described in these pages
was created and produced by **ALESSI**, a leading
provider of home accessories.

THE LEMON SQUEEZER
This juicing tool is used in the kitchen for squeezing citrus fruits to extract the juice. The juice is obtained by cutting fruits into two parts and squeezing against the top cone, using a rotary motion to get the most citrus possible.

THE MILK JUG
The milk jug, made of steel and equipped with a handle and different sized spouts, is used to prepare all hot drinks, thus replacing glass, which can not stand the heat.

THE PESTLE
Made of plastic, wood or marble, the pestle is used in the preparation of "crushed" cocktails, such as the caipirinha family. Generally, it is used to crush mint with sugar and citrus.

THE STRAINER
When preparing cocktails that do not require the use of a shaker, this steel tool is essential to prevent ice being poured into the glass.

CALIPER
It can be used either to handle ice, to place decorations on the rim of the glass or into the drink, thus avoiding the use of hands.

WHISK
This tool is used to effectively mix the ingredients of a cocktail.

THE BLENDER
The blender or food processor is a tool used for blending two or more liquid or solid ingredients. It has different speeds and may be made of plastic or steel. Sometimes the top jar is made of glass. It is an indispensable tool for preparing cocktails of various families: the Caribbean Colada, the Brazilian Batida, American Frozen drinks and sherbets made with ice cream.

THE MOST FAMOUS COCKTAILS

The cocktails in this chapter were carefully selected to represent the trendiest and most popular mixed drinks of the last few years. Even the IBA (the International Bartenders Association), the leading trade association in the world, has included most of the cocktails described on the following pages in its periodically revised list.

The challenge of the IBA is to bring together, in a cocktail recipe book, the world's most consumed drinks, ensuring that standards are codified and that the same characteristics and flavors are maintained the world over. Similarly, we have set out to compile simple and precise recipes that can help you prepare cocktails you would normally order in your favorite pub or bar.

More than anything, this list includes drinks of South American origin:

The Cuba Libre, a very refreshing cocktail, is loved by all because of its simple preparation. There are, perhaps unsurprisingly, many variations; remember, however, to use a good white rum and lime juice, and you will instantly feel like you're on a Cuban beach.

Another very popular cocktail is the Mojito, a white rum-based mixed drink with lime juice, sugar, carbonated water and mint. The strength of this mixture is in the freshness; the secret weapon, however, is the mint and the method of preparation: the Mojito, like all cocktails, must be very well balanced, so that you feel a completeness in its refreshing flavor.

Other popular, pestle-dependent cocktails include the caipirinha, a cocktail of Brazilian origin characterized by the cachaça, a distant relative of rum. It's a very edgy, manly mixed drink, so much so that it is considered the classic "love it or hate it" drink.

The Strawberry Caipiroska is a cocktail that has been very popular for the last decade. It is a mixed drink that appeals to many because of the sweetness of the strawberry (a fruit that is frequently used by bartenders), but with a good dose of vodka (a neutral distillate that is among the popular for cocktail making). It is a cocktail that is especially appreciated by women.

Similarly, the Cosmopolitan, an American drink, owes its fame to Madonna and the television series "Sex and the City". A fresh and slightly sour mixed drink (thanks to the lime juice and the cranberry), its pink color is in honor of the glamorous female drinkers that love it.

There are several versions of the Sex on the Beach, a fresh long drink that is enjoyed from coast to coast. Generally speaking, it is well balanced and not too strong.

The Long Island Ice Tea, on the other hand, has a very high alcohol content, but this may be as a result of its Prohibition-era origins. It is nevertheless very fresh and tasty, with a slight lemon taste.

The B-52, a digestive cocktail, has all the hallmarks of the classic after-dinner drink, thanks to its coffee liqueur, whisky and Grand Marnier (an orange and cognac-based liqueur). It came to prominence in the 1990s as it could be set aflame, offering bar patrons a well-choreographed show.

The Gin Tonic, a long drink by definition, was especially popular in the 1990s, even if its history goes back much further. It can be enjoyed as an aperitif or after-dinner drink with friends. The Gin Tonic can seem like an easy to prepare cocktail, but pitfalls abound, especially in the choice of gin and tonic water.

Like the distillate at its base (tequilla), the Margarita is a made in Mexico cocktail. A unique drink, it is still very much in vogue thanks to a number of fruit-based variations that have sprung up over the years, all of which contributed to the spread of tequilla. A common feature of the Margarita, however, remains the crust of salt on the edge of the cup.

The Martini Cocktail is the symbol of the cocktail. It has, in fact, developed into its own family of cocktails. Despite this, the origin of the drink, as with all great mixed drinks, is lost in the mists of time. Today, the Martini Cocktail remains a must-have on the list of famous international drinks, so much so, in fact, that even its numerous variations appear alongside the classic mix. In all cases, however, the choice of gin is crucial. In addition, there is always the same dispute regarding a garnish: olive or lemon peel?

The Negroni is another drink that is popular all over the world as a great aperitif. A very well balanced drink with a good alcohol content, it promotes the stimulation of gastric mucosa and thus the appetite. It should be served with a slice of orange (not as decoration but as an ingredient itself).

The Rossini, a great thirst-quenching cocktail, is now even used as an aperitif. It is part of the family of sparkling cocktails, or drinks made with dry sparkling wine. Its preparation is very simple, starting with a good strawberry puree, a chilled glass and iced champagne. Ideal as a drink for the holidays, it is much appreciated by female drinkers.

The Skywasser, a fashionable long drink, is part of the so-called soft drinks because it is non-alcoholic. Beautifully rose-colored and very refreshing, it is recommended for the summer. Beloved by children, it allows them to participate in the convivial life of adults.

The Spritz, now called the Italian Spritz by the IBA, is an aperitif of Italian origin, created with Aperol liqueur, soda water, wine and Prosecco. It has become the undisputed king of happy hour (in Italy and elsewhere). Very aromatic, low in alcohol and very refreshing, it goes very well with most appetizers and hors d'oeuvres. Serve in a low glass with a slice of orange.

B-52

INGREDIENTS

COFFEE LIQUEUR
BAILEYS
COINTREAU OR GRAND MARNIER

ORIGINS AND ODDITIES

This cocktail was named after the famous American
bomber aircraft, an emblem of United States military
power.

PREPARATION

Measure 20 ml (4 tsp) of coffee liqueur in a graduated
cylinder, and pour into a shot glass. Measure out
20 ml (4 tsp) of Baileys and 20 ml (4 tsp) of Cointreau
or Grand Marnier and layer the ingredients, in order,
into a shot glass (use a long-handled spoon to slide
each ingredient, separately and gently, into the shot
glass).

SUGGESTED USE

Good as a digestive after a meal.

Coffee Panna Cotta   EASY

ingredients for 4 people
time: 30 minutes + cooling time
(4 hours)

1/2 cup (8 tbsp) sugar
about 1 2/3 cup fresh cream
3 1/2 cups milk
1 2/3 cups coffee
6 gelatin in sheets
whipped cream
ground coffee or chocolate chips for
decoration

In a small bowl, let the gelatine leaves soften in cold water for ten minutes. Pour the milk into a saucepan, add the sugar, coffee and fresh
cream. Heat the ingredients on medium heat, removing everything
from the stove just before it starts to boil. Squeeze the gelatin with your
hands and add to the mixture, stirring vigorously with a whisk, so that
everything is completely dissolved. Pour the mixture into 4 panna cotta
molds and let cool. Refrigerate for at least 4 hours. Serve, with each
portion on a dessert plate or in a bowl, garnished with coffee powder
or dark chocolate chips and accompanied with a slight dash of whipped
cream.

CAIPIRINHA

INGREDIENTS

LIME
WHITE OR CANE SUGAR
CACHAÇA

ORIGINS AND CURIOSITIES

At the beginning of the 1900s, farmers in Brazil (the "caipira", which is the term for people from the countryside. An English equivalent would be "hillbilly") used to drink this now famous drink during cultivation, most probably as a counter to the torrid conditions that often accompanied their hard work.

PREPARATION

Place 2 tbsp of sugar and 1/2 a lime, cut into cubes, in a low tumbler and, using a pestle, crush the whole to form a pulp. Fill a glass with crushed ice and pour 50–60 ml (10–12 tsp) of cachaça (measured in a graduated cylinder). Stir for a few seconds with a long handled spoon to mix the best ingredients. Serve, garnished with 2 short straws.

SUGGESTED USE

Perfect for an after-dinner drink, it is an exceptional evening aperitif.

Beef Churrasco

MEDIUM

ingredients for 4 people
time: 2 hours and 30 minutes

2.2 lbs rib-eye beef
3 sprigs rosemary
2 bunches spring onions
3/4 cup + 1 1/2 tbsp white wine
3 1/3 tbsp vinegar
2 tbsp butter
salt
pepper
baked potatoes

Let the beef sit at room temperature 1 hour before starting preparation. Stab it with a large spit (positioned at 2/3 of the height in relation to the flames, which should be high). Grill for 50 minutes, constantly turning everything carefully. Clean and chop the onions very finely, and cook them in a saucepan with butter over low heat for 10 minutes. Add the salt and pepper, blending first with vinegar and then with wine. Allow to boil and simmer for another 20 minutes. Just before removing from heat, add the rosemary (chopped finely). Remove the spit from the meat and let sit for a few minutes. Slice the meat, not too finely, and place it on a serving dish, accompanied with 2 sauce boats or bowls of the hot onion condiment. Serve immediately, preferably accompanied with diced, oven-roasted potatoes.

COSMOPOLITAN

INGREDIENTS

DRY VODKA   LEMON JUICE
COINTREAU   CRANBERRY JUICE

ORIGINS AND ODDITIES

It has been said that in 1987, a famous Miami
bartender named Cheryl Cook created a cocktail
that would satisfy the taste of women. Cook used
common ingredients, mixing them to create a sweet
pink drink that quickly became one of the most
famous cocktails in the world. It is loved by stars
such as Madonna and the characters in the television
series "Sex and the City".

PREPARATION

Measure 30 ml (2 tbsp) of dry vodka in a graduated
cylinder and pour into a shaker. Repeat with 20 ml
(4 tsp) of Cointreau, 10 ml (2 tsp) of lemon juice and
30 ml (2 tbsp) of cranberry juice. Add some ice cubes
and shake vigorously for a few seconds. Pour into a
chilled cocktail glass (previously chilled in the freezer)
and serve.

SUGGESTED USE

Recommended for the evenings or during
happy hour.

Vogue Risotto with Blueberries   EASY

ingredients for 4 people
time: 45 minutes

1 4/5 cups Carnaroli rice
about 1 cup fresh blueberries
1 glass red wine
5 1/2 tbsp butter
vegetable broth
10 tsp fresh berries
parsley leaves

Wash and clean the fresh blueberries and put them in a saucepan with
2 tbsp of butter. Cook over very low heat for about 10 minutes, until
the blueberries begin to fall apart. Boil the vegetable broth, positioning
it so that it remains on hand throughout the cooking of the risotto.
In a saucepan, melt the remaining butter, add rice and let it roast for a
few minutes, stirring vigorously. Sprinkle with a glass of red wine and
let evaporate. Add 2 ladles of hot broth and continue cooking over
high heat for 15 minutes, adding broth as needed. Add blueberries
(which have been whisked in the mixer) to the saucepan and finish
cooking. Just before serving, remove pan from heat and stir everything with a generous knob of butter. Garnish with fresh berries and
chopped parsley.

CUBA LIBRE

INGREDIENTS

LIGHT RUM
LEMON OR LIME JUICE
COLA

ORIGINS AND ODDITIES

This well-known long drink most certainly got its name in Cuba, though there are numerous stories surrounding its creation. The most accepted dates back to 1898, during celebrations of the cuban island's liberation from Spanish rule. To celebrate their freedom, the Cuban people started adding Coca Cola to the usual rum and lime, thereby honoring the US Army's help in the expulsion of the Iberians. The exclamation "Cuba Libre" (Free Cuba) immediately became the name of the new drink.

PREPARATION

Measure 25 ml (5 tsp) of rum in a graduated cylinder and pour into a clear tumbler filled with ice. Repeat with 20 ml (4 tsp) of lemon or lime juice. Fill almost to the brim with cola and stir for a few seconds. Serve, garnished with 2 long straws and 1 slice of lime or lemon.

SUGGESTED USE

A long drink loved by younger drinkers, it is suitable for any time of day.

Autumn Languor   EASY

ingredients for 6/8 people
time: 40 minutes + cooling time
(2 hours)

1 roll puff pastry
4 cups mascarpone
(original Italian cream cheese)
4 egg yolks
about 24 walnut kernels
6 tbsp sugar
2 tbsp unsweetened cocoa powder
cinnamon powder

Mix the walnuts and sugar in the mixer, then transfer to a bowl. Add the egg yolks and mix well with a whisk. Add the mascarpone, cocoa and a dusting of cinnamon, stirring again until the mixture is homogeneous. Line a cake tin with a baking sheet and spread the dough, with the help of a fingertip, to a thick height of about 3 cm. Combine the mixture, leveling the surface gently. Bake at 356°F (180°C) for about 30 minutes. Remove the cake from the oven and let it cool. Place in refrigerator and let stand for about 2 hours. Serve and garnish as desired with walnuts and cinnamon.

GIN TONIC

INGREDIENTS

GIN
TONIC WATER

ORIGINS AND ODDITIES

To find out how this cocktail was created, you have to go back to the time of British colonialism: to relax, Anglo-Saxon officials would add a generous ration of their beloved English gin to the ubiquitous Indian tonic water (regarded as a natural medicine against malaria).

PREPARATION

Measure 45 ml (3 tbsp) of gin in a graduated cylinder and pour into a tall tumbler filled with ice. Add tonic water almost to the brim and serve, garnished with 2 long straws and 1 slice of lemon or lime.

SUGGESTED USE

This long drink is perfect for every hour of the day and excellent as an aperitif.

Caprese Skewers   EASY

ingredients for 4 people
time: 30 minutes

12 cherry tomatoes
12 cherry mozzarella balls
basil
extra virgin olive oil
salt
pepper
oregano
1/2 a grapefruit

Wash and cut cherry tomatoes in half. Season with salt and let rest in a bowl for 20 minutes. Remove any water and combine with the mozzarella. Season with pepper, extra virgin olive oil and abundant oregano, leaving everything to marinate for 10 minutes. Use medium length toothpicks to skewer the ingredients, alternating between tomatoes and mozzarella and ending with the fresh basil leaves. Cover the grapefruit with aluminum foil to form a base for the skewers, allowing you to serve them in a spectacular fashion.

LONG ISLAND ICE TEA

INGREDIENTS

GIN
LIGHT RUM
DRY VODKA
COINTREAU

LEMON JUICE
SUGAR SYRUP
COLA

ORIGINS AND ODDITIES

Created in Long Island during the prohibition years,
it came to be when drinkers started trying to mask
different spirits, adding in this case cola. The drink
took the final part of its name from the color usually
associated with tea. It can be prepared
in a shaker or directly in a tumbler.

PREPARATION

In a graduated cylinder measure 20 ml (4 tsp) of light
rum and pour into a tumbler filled with ice. Repeat
with 20 ml (4 tsp) of gin, 20 ml (4 tsp) of Cointreau,
20 ml (4 tsp) of dry vodka, 20 ml (4 tsp) of lemon
juice and 20 ml (4 tsp) of sugar syrup.
Add 40 ml (2 3/4 tbsp) of cola and mix the
ingredients, stirring vigorously with a long-handled
spoon for a few seconds. Serve, garnished with
2 long straws and 1/2 a slice of lime or lemon.

SUGGESTED USE

Suitable for all hours of the day but in moderation,
due to the high alcohol content of the drink.

Spicy Chocolate Mousse   EASY

ingredients for 4 people
time: 30 minutes +
cooling time (6 hours)

0.66 lbs (7 oz) dark chocolate
1 1/3 tbsp butter
2/5 cup coffee
4 eggs
chili powder
icing sugar
whipped cream

Melt the chocolate in a bain-marie, stirring constantly to make sure that
it does not stick or form lumps. Remove from the heat and add coffee,
butter, egg yolks and 1/4 tsp of chili powder. Mix well and then leave
the mixture to cool. Meanwhile, whisk the egg whites with 2 tbsp of
icing sugar. Add the prepared sugar and egg whites with the chocolate, stirring vigorously with a whisk until the mixture is smooth and
perfectly mixed. Pour the mousse into 4 small bowls and place them to
cool in the refrigerator for at least 6 hours. Remove from the refrigerator 5 minutes before serving, garnish as desired with a light sprinkling
of whipped cream flavored with coffee.

MARGARITA

INGREDIENTS

TEQUILA
COINTREAU
LEMON OR LIME JUICE

ORIGINS AND ODDITIES

There are several legends about the birth of the Margarita, the most famous tequila-based drink in the world. The most accepted goes back to the mid-'30s, when a man named Danny Tergete mixed tequila, Cointreau and lemon juice on the day of his brother's wedding. He would name his creation Margarita, in honor of the bride, his sister-in-law.

PREPARATION

Measure 45 ml (3 tbsp) of tequila in a graduated cylinder and pour into a shaker. Do the same for 25 ml (5 tsp) of Cointreau and 20 ml (4 tsp) of lemon or lime juice. Add ice cubes and shake vigorously for a few seconds. Rub the rim of a "margarita glass" (a stem glass) with the rind of a lemon or lime, then dip the glass in salt and spin. Pour and serve.

SUGGESTED USE

The Margarita can be a refreshing cocktail at all hours of the day, however, it is especially recommended for happy hour.

Papaya and Ham Rolls

EASY

ingredients for 4 people
time: 30 minutes

1.3 lbs (21 oz) papaya
0.33 lbs (5.3 oz) ham (sliced thinly)
4/5 cup fresh cream
1 big ripe tomato
4 fresh mint leaves
red pepper
juice of 2 lemons
extra virgin olive oil
salt and pepper

Finely shred 4 beautiful fresh mint leaves, combining them all into a bowl. Add the cream and 3 tbsp of lemon juice (about 1 lemon). Mix the ingredients well with the help of a small whisk and let the first sauce stand for 15 minutes. In the meantime, rinse the papaya, and, slicing vertically, remove the seeds and cut into wedges. Then place it on a plate and season it with 1 1/2 tbsp of lemon juice (about 1/2 a lemon). Blend the tomato with a few cloves of papaya. Add the red pepper, remaining lemon juice and 1 tbsp of extra virgin olive oil, pouring the sauce obtained in a second bowl to be served directly on the table. Roll up the slices of ham with the papaya wedges and arrange them as desired on a serving platter and serve, accompanied with both sauces: the red pepper and the sour cream.

MARTINI COCKTAIL

INGREDIENTS

GIN
DRY VERMOUTH

ORIGINS AND ODDITIES

A well-known legend regarding this cocktail recounts
the tale of an Italian bartender (with the surname
Martini) who emigrated to the United States and
created this drink in 1910 in honor of John D.
Rockefeller, a frequent visitor to Martini's bar.

PREPARATION

Measure 80 ml (1/3 cup) of gin in a graduated
cylinder and pour into a transparent pitcher. Repeat
with 10 ml (2 tsp) of dry vermouth and add several
ice cubes. Stir with a long-handled spoon and pour
into a chilled cocktail glass, being careful that the
ice does not slide into the glass. Serve, garnished
with 0.35 oz (10 g) previously rinsed green olives
skewered on a long toothpick and a lemon rind.

SUGGESTED USE

Dry and slightly aromatic, has become the
world's most popular aperitif, and is especially
recommended during happy hour.

Two-Color Caviar Crostini   EASY

ingredients for 4 people
time: 20 minutes

4 thick slices white bread
black caviar
red caviar
butter
chopped parsley

Cut the white bread into slices and toast both sides on a very hot grill.
With a fork, work the butter quickly in a bowl and spread thoroughly
on the crostini (toast slices). With a teaspoon, gently place the black
and red caviar in equal parts on the slices and serve. Sprinkle lightly
with chopped parsley.

MOJITO

INGREDIENTS

LIGHT RUM

WHITE SUGAR OR CANE SUGAR

FRESH MINT

LIME

SODA OR SPARKLING WATER

ORIGINS AND ODDITIES

The legend of this cocktail is based on the infamous pirate Francis Drake (1540–1596), who was said to have loved mixing rum, sugar and mint leaves, ingredients that were believed to alleviate some ailments of the time. Helping to facilitate the dissemination of this cocktail was Ernest Hemingway (1899–1961), who would have bartender Martinez of La Bodeguita del Medio, in Havana, prepare him different Mojitos every day.

PREPARATION

Put 1/2 a lime (cut into cubes) in a tall tumbler. Add 25 g (2 tbsp) of sugar and mash everything with a pestle until it's a pulp. Add mint leaves, pressing gently against the rest. Fill the glass with crushed ice and add 25 ml (5 tsp) of light rum (previously measured in a graduated cylinder). Fill to the rim with soda water and stir for a few seconds with a long-handled spoon, so as to best mix the ingredients. To serve, garnish the drink with 2 straws and a nice long sprig of fresh mint.

SUGGESTED USE

To be enjoyed at all hours of the day. Very suitable as an aperitif.

 Quick Pink Grapefruit and Shrimp Salad

EASY

ingredients for 4 people
time: 20 minutes

0.44 lbs (7 oz) boiled shrimps

0.44 lbs (7 oz) valerian

4 pink grapefruits

4 cherry tomatoes

2 stalks celery

juice of 1 lemon

salt

pepper

white sugar

extra virgin olive oil

Wash the valerian and celery, then cut them into thin slices. Peel the grapefruit, removing even the white membrane also carefully collecting the juice released by the grapefruit in a sauce dish (gravy boat). Add the lemon juice to the gravy boat, 2 tbsp of extra virgin olive oil, salt, pepper and a pinch of sugar. Mix the ingredients vigorously with the help of a small whisk. Arrange a bed of valerian on four salad bowls and lay down (in this order) celery slices, a few cloves of pink grapefruit and 1 tbsp of boiled shrimps. Season with plenty of sauce and serve, garnishing the whole with diced cherry tomatoes.

NEGRONI

INGREDIENTS

GIN
RED VERMOUTH
CAMPARI

ORIGINS AND ODDITIES

The Negroni is an alcoholic cocktail that is typically orange in color. It was created in the 1920s by Count Camillo Negroni in Florence, Italy. Count Negroni was a regular at the Caffè Casoni and he was said to have one day grown tired of the usual American cocktails. As a celebratory nod to a recent London trip, the aristocrat asked the bartender (who was named Fosco Scarselli) to replace the usual soda with a dash of gin. From that day on, the drink that the Count called "the usual", would be known to other bar patrons as "the Negroni," one of the most well-known and beloved Italian cocktails in the world.

PREPARATION

Measure 30 ml (2 tbsp) of gin in a graduated cylinder and pour into a tumbler filled with ice. Repeat, adding 30 ml (2 tbsp) of red vermouth, and 30 ml (2 tbsp) of Campari. Mix together for a few seconds with a long-handled spoon. Garnish with 1/2 an orange slice and serve.

SUGGESTED USE

The Negroni is the aperitif par excellence, but it can also be enjoyed throughout the evening.

Salmon and Leek Pie   MEDIUM

ingredients for 6/8 people
time: 1 hour

1 roll puff pastry
0.55 lbs (8.8 oz) smoked salmon
1 leek
1/2 cup fluid cream
2 eggs
salt
pepper
extra virgin olive oil
chopped parsley

Wash a nice leek and split it in two. Cut the smoked salmon into strips and combine with the leek, and finely grind the whole. Sauté in a large frying pan with 3 tbsp of extra virgin olive oil and the remaining leek, finely chopped. Add the rest of the salmon and cook for a few minutes over medium heat, dillutting the whole with 1/4 cup of warm water. Add any remaining chopped ingredients and continue cooking for another 5 minutes. Remove from heat and let stand. Pour the cream into a bowl and add the eggs. Salt and pepper to your liking, mixing with a whisk. When it cools, add the mixture of salmon and leek, gently combining the ingredients until it is a homogeneous mixture. Line a baking sheet with puff pastry and bake at 430°F (220°C) for 20 minutes. Halfway through cooking, gently add the mixture prepared earlier and finish cooking, until the pie surface is golden and almost solid. Remove from oven and serve, sprinkling each portion with plenty of chopped parsley and bits of raw leek.

ROSSINI

INGREDIENTS

STRAWBERRIES
BRUT SPARKLING WINE OR CHAMPAGNE
STRAWBERRY SYRUP (OPTIONAL)

ORIGINS AND ODDITIES

A variation of the Bellini, the Rossini seems to have
been invented in the mid-twentieth century, in
honor of the famous Italian composer.

PREPARATION

Puree 5–6 medium-sized strawberries with 10 ml
(2 tsp) of strawberry syrup and 30 ml (2 tbsp) of
natural water previously measured in a graduated
cylinder. Separate 30 ml (2 tbsp) of the puree and
pour it in a chilled cup (previously chilled in the
freezer). Add 90 ml (6 tbsp) of well-chilled brut
sparkling wine and stir gently with a long-handle
spoon. To serve, garnish as desired with fresh
strawberries.

SUGGESTED USE

To be enjoyed at any hour of the day,
the Rossini is excellent as an aperitif.

Ham Mousse

EASY

ingredients for 4 people
time: 45 minutes

0.53 lbs (8.5 oz) ham
1/3 cup flour
4 tbsp butter
3/4 cup + 1 1/2 tbsp milk
grated nutmeg
3 tbsp + 1 tsp (1/5 cup) cream
1.41 oz (1/3 cup + 1 tbsp) grated
cheese
2 eggs
salt
pepper
lettuce leaves
1 fennel

Heat the milk in a saucepan, without bringing it to a boil. Meanwhile,
cut the ham into small cubes and mix in a mixer. Melt the butter in a
saucepan, combining the sifted flour and milk, stirring vigorously with
a whisk and cook for another 5 minutes. Remove from heat and allow
to cool before adding the ham, grated cheese, cream and egg. Mix
everything well until the mixture is homogeneous. Butter 4 ramekins
and fill with prepared pudding, baking in the oven for 25 minutes at
356°F (180°C). When the mousse is almost solid, remove from the oven
and let it cool. Remove from the molds and serve on a bed of lettuce
and raw fennel, cut into thin strips (previously seasoned to taste).

SEX ON THE BEACH

INGREDIENTS

DRY VODKA
PEACH LIQUEUR

ORANGE JUICE
CRANBERRY JUICE

ORIGINS AND ODDITIES

A cocktail popular with younger drinkers, it was
created around the late 1980s, when the use of
the term "sex" with a drink ceased to be taboo
(the 1970s had already seen the drinks "Fun on
the Beach" and "Peach on the Beach").

PREPARATION

Pour 30 ml (2 tbsp) of dry vodka, 30 ml (2 tbsp)
of peach liqueur, 50 ml (3 1/3 tbsp) of orange juice
and 50 ml (3 1/3 tbsp) of cranberry juice (measured
previously in a graduated cylinder) into a shaker.
Add a few ice cubes and shake vigorously. Pour into
a tall tumbler filled with ice and serve, adding 2 long
straws. Garnish with slices of citrus fruit to taste.

SUGGESTED USE

An excellent long drink that can be enjoyed at any
hour of the day.

Peach Strudel

EASY

ingredients for 6/8 people
time: 1 hour

1 roll puff pastry
4 nectarines
8 amaretti cookies
0.22 lbs (3.5 oz) dark chocolate
flakes or chips
sugar
butter
juice of 1/2 a lemon
icing sugar

Wash the peaches and remove the pits, and, without peeling them,
blend 2 of them. Add the amaretti cookies and 1 tbsp of lemon juice
and blend again until the mixture is creamy and smooth. Roll out the
puff pastry and cover it with a generous layer of peach cream. Cut the
remaining peaches in slices and distribute the cream vertically. Sprinkle
everything with dark chocolate flakes (mixed previously with 1 tbsp of
white sugar). Close the dough around the cream and gently lay the strudel on a baking sheet lined with baking paper, brush the surface with
plenty of melted butter mixed with sugar, so that it browns nicely. Bake
at 400°F (200°C) for 25 minutes. Let cool (do not serve the strudel too
hot), garnished with a dusting of icing sugar.

SKYWASSER

INGREDIENTS

RASPBERRY SYRUP
LEMON OR LIME JUICE
SODA WATER OR SPARKLING WATER

ORIGINS AND ODDITIES

Initially served in a popular resort in the Alps (usually after a hard day of skiing — skywasser literally means "ski water"), this drink, which was much-loved by sportsmen, soon revealed remarkable invigoriting properties provided by its original ingredients: lemon juice, raspberry syrup, kirsch (cherry liqueur) and a pot of hot water. However, it soon proved itself too strong for a larger female audience, and with time, the Skywasser would come to be prepared with soda water and ice (instead of alcohol and hot-water).

PREPARATION

Measure 20 ml (4 tsp) of raspberry syrup in a graduated cylinder and pour into a tall tumbler filled with ice. Repeat with 30 ml (2 tbsp) of lemon juice, filling almost to the brim with soda water. Stir gently with a long handled spoon and serve, garnished with 2 long straws, 1/2 a slice of lemon and 2 cocktail cherries.

SUGGESTED USE

A great refreshing drink, this cocktail is recommended throughout the summer.

Melon, Berry and Basil Salad   EASY

ingredients for 4 people
time: 20 minutes + cooling time
(2 hours)

1 ripe melon
about 1 cup berries
1 vanilla sachet
sugar
zest of 1/2 a lemon
juice of 1/2 a lemon
fresh basil leaves
strawberries

Pour 1/2 cup of warm water into a saucepan and let the vanilla dissolve. Add the grated zest of 1/2 a lemon, 2 tbsp of sugar. Boil on medium heat for 10 minutes, until it turns into a syrupy sauce. Remove from heat and let cool. Meanwhile, rinse and open the melon, removing the seeds and skin. Cut into cubes and place in a large glass bowl. Add the washed and dried berries and syrup. Sprinkling basil leaves (cut into thin strips) and mix gently. Let rest in refrigerator for at least 2 hours. Serve in a salad bowl (pre-chilled in the freezer), garnished with fresh strawberries.

SPRITZ

INGREDIENTS

APEROL
DRY SPARKLING WINE
SODA OR SPARKLING WATER

ORIGINS AND ODDITIES

The legend says that during their stay in Triveneto, Austrian soldiers found the local wines to be very strong. As a result, they started to sprinkle soda water in the wine to lower the alcohol content. The new mixture was therefore called Spritz, which in German means "spray". Over the years, bartenders in Venetian cities also started adding aperitifs to wine (including Aperol, Bitter, Campari, Cynar, etc.).

PREPARATION

Measure 30 ml (2 tbsp) of Aperol in a graduated cylinder and pour into a tumbler filled with ice. Repeat with dry sparkling wine and soda. Stir gently for a few seconds and serve, garnished with 2 short straws and 1/2 an orange slice.

SUGGESTED USE

A light aperitif with low alcohol content, it is suitable for every hour of the day, but especially during happy hour.

Tomatoes au Gratin   EASY

ingredients for 4 people
time: 30 minutes

4 big tomatoes (not too ripe)
4 salted anchovies
1 1/4 cups breadcrumbs
about 4 tbsp capers
1 onion
parsley
basil
extra virgin olive oil
salt
pepper
sunflower seed oil

Wash, dry and cut the tomatoes in half. Remove the seeds and season the inside with salt and pepper. Finely chop an onion and let it dry in a frying pan with 2 tbsp of extra virgin olive oil. Drain, then roast the breadcrumbs in the remaining liquid for a few minutes over low heat. In a bowl put the onion, chopped parsley, chopped anchovies, capers (washed abundantly), roasted breadcrumbs, salt and pepper to taste. Work the mixture with a wooden spoon until it is homogeneous. Stuff the tomatoes with the mixture thoroughly and place them carefully on a baking tray lightly greased in a seed oil. Bake the tomatoes at 356°F (180°C) for 10 minutes and serve on a platter, garnished with beautiful sprigs of fresh basil.

STRAWBERRY CAIPIROSKA

INGREDIENTS

DRY VODKA
FRESH STRAWBERRIES
LIME

WHITE OR CANE SUGAR
STRAWBERRY OR
SUGAR SYRUP

ORIGINS AND ODDITIES

The Caipiroska is a modern take on the Caipirinha,
Brazil's famous cocktail originally made of cachaça
(distilled sugar cane). The preparation and the
ingredients of the two drinks are the same, with
only the alcohol-base changing: for the Caipiroska
it is dry vodka, for the Caipirinha it is cachaça.

PREPARATION

Dice 1/2 a lime and lay the bits down in a low tumbler.
Add 30 g (2 1/2 tbsp) of sugar, 20 ml (4 tsp)
sugar or strawberry syrup and 3–4 fresh strawberries.
Grind everything with a pestle until it is a pulp.
Add crushed ice and 50–60 ml (10–12 tsp) of dry
vodka previously measured in a graduated cylinder.
Stir for a few seconds with a long handled spoon
to best mix the ingredients. Serve, garnished with
2 short straws and beautiful fresh strawberries.

SUGGESTED USE

This drink is suitable for all times of the day, and
is well-loved by younger drinkers, particularly those
who make a habit of happy hour.

Cheerful Crab and Arugula Fusilli   EASY

ingredients for 4 people
time: 45 minutes

0.88 lbs (14 oz) fusilli
12 frozen crab meat sticks
1/2 a melon (not too ripe)
0.11 lbs (1.76 oz) arugula (rocket)
salt
extra virgin olive oil
salt and pepper

Heat 2 1/8 cups of water in a saucepan and dip the crab meat into
the water. Once thawed, drain and cut the crab into slices of equal
thickness. Wash and open the melon, removing the seeds and peel,
cutting into cubes. Wash and dry the arugula, slicing it very thinly.
Cook the pasta in boiling, salted water until al dente and drain. After
letting it cool under running cold water, place the pasta in a large pan
and add the slices of crab, arugula and diced melon. Mix well with
spoon, and before serving, season with salt, pepper and plenty of
extra virgin olive oil.

GIN-BASED COCKTAILS

Is there anything more British than horse racing? The answer is gin, which casually crosses time and fashions. Its popularity in the last century is a testament to her majesty the Queen Mother, who up to her last day helped form a cult appreciation around a drink like the Gin Tonic, which she sipped after afternoon tea.

Gin is one of the most cosmopolitan spirits that can be found, as it is now produced around the world, from England to Holland, Spain, Germany, India and Italy.

But stories related to its origins jump from country to country, age to age: from medieval monks to Sylvius Franciscus of Leiden, the Dutch scientist who invented the juniper distillate, up until the Thirty Years' War (1618-1648), from which British troops returned home with barrels of Dutch courage, the ancestor to today's gin.

Originally, the spirit was considered a medical remedy for digestion, and was called Jenever. It was obtained by distiling juniper and alcohol. It served as a remedy for kidney and stomach problems and was used for this purpose throughout the seventeenth century.

In 1698 the English king William III of Orange stopped the importation of spirits from Catholic countries, strongly pushing the production of local spirits, like gin. This helped increase the consumption of gin, which grew to such an extent that it become a social evil, eventually receiving the nickname "Bad Boy".

Around 1720, one quarter of the population of London was involved in the production or sale of gin, and in those same years England produced 70 million gallons of gin for a population of 6 million inhabitants. In 1736, the British government launched the Gin Act, which imposed severe restrictions on both the production and consumption of gin, but this only led to widespread smuggling.

In subsequent years, the introduction of the column distiller led to an improvement in production techniques, with the end result of a healthier and more refined distillate. The spread of gin in the world keep pace with the expansion of the British Empire and many new countries began to appreciate this distillate.

In the era of Prohibition (1919-1933) in the United States, gin proved easier to produce than whisky, because it did not require aging, and homemade production of so-called "bathtub gin" was widespread. Today, gin is an internationally popular distillate, partly because its ingredients come from all over the world.

There are two methods to produce: distillation or flavoring of a spirit.

There are three techniques used:
- distillation

- percolation

- maceration

For distillation, a cereal like grain is used, to which juniper berries and other botanical elements (up to 10-15) are carefully add: ginger, angelica, cardamom, etc. In addition to these elements, water also plays a role, as it must be neutral and demineralized. There are two distillation methods: continuous or discontinuous.

The first involves the use of a distillation column (which consists of an analyzer and rectifier); the second one uses a series of alembic stills, which redistill the spirit from the preceding alembic. The result is a very alcoholic, pure liquid at a continuous distillation. In percolation, instead, we have a tank filled with a water-alcohol solution in which a basket, containing herbs, is suspended in. The vapors obtained from the herbs release aromas that fall to the bottom and mix in with the solution. Maceration is used when you want to get the highest quality possible from herbs. Gin manufacturers in each country use these mthods, although the "London Dry Gin" distillation column remains the most widely practiced option.

The many existing types of gin on the market today differ in the quality and quantity of spices used, the type of grain, the alcohol content and flavor. A highly important and unique characteristic of every brand is the choice and amount of selected botanical elements.

Types of gin:

London Dry Gin is the classic gin and the most popular. It was created in the nineteenth century

Plymouth Gin, dry and intensely flavored, with a wide aroma, it is the only gin to have a sort of legal protection. Its ingredients are called the Magnificent Seven

Old Tom Gin, English, colorless, sweet taste as sugar syrup is added

Sloe Gin, flavored with wild sloes, violet-colored

Damson Gin, flavored with plums

Golden Gin, aged in oak barrels used for sherry, amber-colored

Orange and Lemon Gin, flavored with citrus essences

Jenever, produced in Holland using malt for whisky

Gin is an excellent distillate for cocktails: An example is the Martini Cocktail, the cocktail par excellence. Already in 1874, gin was being used in the Martinez cocktail, which mixed gin and sweet vermouth. The Martini Hemingway, a variant of the famous cocktail, famous cocktail, owes its name to the famous writer, who, as a great admirer of gin, preferred to drink it very dry.

Gin is popular for its extraordinary mixability and its ability to work well with many products, so much so that the distillate is the most cited in IBA (International Bartenders Association) international drinks recipes. Up until the 1990s, gin played a main role in apperitifs and long drinks cocktails, before vodka established itself as a viable alternative. A case in point, the Vodka Martini, a variant of the famous Martini Cocktail recipe.

BLUE ANGEL

INGREDIENTS

GIN

COINTREAU

BLUE CURAÇAO

LEMON OR LIME JUICE

ORIGINS AND ODDITIES

Legend has it that this cocktail was created in honor of actress and singer Marlene Dietrich, who starred in Josef von Sternberg's *Blue Angel*, shot in 1930.

PREPARATION

Measure 30 ml (2 tbsp) of gin in a graduated cylinder and pour in a shaker. Repeat with 20 ml (4 tsp) of Cointreau, 20 ml (4 tsp) of Blue Curaçao and 20 ml (4 tsp) of lemon juice. Add some ice cubes and shake vigorously for a few seconds. Pour into a cocktail glass (pre-cooled in the freezer) and serve.

SUGGESTED USE

A delicious digestif, it can be enjoyed throughout the evening.

 Strawberry Ricotta Tart   EASY

ingredients for 6/8 people
time: 2 hours

0.80 lbs (12.6 oz) ricotta cheese
0.44 lbs (7 oz) cereal biscuits
8 1/2 tbsp (1/2 cup) butter
1/2 cup + 1 tbsp sugar
0.26 lbs (4.2 oz) strawberry jam
1/2 cup + 2 tsp flour
3 tbsp + 1 tsp (1/5 cup) fresh cream
4 eggs
fresh strawberries
whipped cream
icing sugar

In a large bowl, add softened butter and crumbled cookies. Mix well and pour the mixture into a detachable cake tin with a rim diameter of about 20 cm. Heat the strawberry jam and distribute it on the base of the tin. Mix the cottage cheese, flour, sugar and egg yolks in a mixer. Add the whipped cream and egg whites, incorporating everything very gently. Pour the batter into the cake tin and bake at 320°F (160°C) for about 45 minutes. Let the pie cool. Serve, garnished as desired with the icing sugar, sliced strawberries and whipped cream.

BRONX

INGREDIENTS

GIN   DRY VERMOUTH
RED VERMOUTH   ORANGE JUICE

ORIGINS AND ODDITIES

The story goes that Joseph S. Sormani, a
bartender of Italian descent, created this drink
at the beginning of the 1900s in Philadelphia
(a city that he loved to visit). Sormani would
eventually introduce this cocktail in his Bronx
neighborhood. It was an instant success.

PREPARATION

Measure 30 ml (2 tbsp) of gin in a graduated cylinder
and pour in a shaker. Repeat with 20 ml
(4 tsp) of red vermouth, 20 ml (4 tsp) of dry vermouth
and 20 ml (4 tsp) of orange juice. Add some ice
cubes and shake vigorously for a few seconds. Pour
into a cup (pre cooled in the freezer) and serve.

SUGGESTED USE

The Bronx is an excellent aperitif.

Gorgonzola Pear Crostini   EASY

ingredients for 4 people
time: 1 hour

8 slices white bread
0.44 lbs (7 oz) sweet gorgonzola
cheese
4/5 cup fluid cream
2 ripe pears
salt
pepper

Remove the gorgonzola's crust and place in a bowl, working vigorously with a wooden spoon until creamy. With a whisk, whip the cream
and add the gorgonzola, stirring gently. Season with salt and pepper
as desired and let the mixture rest in the refrigerator for 20 minutes.
Wash and clean the pears, then cut into thin long slices. Remove the
crust from the bread slices and grill (or toast). Remove the mousse from
the refrigerator and spread it on the toast. Garnish with slices of pear
and serve.

CARDINALE

INGREDIENTS

GIN
CAMPARI
DRY VERMOUTH

ORIGINS AND ODDITIES

It seems it was indeed a cardinal who, during
a stay in Rome, asked a bartender to create this
deeply red-colored cocktail. Since he often wore
elegant clothes of a similar tone, the cocktail was
named in his honor.

PREPARATION

Measure 40 ml (2 3/4 tbsp) of gin in a graduated
cylinder and pour into a glass carafe. Repeat with
30 ml (2 tbsp) of dry vermouth and 20 ml (4 tsp)
of Campari. Add a few ice cubes and stir with a long-
handled spoon for a few seconds. Serve the drink
in a cocktail glass (pre-chilled in the freezer). When
pouring, be careful to hold the ice back in
the carafe with the help of the spoon.

SUGGESTED USE

Perfect as an aperitif.

Provolone Canapés   EASY

ingredients for 4 people
time: 30 minutes

8 slices white bread
0.55 lbs (8.8 oz) provola cheese
4 anchovies
2 tomatoes
salt
pepper
extra virgin olive oil
chopped parsley
arugula (rocket)

Remove the crust from the slices of bread and cut in half, resulting
in triangles. Toast the triangles. Arrange on a baking tray and on each
canapé, place a small provola (sliced in a fan shape), 1/2 an anchovy
fillet and tomatoes (previously washed and cut into cubes). Season
with salt and pepper to taste. Bake at 356°F (180°C) until the cheese is
almost completely melted. Arrange the canapés on a bed of arugula
and serve hot, drizzled with extra virgin olive oil and a sprinkling of
chopped parsley.

CARUSO

INGREDIENTS

GIN
DRY VERMOUTH DRY
CRÈME DE MENTHE VERTE
(GREEN MINT LIQUEUR)

ORIGINS AND ODDITIES

This cocktail, created in the mid-'20s, was dedicated
to the famous Italian tenor Enrico Caruso.

PREPARATION

Measure 30 ml (2 tbsp) of gin in a graduated cylinder
and pour in a shaker. Repeat with 30 ml
(2 tbsp) of dry vermouth and 30 ml (2 tbsp) of crème
de menthe verte. Add a few ice cubes and shake
vigorously for a few seconds. Serve in a cocktail glass
(pre-cooled in the freezer).

SUGGESTED USE

Enjoyable after dinner and on summer nights.

Chocolate Morsels   EASY

ingredients for 4 people
time: 1 hour and 30 minutes

0.44 lbs (7 oz) white chocolate
flakes or chips
0.11 lbs (1.76 oz) candied ginger
0.22 lbs (3.5 oz) toasted almonds
0.33 lbs (5.3 oz) dark chocolate
flakes or chips

Finely chop the toasted almonds and candied ginger. Melt the white
chocolate in a bain-marie, adding the ginger and almonds. Mix
thoroughly with the help of a wooden spoon. Remove from the heat,
and with a teaspoon, place balls of the mixture on a plate covered
with wax paper, leaving them to solidify in the fridge. Dissolve the
dark chocolate in a bain-marie. Once solid, skewer the balls with a
long toothpick, completely immersing them for a few seconds in
the melted dark chocolate, being careful to drain off the excess. Re-
arrange the balls on a plate covered with waxed paper and let everything harden. Serve, garnished as desired with whipped cream,
caramel or hazelnut flakes.

CHEROKEE

INGREDIENTS

GIN   GRAPEFRUIT JUICE
CAMPARI   GRENADINE SYRUP
ORANGE JUICE

ORIGINS AND ODDITIES

A modern drink, the Cherokee's amber color
is a reminder of the dark skin tones of the
Cherokee Indians.

PREPARATION

Measure 30 ml (2 tbsp) of gin in a graduated cylinder
and pour into a tall tumbler filled with
ice. Repeat with 20 ml (4 tsp) of Campari, 70 ml
(4 tbsp + 2 tsp) of orange juice, 30 ml (2 tbsp)
of grapefruit juice and 10 ml (2 tsp) of grenadine
syrup. Mix the ingredients well with a long-handled
spoon and serve, garnished with 2 long straws,
2 cocktail cherries, 1 sprig of mint and 2 orange
slices.

SUGGESTED USE

This long drink is enjoyed around the world,
most especially at happy hour.

Shrimp Skewers   EASY

ingredients for 4 people
time: 40 minutes

0.88 lbs (14 oz) shrimp tails
3 1/2 tbsp grated cheese
1 cup breadcrumbs
chives
sage
mint
rosemary
salt
pepper
extra virgin olive oil
lemon wedges
chopped parsley

Finely chop all the herbs and place them in a soup bowl. Combine
breadcrumbs, grated cheese, salt and pepper. Wash the shrimp tails
and remove first the shell, then the dark filament along their backs.
Heavily bread them and stick them on medium length toothpicks.
Heat the hotplate and lay the shrimp skewers down, drizzling with
extra virgin olive oil during cooking. Cook the shrimp 5 minutes per
side and serve, accompanied with the chopped parsley and lemon
wedges.

GIN AND IT

INGREDIENTS

GIN
RED VERMOUTH

ORIGINS AND ODDITIES

Originally created in the 1930s, this drink was at that time known as the Fifty-Fifty. Its name change, and the "It", was due to the use of Italian red vermouth, an ingredient that differentiates the Gin and It from its brother, the Gin and French, which uses French dry vermouth.

PREPARATION

Measure 65 ml (13 tsp) of gin in a graduated cylinder and pour into a glass carafe. Repeat
with 25 ml (5 tsp) of red vermouth. Add some ice cubes and mix together with a long-handled spoon. Pour into a cup (previously chilled in the freezer), holding the ice in the carafe with the spoon. Serve.

SUGGESTED USE

Excellent as an aperitif.

Soft Cheese Pizzas   EASY

ingredients for 4 people
time: 1 hour

0.88 lbs (14 oz) of bread dough
0.44 lbs (7 oz) soft cheese
8 thin slices of smoked bacon
(pancetta)
sage leaves
extra virgin olive oil
butter
salt and pepper

Roll out the dough until you get a rectangle. Place in a baking pan (previously greased with olive oil), and let it rest for about 20 minutes. In the meantime, cut the bacon into strips, letting it brown in a saucepan for a few minutes with a knob of butter. Chop the sage and break up the cheese bread dough. Put both in the pan and distribute the cheese, sage and bacon evenly. Bake at 430°F (220°C) for about 20 minutes and serve in small slices.

GIN FIZZ

INGREDIENTS

GIN
LEMON JUICE
SUGAR SYRUP

SODA WATER OR
SPARKLING WATER

ORIGINS AND ODDITIES

The Gin Fizz was created in the United States around the 1920s (in the heyday of the Charleston), when along the Atlantic coast of Carolina, dockers would mix gin, lemon and soda water.

PREPARATION

Measure 45 ml (3 tbsp) of gin in a graduated cylinder and pour into a shaker. Repeat with 30 ml (2 tbsp) of lemon juice and 20 ml (4 tsp) of sugar syrup. Add some ice cubes and shake for a few seconds. Pour into a tall tumbler and fill almost to the brim with soda water. Stir gently with a long handled spoon and serve, garnished with 2 long straws, 2 cocktail cherries and 1/2 a slice of lemon.

SUGGESTED USE

This long drink can be enjoyed at all hours of the day, but it is ideal during the hottest hours. It has excellent digestive properties.

Caramelized Pineapple

EASY

ingredients for 4 people
time: 30 minutes

1 ripe pineapple
8 tbsp (1/2 cup) brown sugar
2 lemons
2 yogurt vanilla
cinnamon powder

Peel a ripe pineapple and cut it in half. Core the middle, then cut it into thin slices. In a small saucepan, caramelize brown sugar with the juice of 1 lemon. With the help of a fork, put the pineapple slices in the pan, caramelizing each side. Lay it all on a baking sheet lined with baking paper. Bake at 400°F (200°C) for a few minutes, waiting for the sugar to entirely crystallize. Place the pineapple on a serving dish and sprinkle with cinnamon and serve, accompanied with a sauce boat filled with vanilla yogurt.

GIN LEMON

INGREDIENTS

GIN
LEMON SODA

ORIGINS AND ODDITIES

There is no officially recognized story regarding the creation of this famous drink. It could, however, be a simple revisiting of the Singapore Sling (formerly called the Gin Sling).

PREPARATION

Measure 45 ml (3 tbsp) of gin in a graduated cylinder and pour into a tall tumbler filled with ice. Fill almost to the brim with lemon soda and serve, garnished with 2 long straws.

SUGGESTED USE

Magnificently refreshing, the Gin Lemon is suitable for all hours of the day.

Pineapple Fritters   EASY

ingredients for 4 people
time: 30 minutes

6 slices pineapple in syrup
1 egg
2/3 cup flour
milk
butter
salt
sunflower seed oil
icing sugar

Beat the eggs in a bowl, then combine with the flour, a knob of butter, a pinch of salt and milk. Halve the pineapple slices, and, with the help of a fork, dip them thoroughly in the batter. Fry in boiling sunflower seed oil, and then lay them on two sheets of paper towels. Serve hot, sprinkling the fritters with icing sugar.

LAY OFF

INGREDIENTS

GIN

WHITE VERMOUTH

CAMPARI

ORANGE JUICE

ORIGINS AND ODDITIES

A drink that was introduced at a competition held at the *Grand Hotel di Gardone Riviera* (in Lake Garda, Italy). It finished in third place.

PREPARATION

Measure 30 ml (2 tbsp) of gin in a graduated cylinder and pour into a shaker. Repeat with 30 ml (2 tbsp) of orange juice, 20 ml (4 tsp) of white vermouth and 10 ml (2 tsp) of Campari. Add a few ice cubes and shake for a few seconds. Serve in a cocktail glass (pre-chilled in the freezer), garnishing with 1 cocktail cherry and 1 orange slice.

SUGGESTED USE

Perfect as an aperitif, it can be enjoyed at all hours of the day.

Homemade Olive Bread Sticks

EASY

ingredients for 4 people
time: 2 hours

4 cups white flour
fresh yeast
3/4 cup + 1 1/2 tbsp warm water
table salt
coarse salt
extra virgin olive oil
0.39 lbs (6.35 oz, about 41) pitted black olives

Dissolve a knob of fresh yeast in warm water and pour into a bowl. Combine the remaining water and flour, mixing until it is a homogeneous mixture. Shape into a ball and let rest for 40 minutes or until the dough doubles in volume. Chop the olives and mix with the rest, adding 1 1/2 tsp of salt and 5 1/4 tsp of extra virgin olive oil. Divide the dough into balls, then lengthen them to form breadsticks. Arrange the breadsticks on a baking sheet lined with baking paper and let rise for another 30 minutes. Brush with extra virgin olive oil and sprinkle with coarse salt. Bake breadsticks for 20 minutes at 430°F (220°C). Serve cold.

NEW FRED ROSE

INGREDIENTS

GIN   LIMONCELLO
MANDARINETTO ISOLABELLA   CAMPARI

ORIGINS AND ODDITIES

It's been said that this cocktail was created
by a bartender named Fred, in honor of Rose,
a girl he was smitten with.

PREPARATION

Measure 30 ml (2 tbsp) of gin in a graduated cylinder
and pour into a shaker. Repeat with 30 ml
(2 tbsp) of Mandarinetto Isolabella, 20 ml (4 tsp) of
Campari and 10 ml (2 tsp) of limoncello. Add some
ice cubes and shake vigorously for a few seconds.
Pour into a cocktail glass (pre-chilled in the freezer)
and serve, garnished with 1 slice of lemon or lime
and 1 cherry.

SUGGESTED USE

This very refreshing drink can be enjoyed
throughout the day. Also recommended
as an aperitif.

Salmon Surprise   EASY

ingredients for 4 people
time: 1 hour and 30 minutes

0.66 lbs (10.5 oz, about 2 small or about
1 1/2 medium) potatoes
0.44 lbs (7.05 oz) smoked salmon
1/3 cup + 1 tbsp flour
0.22 lbs (3.5 oz, 4 thick slices) stale bread
extra virgin olive oil
sunflower seed oil
sesame seeds
salt and pepper

Wash and peel the potatoes, then boil them in salted water. Drain
them and cool under running cold water. Finely shred the salmon
and wring out the wet stale bread (previously soaked with water). In
a bowl mash the potatoes with the help of a large fork and add the
bread, salmon, a spoonful of extra virgin olive oil, flour, and salt and
pepper to taste. After mixing them all together, form patties the size
of walnuts with your hands, then roll in sesame seeds. Fry the balls
in abundant sunflower seed oil for about 5 minutes. When the outer
surface of the salmon is golden, arrange them on a tray covered with
absorbent paper. Serve hot.

PALM BEACH

INGREDIENTS

GIN
CAMPARI
PINEAPPLE JUICE

ORIGINS AND ODDITIES

Created in the 1950s, the Palm Beach seems
to have been the welcome cocktail of exclusive
seaside resorts located on the Atlantic coast
of Florida.

PREPARATION

Measure 40 ml (2 3/4 tbsp) of gin in a graduated
cylinder and pour into a transparent shaker.
Repeat with 30 ml (2 tbsp) of Campari and
90 ml (6 tbsp) of pineapple juice. Add ice cubes
and shake vigorously for a few seconds. Pour the
drink into a tall tumbler filled with ice and serve,
garnished with 1/2 a slice of pineapple, 2 cocktail
cherries and 2 long straws.

SUGGESTED USE

Perfect as an aperitif, it can be enjoyed
throughout the day.

Cuttlefish Carpaccio   EASY

ingredients for 4 people
time: 2 hours

0.88 lbs (14 oz) medium-large
(tentacle-free) fresh cuttlefish
0.44 lbs (7 oz) Parmigiano Reggiano
flakes
1 celery heart
juice of 1 lemon
extra virgin olive oil
salt and pepper

Clean the cuttlefish, carefully discarding the blackish skin and wash
in abundant cold water. Boil them in salted water until they are al
dente. Drain, and, after being cooled under running water, place
them in the refrigerator. Meanwhile, clean, wash and chop the
celery into thin rings. Finally, slice the cuttlefish, placing it on a nice
serving dish. Sprinkle with Parmigiano Reggiano and celery (previously sliced). Season with plenty of extra virgin olive oil, the juice of
1 lemon, salt and pepper and let rest for 30 minutes before serving,
so that the carpaccio can best absorb the dressing.

PARADISE

INGREDIENTS

GIN
APRICOT BRANDY (APRICOT LIQUEUR)
ORANGE JUICE

ORIGINS AND ODDITIES

According to legend, this cocktail, originally named
Houla-Houla in honor of Hawaii, was created around
the 1920s in England and later renamed Paradise.

PREPARATION

Measure 40 ml (2 3/4 tbsp) of gin in a graduated
cylinder and pour into a shaker. Repeat with 30 ml
(2 tbsp) of Apricot Brandy and 20 ml (4 tsp) of orange
juice. Add ice cubes and shake vigorously for a few
seconds. Pour into a cup (pre-chilled in the freezer)
and serve, garnished with 1/2 an orange slice.

SUGGESTED USE

A fantastic drink, the Paradise can be enjoyed
at all hours of the day.

Aphrodisiac Fruit Salad   EASY

ingredients for 4 people
time: 20 minutes

4 slices pineapple
1 slice watermelon
2 peaches
1 kiwi
1 mango
1 red orange
red pepper flakes
apricot brandy
sugar
apricot or orange ice cream

Wash all the fruit thoroughly, cutting them into cubes and placing
them in a bowl. Add 1 tbsp of sugar, 1 tbsp of of Apricot Brandy and a
slight sprinkle of pepper flakes. Stir gently and serve in 4 cups (previously chilled in the freezer). Add a generous scoop of apricot or orange
ice cream to each salad.

PINK LADY

INGREDIENTS

GIN

COINTREAU

LEMON JUICE

GRENADINE SYRUP

ORIGINS AND ODDITIES

A variation of the more famous White Lady, this cocktail was created in the 1920s in Great Britain in honor of the ladies of the time.

PREPARATION

Measure 30 ml (2 tbsp) in a graduated cylinder and pour into a shaker. Repeat with 25 ml (5 tsp) of Cointreau, 25 ml (5 tsp) of lemon juice and 10 ml (2 tsp) of grenadine syrup. Add a few ice cubes and shake vigorously for a few seconds. Serve in a cocktail glass (pre-cooled in the freezer).

SUGGESTED USE

This is considered a purely evening drink.

Cage Apples

EASY

ingredients for 4 people
time: 1 hour

0.44 lbs (7 oz) puff pastry
2 rennet apples
2 tbsp cane sugar
2 tbsp cinnamon
4 amaretti cookies
4 tsp apricot jam
1 egg
icing sugar

Roll out the pastry to form a thin rectangle and with a knife divide into 4 squares. Wash and peel the apples, removing the cores. At the center of each square of pastry lay 1 amaretto and cover with 1 tsp of jam and a dusting of cinnamon. Cover with half the apple and wrap it in puff pastry to create a little bundle, using the egg (previously beaten in a soup bowl) as a glue. Brush the remaining egg on the bundles, so that, once baked, they have a nice golden color. Bake at 356°F (180°C) for about 25 minutes, making sure the pastry does not burn. Arrange the cage apples on a serving dish and sprinkle with plenty of icing sugar. Serve cold.

SINGAPORE SLING

INGREDIENTS

GIN   GRENADINE SYRUP
CHERRY BRANDY   LEMON JUICE
COINTREAU   SODA WATER

ORIGINS AND ODDITIES

This cocktail was created in 1915 by Ngiam Tong
Boon for the luxurious Raffles Hotel in Singapore,
which, at the time, was frequented by distinguished
personalities from the world of literature, including
Kipling, Maugham, and Hesse. Its most well-known
recipe is presented here.

PREPARATION

Measure 20 ml (4 tsp) of gin in a graduated
cylinder and pour into a shaker. Repeat with 20 ml
(4 tsp) of cherry brandy, 20 ml (4 tsp) of Cointreau,
10 ml (2 tsp) of grenadine syrup and 30 ml (2 tbsp)
of lemon juice. Shake vigorously for a few seconds
and pour into a tumbler filled with ice. Fill almost
to the brim with soda water, then stir with a
long-handled spoon. Serve, garnished with 2 long
straws, 1/2 a slice of pineapple and 2 cocktail cherries.

SUGGESTED USE

A long drink that can cheer you up at all hours
of the day.

Ham and Melon in Glasses
EASY

ingredients for 4 people
time: 20 minutes

1 ripe melon
0.88 lbs (14 oz, 4 slices) thinly-sliced
cured ham

Put the melon in the refrigerator for at least 2 hours before starting
preparation. Three-quarters of an hour before serving, cut the melon
in half lengthwise, removing seeds and the peel from each slice. Then
cut the slices into 5 cm long strips, repeating the operation with the
ham. Fill 4 wine glasses, alternating 2 layers of melon with 2 layers of
cured ham. Keep them cool until they are ready to serve.

WHITE LADY

INGREDIENTS

GIN
COINTREAU
LEMON JUICE

ORIGINS AND ODDITIES

As legend has it, the White Lady was created
in the 1920s by Harry MacElhone, a well-known
American barman who was, at that time,
residing in Paris. Attending a conference
at a famous hotel in the French capital,
MacElhone encountered a lady who had fallen ill.
The lady was dressed all in white. As the story
goes, MacElhone created a drink that helped the
woman recover, a drink that would soon be
named in her honor.

PREPARATION

Measure 40 ml (2 3/4 tbsp) of gin in a graduated
cylinder and pour into a shaker. Repeat with 30 ml
(2 tbsp) of Cointreau and 20 ml (4 tsp) of lemon
juice. Add some ice cubes and shake vigorously for a
few seconds. Pour into a cocktail glass
(pre-cooled in the freezer) and serve.

SUGGESTED USE

The White Lady is generally considered a refined
cocktail with effective digestive properties, and
is thus recommended for elegant evenings.

Lemon Meringue

MEDIUM

ingredients for 4 people
time: 1 hour

4 egg whites
1 cup (16 tbsp) sugar
zest of 2 lemons
0.26 lbs (4.2 oz) blanched almonds

Mix the almonds in a mixer. Work the egg whites and sugar vigorously
with a whisk until the mixture is firm. Add the almonds and mix gently
with a spoon. Repeat with the grated lemon zest until the mixture is
homogeneous. Line a baking tray with greaseproof paper and, using a
pastry bag, shape the meringues to your preference, making sure to
maintain their size. Bake at 250°F (120°C) for about 30 minutes, preferably at the bottom of the oven.

VODKA-BASED COCKTAILS

Russia and Poland are two countries that claim to have invented vodka (or wodka).

In Poland, vodka was initially used in the preparation of gunpowder for muskets. The first reports of this spirit date back to the fourteenth century, though the first written documents only appeared a century later. "Wodka" originated from a spirit called "okowita" (from the Latin *aqua vitae*), and was used as a beverage and for medicinal purposes. It was so popular, in fact, that a document from 1534 recommended a flavored version as a pain remedy for various ailments (it was also recommended as an after-shave lotion). The production and sale of this distillate was liberalized in Poland in 1546, establishing its growth and continual success. In the mid-nineteenth century, Polish distilleries began marketing vodka in Northern European countries, including Russia, where the production and commercialization of vodka began around the fourteenth century. Seeing its popularity, Czar Ivan the Terrible established a government monopoly on vodka production in 1540, which reserved production rights to the Russian nobility. This led to an increase in illegal production and sales in the general population.

Over the years, official distilleries improved production techniques, moving from simple distillation to a multiple system, until finally using charcoal filtration to obtain maximum purification.

Between the seventeenth and eighteenth century, production increased, both in quantity and quality, thanks to the importation of modern alembics from Western Europe. The production of vodka in Russia, however, continued to follow two paths: quality spirits reserved for the upper classes and that of a decidedly lower quality, which was destined for the lower classes.

In the nineteenth century chemist Dmitry Mendeleev (inventor of the periodic table of elements) developed standards for vodka, establishing an alcoholic content of 40%. Since the beginning of the twentieth century, company Moskovskaya has been the standard bear-

er of Vodka production, marketing a vodka produced with natural rye and distilled water.

Vodka is an infusion of sugars that undergoes the process of fermentation and distillation. The relatively simple manufacturing and technology, however, go hand in hand with the selection of raw materials, such as grains, molasses, potatoes, beets, grapes and rice. There are a number of natural ingredients that can be used as a base, although wheat and rye are the most commonly used. Another key element is the purity of water, which must be unpolluted and demineralized.

Every distiller has his preferences: quality Russian vodka, for example, is obtained from the malt of fermented rye with selected yeasts. Depending on the brand, these ingredients are then complimented with different proportions of oats, wheat, barley and buckwheat. Equally important, however, is the alembic: this can be done with a distiller or a batch distillation column.

After distillation and a partial dilution with distilled water, the liquid obtained is filtered through charcoal (birch), to free the spirit from any odors and aldehydes. The result is colorless, with well-defined aromas. The resulting vodka is ready for commercialization and is not usually aged, though it may be flavored with spices, herbs, fruit.

There is no universal classification for vodka, as each country has a way of distinguishing qualities and characteristics.

When it comes to mixed drinks, however, vodka is something of an uncontested queen. Due to its neutrality, it can be combined smoothly with an infinite number of flavors. No wonder then that it occupies a prominent place at IBA competitions and cocktails. Some of the most famous cocktails made with vodka include: Sex on the Beach, Cosmopolitan, Caipiroska, Moskow Mule.

Vodka, though, can also be enjoyed on its own: chilled in ad hoc glasses and immersed in ice, it can be a smooth delight.

ALABAMA SLAMMER

INGREDIENTS

DRY VODKA
DISARONNO AMARETTO
SOUTHERN COMFORT

ORANGE JUICE
GRENADINE SYRUP

ORIGINS AND ODDITIES

The origins of this drink are still unclear, mainly
because none of its ingredients are originally from
Alabama. This certainly has not slowed its rise,
which began in the mid-'90s, and has since turned
it into one of the most well-known and popular
cocktails in the world.

PREPARATION

Measure 20 ml (4 tsp) of vodka in a graduated
cylinder and pour into a shaker. Repeat with
20 ml (4 tsp) of Disaronno Amaretto, 20 ml (4 tsp)
of Southern Comfort, 90 ml (6 tbsp) of orange juice
and 10 ml (2 tsp) of grenadine syrup. Add some
ice cubes and shake vigorously for a few seconds.
Pour into a tall tumbler filled with ice and serve,
garnished with 1/2 an orange slice, 2 cherries and
2 long straws.

SUGGESTED USE

A long refreshing drink suitable for all hours of the
afternoon and evening.

 Amaretto Sweets   EASY

ingredients for 6/8 people
time: 1 hour and 15 minutes

1 cup (16 tbsp) sugar
0.55 lbs (8.8 oz) amaretti cookies
3/4 cup breadcrumbs
7 eggs
1 lemon
1/2 a sachet baking powder
1 shot glass amaretto liqueur
flour
butter
icing sugar

Mix the amaretti cookies in a mixer. In a bowl, mix the egg yolks with
sugar for a few minutes. Combine the egg whites until it stiffens, stirring
gently from bottom to top. Add the amaretto and the breadcrumbs,
softening the mixture with the rum and the juice of 1 lemon. Add the
grated lemon rind and baking powder, giving it a final mix. Grease and
flour a cake pan and pour the mixture into it. Bake at 356°F (180°C) for
about 45 minutes. Garnished as desired plenty of icing sugar.

APPLE MARTINI

INGREDIENTS

DRY VODKA
APPLE LIQUEUR
COINTREAU

ORIGINS AND ODDITIES

One of the most popular variations of the classic
Martini Cocktail was created in New York in the
late 1980s and soon became very popular among
younger drinkers.

PREPARATION

Measure 50 ml (3 1/3 tbsp) of vodka in a graduated
cylinder and pour into a shaker. Repeat with 20 ml
(4 tsp) of apple liqueur and 20 ml (4 tsp) of Cointreau.
Add ice cubes and stir for a few seconds. Pour into
a cup (pre-chilled in the freezer) and serve.

SUGGESTED USE

Usually served as an aperitif, it can easily
be enjoyed throughout the day.

Delicate Salad   EASY

ingredients for 4 people
time: 1 hour

0.66 lbs (10.5 oz, about 5 cups) fresh
porcini mushrooms
2 green apples
2 bunches of arugula (rocket)
16 walnut kernels
juice of 1 lemon
extra virgin olive oil
salt
white pepper

Remove the base of the mushrooms and clean them properly,
removing any earth with the help of a brush. Cut horizontally into thin
slices of the same thickness and repeat the operation with the apples, leaving the peel. Wash and coarsely chop the arugula and season
generously with a simple sauce made by mixing the lemon juice, extra
virgin olive oil, salt and white pepper in a bowl. Then place the salad on
a nice serving dish and lay slices of mushroom in a spectacular fashion,
alternating with slices of green apple. Distribute evenly on the surface
the walnut kernels, divided in half, and let rest in refrigerator for 30
minutes before serving.

BLACK RUSSIAN

INGREDIENTS

DRY VODKA
COFFEE LIQUEUR

ORIGINS AND ODDITIES

The birth of this cocktail is traced back to 1949,
when Gustave Tops, a barman at the Metropole
hotel in Brussels, created a new drink in honor of the
United States Ambassador's visit to Luxembourg.

PREPARATION

Measure 55 ml (3 3/4 tbsp) of vodka dry in a
graduated cylinder, and pour into a tumbler filled
with ice. Repeat with 35 ml (2 tbsp + 1 tsp) of coffee
liqueur. Mix with a long-handled spoon and serve,
garnished with 2 short straws.

SUGGESTED USE

A drink with excellent digestive properties,
it is enjoyed by many throughout the evening.

 ## Coffee Cremini

EASY

ingredients for 4 people
time: 1 hour

scant 2 cups cream
9 tsp coffee powder
0.22 lbs (3.5 oz) dark chocolate
4 egg yolks
1 tbsp sugar

for the sauce:
0.11 lbs (1.76 oz) dark chocolate
cinnamon
whipped cream

Bring the coffee and cream to a boil in a saucepan. Remove from
heat and pass it through a colander. Add the chopped chocolate and
sugar. Add the egg yolks one at a time, without stirring. Divide the
mixture into 4 ramekins and place them carefully on a baking pan
filled with hot water (the water should cover up to 2/3 of the ramekins). Cover them with a sheet of aluminum foil and bake at 356°F
(180°C) for 25 minutes. Meanwhile prepare the sauce, melting the
chocolate in a bain marie, adding cinnamon to taste. Remove the
cremini from the oven and serve then warm with the sauce as an
accompaniment. Garnish with a sprinkle of cinnamon and whipped
cream.

BLUE LAGOON

INGREDIENTS

DRY VODKA
BLUE CURAÇAO
LEMON JUICE

ORIGINS AND ODDITIES

Created in England in the 1950s, in the following
decades, the Blue Lagoon became one of the
most frequently mentioned cocktails in the most
important international cookbooks.

PREPARATION

Measure 40 ml (2 3/4 tbsp) of vodka in a graduated
cylinder and pour into a shaker. Repeat with 30 ml
(2 tbsp) of lemon juice and 20 ml (4 tsp) of Blue
Curaçao. Add some ice cubes and shake vigorously
for a few seconds. Pour into a pre-chilled cup and
serve, garnished with 1 slice of lemon.

SUGGESTED USE

This sublime digestive can be consumed throughout
the day.

Mandarin Sweets

EASY

ingredients for 4 people
time: 2 hours and 45 minutes

8 4/5 tbsp softened butter
4/5 cup icing sugar
2 tbsp grated tangerine peel
2 tbsp tangerine juice
2 cups flour
baking powder (a tip of teaspoon)
2 tsp poppy seeds
1 egg
pearl sugar

In a bowl, work the butter and icing sugar until creamy. Add the
zest and tangerine juice. Combine the flour a little at a time with
the baking powder, working continuously. Finish by adding poppy
seeds. Shape into a ball and lay the dough on a plate, covered with a
damp cloth. Let it rest in the refrigerator for a couple of hours. Flour
the work surface and roll out the dough with a rolling pin. Cut the
biscuits according to your preferred form, and lay them on a baking
sheet lined with parchment paper. Brush with egg and sprinkle with
the pearl sugar. Bake at 356°F (180°C) for 15 minutes, until the edges
do not appear golden. Remove from the oven and serve, sprinkling
everything with icing sugar.

CAIPIROSKA

INGREDIENTS

DRY VODKA
LIME
WHITE OR CANE SUGAR

ORIGINS AND ODDITIES

This is a modern reinterpretation of the famous
Brazilian Caipirinha, which, over the years, has become
one of the most popular drinks in the world.

PREPARATION

Cut 1/2 a lime into cubes, place in a low tumbler and
add 25 g (2 tbsp) of sugar. With a pestle, crush
it all up to make a pulp. Fill the glass with crushed ice
and pour in 50–60 ml (10–12 tsp) of vodka previously
measured in a graduated cylinder.
Stir for a few seconds with a long-handled spoon, to
best mix the ingredients. Serve, garnished with
2 short straws.

SUGGESTED USE

A great drink to be enjoyed at all hours of the day, it
is much loved by younger drinkers and very popular
during happy hour.

 Bruschetta with Capers   EASY

ingredients for 4 people
time: 20 minutes

4 big slices white bread
4 egg yolks
4 tbsp grated cheese
1/2 a mackerel in oil
1.4 oz (about 4 1/2 tbsp) of salted
capers
4 black pitted olives

Finely chop the mackerel and the capers. Put them in a bowl with the
egg yolks and the grated cheese. Mix well. Chop the olives. Spread
the cream on the slices of bread and place the olive bits on top. Heat
in hot oven at 430°F (220°C) for 5 minutes and serve.

GODMOTHER

INGREDIENTS

DRY VODKA
DISARONNO AMARETTO

ORIGINS AND ODDITIES

Created in the United States in the wake of the
Godfather's success, the Godmother, while still
a strong, aromatic drink, had a smoother taste
that was more suitable to the palate of women.

PREPARATION

Measure 55 ml (3 3/4 tbsp) of vodka in a graduated
cylinder and pour into a tumbler filled with ice.
Repeat with 35 ml (2 tbsp + 1 tsp) of Disaronno
Amaretto. Stir with a long-handled spoon and serve.

SUGGESTED USE

An enjoyable digestif, it is suitable for all hours
of the evening.

Mango Flambé   EASY

ingredients for 4 people
time: 30 minutes

4 mangoes
2 1/2 tbsp sugar
zest of 1 orange
juice of 2 oranges
juice of 2 lemons
2 tsp cointreau
2 tsp rum
butter

Wash and peel the mangoes and cut them in half, removing the
core. In a saucepan, melt the butter and add sugar and orange zests.
Drench with Cointreau and stir carefully. Far from the flame, add
the orange and lemon juice, bringing the sauce to a boil. Add the
mangoes and rum, letting flame up again in an abundant fashion.
Serve as soon as the flame goes out.

HARVEY WALLBANGER

INGREDIENTS

DRY VODKA
ORANGE JUICE
GALLIANO LIQUEUR

ORIGINS AND ODDITIES

This cocktail was created in the United States around the 1950s. It is said to have been named after the movie *Harvey*. In the film, Harvey the rabbit repeatedly slams against the wall, and the only one able to see him is the main character, played by James Stewart. For this reason, his family believes he is crazy.

PREPARATION

Measure 50 ml (3 1/3 tbsp) of vodka in a graduated cylinder and pour into a tumbler filled with ice. Repeat with 90 ml (6 tbsp) of orange juice and stir with a long-handled spoon. Measure 20 ml (4 tsp) of Galliano liqueur in a graduated cylinder and lay it on the other ingredients with the help of the spoon. Serve, garnished with 2 long straws, 2 cherries and 1/2 an orange slice.

SUGGESTED USE

This long drink can pleasantly surprise you at all hours of the day.

 Orange Tarts

EASY

ingredients for 4 people
time: 45 minutes

0.66 lbs (10.5 oz) shortcrust pastry
1 1/4 cup orange marmalade
0.22 lbs (3.5 oz) dark chocolate flakes or chips
flour
butter
icing sugar

Flour the work surface, and, with the help of a rolling pin, roll out the pastry until you get a thin sheet. Grease and flour 4 tart molds with the pastry. Prick with a fork and sprinkle the bottom with a layer of dark chocolate chips. Gently add 1 tbsp of orange marmalade and bake for about 20 minutes at 356°F (180°C). To serve, sprinkle with icing sugar.

KAMIKAZE

INGREDIENTS

DRY VODKA
COINTREAU
LEMON JUICE

ORIGINS AND ODDITIES

The name of this cocktail is probably derived from
the Japanese Kamikaze, suicide attacks by military
aviators during World War II. Pilots would try
to crash their aircrafts into enemy ships in an
attempt to sink them.

PREPARATION

Measure 40 ml (2 3/4 tbsp) of vodka in a graduated
cylinder and pour into a shaker. Repeat with 30 ml
(2 tbsp) of Cointreau and 20 ml (4 tsp) of lemon
juice. Add a few ice cubes and shake vigorously
for a few seconds. Serve in a cocktail glass
(pre-chilled in the freezer).

SUGGESTED USE

Good as a digestive, this cocktail, which is very high
in alcohol content, is especially recommended for
lively evenings at the disco.

Bellavista Watermelon   EASY

ingredients for 4 people
time: 30 minutes

1/4 of a watermelon
0.44 lbs (7 oz) fresh blackberries
0.44 lbs (7 oz) fresh raspberries
10 mint leaves
1 tbsp icing sugar
1 shot glass iced vodka

Wash and thinly slice the watermelon, trying to eliminate the majority
of seeds. Wash the blackberries and raspberries in running water,
then let them dry on sheets of absorbent paper. Remove the watermelon rind and cut each slice in half until you have small triangles.
Place on a bed of crushed ice. In a bowl, mix the berries with mint
leaves. Combine the icing sugar and vodka, using a spoon to lay it all
gently on the slices of watermelon. Serve immediately.

NEGROSKI

INGREDIENTS

DRY VODKA
CAMPARI
RED VERMOUTH

ORIGINS AND ODDITIES

A modern variation of the famous Negroni,
with gin replaced by dry vodka.

PREPARATION

Measure 30 ml (2 tbsp) of vodka in a graduated
cylinder and pour into a tumbler filled with ice.
Repeat with 30 ml (2 tbsp) of Campari and 30 ml
(2 tbsp) of red vermouth. Stir with a long-handled
spoon and serve, garnished with 1 orange slice.

SUGGESTED USE

It is a valid alternative to the Negroni cocktail.

Mignon Hamburgers

EASY

ingredients for 4 people
time: 30 minutes

1.3 lbs (21 oz) minced lean beef
1 tsp mustard
2 tbsp ketchup
1 onion
3 eggs
salt
pepper
flour
sunflower seed oil
matchstick french fried potatoes

In a large bowl, mix the ground beef with the eggs using your hands.
Combine the sauce with the finely chopped onion and mix well until everything is smooth and perfectly mixed. Repeat the operation,
after adding salt and pepper, to obtain a homogeneous and well seasoned preparation. With your hands, make small balls of meat, eventually flattening them out to form the classic burger shape. Lightly
flour the burgers and fry them in a pan drizzled with a bit of seed oil
at high heat, turning them occasionally. Serve the burgers piping hot,
accompanied with matchstick french fried potatoes.

SALLY

INGREDIENTS

DRY VODKA   CAMPARI
APEROL   MANDARINETTO ISOLABELLA

ORIGINS AND ODDITIES
This new drink, created by Italian barman Giangranco Di Niso, came in first place in a national 2003 cocktail competition.

PREPARATION
Measure 30 ml (2 tbsp) of vodka in a graduated cylinder and pour into a tumbler filled with ice. Repeat with 30 ml (2 tbsp) of Aperol, 20 ml (4 tsp) of Mandarinetto Isolabella and 10 ml (2 tsp) of Campari. Stir with a long-handled spoon, garnish with 1/2 an orange slice and 2 cherries. Serve.

SUGGESTED USE
A delicious appetizer that will brighten your summer evenings.

Savory Cream Puffs   EASY

ingredients for 4 people
time: 30 minutes

0.26 lbs (4.2 oz) sweet gorgonzola
0.08 lbs (1.41 oz) hazelnuts
16 large puffs
1 tsp paprika
salt and pepper

Finely chop the hazelnuts and season with the paprika, salt and pepper. Work the gorgonzola strongly in a bowl with a wooden spoon, to obtain a smooth cream. Add the seasoned hazelnuts and mix it all further. Abundantly stuff the puffs with the creamy mixture, using a pastry bag, then bake them in the oven for a few minutes at 356°F (180°C). Serve hot.

SAMOA

INGREDIENTS

DRY VODKA
PEACH LIQUEUR
CAMPARI

ORIGINS AND ODDITIES

It seems that this drink was invented around the mid-'80s in a New York City bar when a couple wanted a new drink. The bartender named the resulting cocktail in honor of the island where the lovers had just spent a wonderful holiday.

PREPARATION

Measure 50 ml (3 1/3 tbsp) of vodka in a graduated cylinder and pour into a carafe. Repeat with 20 ml (4 tsp) of Campari and 20 ml (4 tsp) of peach liqueur. Add some ice cubes and stir with a long-handled spoon for several seconds. Pour into a cup (pre-chilled in the freezer), holding the ice back with the help of the spoon. To serve, garnish with 1/2 an orange slice and 1 cherry.

SUGGESTED USE

Excellent as an aperitif and during celebratory summer nights.

 Russian Salad EASY

ingredients for 4 people
time: 2 hours and 30 minutes

0.66 lbs (10.5 oz, about 2 cups) peas
0.66 lbs (10.5 oz, about 2 small
or about 1 1/2 medium) potatoes
0.66 lbs (10.5 oz, about 6 small)
carrots
1 1/4 cup mayonnaise
salt
pepper
parsley

Wash and peel the potatoes and carrots, cutting into pea-sized cubes. Place them in separate pots and boil in salted water. Once the vegetables are cooked, drain and leave to cool. Add the mayonnaise to the vegetables and mix well with a spoon. Season with salt and pepper and let rest in refrigerator for at least 1 hour. Serve your Russian salad on a serving dish, sprinkling chopped parsley to taste.

SEA BREEZE

INGREDIENTS

DRY VODKA
GRAPEFRUIT JUICE
CRANBERRY JUICE

ORIGINS AND ODDITIES

Created around the late 1920s, this drink initially
counted grenadine among its ingredients instead
of cranberry juice.

PREPARATION

Measure 50 ml (3 1/3 tbsp) of vodka in a graduated
cylinder and pour into a tall tumbler filled with ice.
Repeat with 50 ml (3 1/3 tbsp) of grapefruit juice
and 60 ml (1/4 cup) of cranberry juice. Mix the
ingredients well with a long-handled spoon and
serve, garnished with 2 long straws and 1 slice
of lemon.

SUGGESTED USE

This long drink can be enjoyed at all hours of the day.

Stuffed Grapefruits   EASY

ingredients for 4 people
time: 1 hour and 30 minutes

4 grapefruits
3/8 cup rice
salt
3 tbsp sugar
1 sachet vanilla sugar
lemon juice
4 shot glasses grand marnier
4 tbsp black cherries in syrup
whipped cream

Cut the grapefruits at 2/3 of their height and empty them, being
careful not to damage the skin. Cut the pulp into small cubes. Cook
the rice in salted water and cool under running cold water. In a bowl,
mix the rice with sugar, vanilla sugar, lemon juice, Grand Marnier and
diced grapefruit. Stuff each grapefruit with a spoonful of cherry syrup, then fill to the brim with the rice mixture. Let stand in refrigerator for 30 minutes and serve, garnished with sour cherries and tufts
of whipped cream.

VODKA MARTINI BOND

INGREDIENTS

DRY VODKA
DRY VERMOUTH

ORIGINS AND ODDITIES

A successful remake of the classic Martini Cocktail.
It was named after the famous agent 007, who
in his films often orders a Martini Cocktail with
two variations: shaken, not stirred, and with dry
vodka replacing gin.

PREPARATION

Measure 75 ml (5 tbsp) of vodka in a graduated
cylinder and pour into a shaker. Repeat with 15 ml
(1 tbsp) of dry vermouth. Add a few ice cubes and
shake vigorously for a few seconds. Pour into
a pre-chilled cocktail glass and serve, garnished
with a lemon rind and 2–3 green olives, skewered on
a long toothpick.

SUGGESTED USE

Very dry and very strong, this remains one of the
most popular drinks in the world.

Czarina Small Dumplings   EASY

ingredients for 4 people
time: 45 minutes

0.88 lbs (14 oz) potato small dumplings
0.13 lbs (2.1 oz) black caviar
0.33 lbs (5.3 oz) smoked salmon
dry vodka
butter
cooking cream
chopped parsley
salt and pepper

In a pan, melt a little butter and fry the smoked salmon, cut into
strips, for few minutes. Add plenty of dry vodka, cooking cream and
the caviar. Continue to cook until all ingredients are mixed. When the
sauce is ready, add salt and pepper to taste. Boil the gnocchi in salted water and transfer them directly into the sauce. Before serving,
sprinkle everything with the crushed parsley.

VODKA SOUR PASSION

INGREDIENTS

DRY VODKA
LEMON JUICE

SUGAR SYRUP AND PASSION
FRUIT SYRUP (OR JUICE)

ORIGINS AND ODDITIES
A drink that came from the famous Whisky Sour, it was created in the late 1980s and has, since then, never ceased being a popular drink among the most trendy young people.

PREPARATION
Measure 40 ml (2 3/4 tbsp) of vodka in a graduated cylinder and pour into a shaker. Repeat with 20 ml (4 tsp) of lemon juice, 10 ml (2 tsp) of sugar syrup and 20 ml (4 tsp) of passion fruit juice of syrup. Add some ice cubes and shake for a few seconds. Pour into a cup, pre-chilled in the freezer.

SUGGESTED USE
Commonly considered an aphrodisiac, it is a digestive drink loved by young people and most often consumed during the evenings for relaxation and fun.

Crêpes Suzette

MEDIUM

ingredients for 4 people
time: 1 hour and 30 minutes

1 2/3 cups flour
2/3 cup butter
2 1/8 cups milk
1 shot glass grand marnier
1/2 cup (8 tbsp) sugar
2 eggs
salt
zest of 1 lemon
icing sugar

Break the eggs into a large bowl and work them with a whisk, adding a pinch of salt, 1 tbsp of sugar and flour. While still mixing, add 1 1/3 tbsp of melted, almost cold, butter, and about 1 cup of milk. Continue to work the ingredients with a whisk, until the mixture is smooth. Add the remaining milk and leave to rest in a cool place for 30 minutes. In a crêpes pan, melt a knob of butter and pour a ladle of the batter, spreading it evenly with the flick of the wrist. When the crêpe starts to brown, turn it on the other side. Continue to cook for no more than 1 minute and remove from heat. Repeat for the number of crêpes needed, stacking them in a bowl, so they stay warm. In a small saucepan, melt 1/3 cup of butter and add the remaining sugar and Grand Marnier. Continue to cook over low heat until you get a kind of syrup. Fold the crêpes in four and lay them in a frying pan, basting with a bit of syrup and a few drops of Grand Marnier. Let the flame rise, and, as soon as the heat diminishes, serve hot, garnished with icing sugar and lemon zest.

WHITE SPIDER

INGREDIENTS

DRY VODKA
CRÈME DE MENTHE BLANCHE
(WHITE MINT LIQUEUR)

ORIGINS AND ODDITIES

Created in America in the late 1960s, it was
developed as a remedy to hot summer evenings.
In Northern Europe, the dose of vodka is usually
increased at the expense of the mint.

PREPARATION

Measure 50 ml (3 1/3 tbsp) of vodka in a graduated
cylinder and pour into a tumbler filled with ice.
Repeat with 40 ml (2 3/4 tbsp) of crème de menthe
blanche. Mix with a long-handled spoon and serve,
garnished with a nice sprig of fresh mint and 2 short
straws.

SUGGESTED USE

A refreshing drink, it is very effective as a digestive.

 Mint Pudding   EASY

ingredients for 6/8 people
time: 30 minutes +
cooling time (3 hours)

6 egg yolks
1 cup (16 tbsp) sugar
2 1/2 cups milk
4 tbsp mint syrup
1 tbsp flour
vanilla
fresh mint

Boil the milk, and, once removed from heat, add the vanilla. Mix
thoroughly and let stand for 5 minutes. Pour the mint syrup into
the milk and mix again. In a bowl, beat the sugar with the yolks, then
add the flour and milk. Pour into a saucepan and put it back on the
heat for a few minutes. Stir constantly, being careful that the mixture
does not come to boil. Remove from heat and let the cream cool.
When it has cooled, pour into a pudding mold and let them sit in
the refrigerator for at least 3 hours. Just before serving, remove the
pudding from the mold, decorate as desired with fresh mint leaves
and mint syrup.

RUM-BASED COCKTAILS

The production of rum from sugar cane began on the island of Barbados in the seventeenth century, thanks to the Dutch and their knowledge of distillation. The great colonial empires – French, English and Spanish – began to work the sugarcane to obtain a raw and very coarse product, which they gave to slaves and sailors in the form of a daily ration. Though they all called it rum (or ron), the distillation process differed, with each country applying knowledge and techniques related to their national spirits: French distillers used the production methods of cognac; the British used the gin distiller; and the Spanish had the soleras method. These styles are still readily apparent.

Between the mid-eighteenth and mid-nineteenth century, rum began to be appreciated and it spread to much of Europe, its production, becoming, in the process, a real business. The arrival in Europe of the phylloxera, an insect that destroyed European vineyards in the mid-nineteenth century and deprived the military of their daily ration of cognac, meant that France requisitioned rum from Martinique and Guadeloupe (they were the first manufacturers in the world, with production going back to the twentieth century) and allocated it to its military.

At the beginning of the twentieth century, the spread of beets and beet sugar brought down the price of cane sugar, and resulted in an economic crisis in many Caribbean countries. In the 1930s, Prohibition slowed the spread of rum in the United States.

Rum has had to deal with spirits that were considered more noble and refined, remaining for decades as something used only in mixed drinks and cocktails. It is only recently that aged rum has been considered on the same plane as cognac and whisky.

The production of rum begins with the harvest (cut) in a sugar cane plantation, which is done by hand in the period between February and July. The cut has to be performed between the first and fourth node because this is the point where there is the maximum concentration of sugar. Within 24 hours the canes are taken to a sugar refinery to prevent spontaneous fermentation.

From the crushed cane, the first juice is obtained, as is bagasse, a waste material used in the production of cachaça (a Brazilian distillate). Once the juice is worked, you get crystallized sugar and molasses that contain non-crystallized sugar.

The molasses are then sent to the distillery and, depending on the style of production, there are a number of options for raw materials, distillation and aging methods. Industrial rum is produced from molasses while French rum is distilled from the first juice (vesou). The

distillation method is the second step that can be distinguished according to the style of production, with two different types of stills: discontinous and continous alembic stills.

During the distillation process, the head and tail are eliminated (because they are rich in noxious alcohol) and the heart is kept. The resulting liquid has an alcohol content ranging from 65% vol to 95% vol based on the alembic. At this point, a method of aging is selected, with it often depending on the product you want to sell.

It is a widespread opinion that the quality of rum increases with the amount of years spent in the barrel. Rum is colorless before aging, and it acquires its color from prolonged contact with the slats of the barrels. Rum is aged in barrels that have already been used in the aging process of other products. For example, French rum barrels are previously used in the aging of cognac, while British rum barrels previously contained sherry.

An interesting fact is that a year of aging in the Caribbean is equivalent to 2-3 years in Scotland, thanks to the tropical climate. On the other hand, the same tropical climate means that the heart of the distillate evaporates in large quantities, freeing the so-called "Part of the Angels."

Most rums on the market are a blend of different aged rums, which are assembled to ensure a certain continuity of sensory characteristics for a certain brand. Rums, aside from those derived from the former colonial powers, are divided into agricultural and industrial products, and then subdivided in turn into light rum and dark rum.

Before hitting the market, clear rum undergoes at least one year of aging and appears delicate and light. Dark rum differs mostly by the addition of caramel, making it sweeter and preferable in cocktails and mixes.

There are no specific glasses used for rum, but it is well to serve it in a large balloon glass to facilitate oxygenation and to free the entire panel of aromas and flavors. It's important, however, to select the right rum for what you plan to use it for. In cocktails, industrial rum is preferred by the general public for its convenience and immediacy of taste.

Industrial light rums are often used in fresh cocktails, such as the famous Mojito, Daiquiri, Piña Colada, Bacardi, and Planter's Punch. Industrial dark rums are preferably used with soft drinks, for example, it combines with coca-cola to form the very famous Cuba Libre, a cocktail invented in Cuba to celebrate independence from Spanish rule.

Agricultural rums are used only for tasting because they are characterized by a pronounced, intense flavor that is almost harsh. They can be used in cocktails, but it is advisable to use drops, only to strengthen the scent of a cocktail.

BACARDI

INGREDIENTS

BACARDI WHITE RUM
LEMON OR LIME JUICE
GRENADINE SYRUP

ORIGINS AND ODDITIES

This cocktail seems to have been created in the
United States around 1917, when the ingredients
of a rum Daiquiri were enlivened with a new
addition: Bacardi, Cuban rum named after the
entrepreneur who brought it to market.

PREPARATION

Measure 50 ml (3 1/3 tbsp) of Bacardi white rum in
a graduated cylinder and pour into a shaker. Repeat
with 30 ml (2 tbsp) of lemon or lime juice and 10 ml
(2 tsp) of grenadine syrup. Add some ice cubes and
shake vigorously for a few seconds. Pour into a glass
(pre-chilled in the freezer) and serve.

SUGGESTED USE

An exquisite digestive that can be enjoyed
throughout the evening.

Lemon Meringue

MEDIUM

ingredients for 6/8 people
time: 2 hours and 30 minutes

1 5/8 cups (22 tbsp) sugar
4 eggs
3/4 cup butter
1 2/3 cups flour
juice of 3 lemons
zest of 3 lemons

In a large bowl, work the flour with the butter. In a bowl, using a whisk,
amalgamate the grated zest from 1 lemon with 5 tbsp (1/3 cup) of
sugar and 1 egg. When you get an even homogeneous froth, merge
with the mixture in the terrine. Mix everything and cover with plastic wrap. Leave to rest in the refrigerator for roughly an hour. Work
1/4 cup + 3 tbsp of sugar with 3 yolks. Add the other lemon zest and
cook everything in a bain-marie without letting it boil. Remove from
the heat and let cool. With a rolling pin, roll your dough on oven paper.
Cut a circle and line a cake tin. Lightly pierce the bottom with a fork
and fill abundantly with beans, covering everything with oven paper.
Bake at 400°F (200°C) for 30 minutes. Remove the paper and beans and
continue cooking for other 10 minutes. Beat with the rest of the sugar
the remaining egg whites until firm, and pour into the cooked base.
Bake for another 5 minutes at 400°F (200°C).

BAHAMA MAMA

INGREDIENTS

DARK RUM
MALIBU LIQUEUR
PINEAPPLE JUICE

BANANA CREAM
ORANGE JUICE
GRENADINE SYRUP

ORIGINS AND ODDITIES

This drink was born on the beaches of Malibu, where it quickly became popular among the swimmers in the area.

PREPARATION

Measure 20 ml (4 tsp) of rum in a graduated cylinder and pour in a shaker. Repeat with 20 ml (4 tsp) of Malibu liqueur, 20 ml (4 tsp) of banana cream, 30 ml (2 tbsp) of orange juice, 60 ml (1/4 cup) of pineapple juice and 10 ml (2 tsp) of grenadine syrup. Add some ice cubes and shake vigorously for a few seconds. Pour into a tall tumbler filled with ice, garnish with 1/2 pineapple slices, 1/2 an orange slice, 2 cherries and 2 long straws.

SUGGESTED USE

A good long drink that can be enjoyed at any hour of the day.

Summer Breeze

EASY

ingredients for 6/8 people
time: 30 minutes +
cooling time (2 hours)

0.44 lbs (7 oz) biscuits
1/2 cup (8 tbsp) sugar
7 tbsp butter
3/8 cup (6 tbsp) coconut flour
1/5 cup milk
0.88 lbs (14 oz) fresh ricotta
1 cup batida de coco
1 vial vanilla flavoring
shredded coconut

In a bowl, soften the coconut flour, adding 1 1/3 tbsp of milk. Work the butter until creamy and add, in order, sugar, the batida, the ricotta, and finally the coconut (including milk that has deposited on the bottom of the bowl). Mix well, until the mixture is homogeneous. In a soup plate, pour the remaining milk, diluted with 1 tsp of vanilla flavoring. In a pan, pour a layer of cream, covering it with ladyfingers soaked in flavored milk. Repeat, creating the second layer of the cake. Top with a generous layer of cream. Let stand in refrigerator for 2 hours, and, a second before serving, sprinkle with the grated coconut.

CAIPIRISSIMA

INGREDIENTS

WHITE RUM
LIME
WHITE SUGAR OR CANE SUGAR

ORIGINS AND ODDITIES

A variation of the more famous Caipirinha, this drink seems to have been designed to meet the growing demands of female drinkers, who love the delicate flavor of rum.

PREPARATION

Place 1/2 a lime, cut into cubes, in a low tumbler. Add 25 g (2 tbsp) of sugar and crush it all with a pestle until it's a pulp. Add crushed ice and 50–60 ml (10–12 tsp) of rum previously measured in a graduated cylinder. Stir for a few seconds with a long-handled spoon, to best mix the ingredients, Serve, garnished with 2 short straws.

SUGGESTED USE

An excellent refreshing drink that can be adapted for use from morning to night.

Ginger-Marinated Swordfish   EASY

ingredients for 4 people
time: 3 hours and 30 minutes

0.88 lbs (14 oz) thinly sliced fresh swordfish (classic carpaccio style)
1 small fresh ginger root
fresh basil
4 lemons
4 tbsp extra virgin olive oil
salt and pepper

Thoroughly rinse and squeeze the lemons, pouring the juice into a rectangular terracotta bowl that will allow you to fully immerse the swordfish carpaccio. Let it marinate for 3 hours. Drain the swordfish, blotting, if necessary with paper towels and place it on a serving plate. Clean the ginger and grate into a gravy boat. Combine the extra virgin olive oil, salt and pepper to taste, then mix it all with a fork. Sprinkle the swordfish with plenty of ginger sauce, garnishing with beautiful fresh basil leaves and small triangles of lemon. Serve.

CARIBBEAN COFFEE

INGREDIENTS

DARK RUM
COFFEE LIQUEUR
CANE OR WHITE SUGAR

LONG COFFEE
CREAM

ORIGINS AND CURIOSITIES

A variation of the more famous Irish Coffee, this drink was created in the 1950s in the only place where rum is typically distilled: the Caribbean Islands.

PREPARATION

Measure 40 ml (2 3/4 tbsp) of rum in a graduated cylinder and pour it into a milk jug, repeating the operation with 20 ml (4 tsp) of coffee liqueur. Combine 1 tbsp of sugar and 1 long coffee. Bring to a boil, stirring occasionally. Pour into a heat resistant mug and, just before serving, add 40 ml (2 3/4 tbsp) of cream (previously measured in a graduated cylinder), using the edge of the teaspoon, so that it remains separate from the rest.

SUGGESTED USE

A drink with strong tonic properties, it is recommended during the cooler times of the year.

Coffee Flames   EASY

ingredients for 4 people
time: 45 minutes +
cooling time (3 hours)

10.58 oz (10.5 oz) dark chocolate
5 abundant tsbp instant coffee
6 tbsp + 2 tsp (2/5 cup) fresh cream
sweet coffee beans

Coarsely chop the chocolate and melt in a bain-marie. In a saucepan, pour the cream and dilute it with coffee. Heat over a low heat without let it boil, then add the melted chocolate, mixing the ingredients continously with a whisk. Remove from heat and let cool. Fill a pastry bag (with a serrated spout) with the mixture and squeeze it in small clumps in paper cups. Garnish with the extremities of the chocolates with a coffee bean. Store in the fridge for at least 3 hours before serving.

RUM AND PEAR SHOOTER
(RUM AND PEAR CHUPITO)

INGREDIENTS

DARK RUM
PEAR JUICE

ORIGINS AND ODDITIES
Created as a late evening drink around the 1980s,
it would soon became much loved among the
newest generations of cocktail drinkers.

PREPARATION
Measure 30 ml (2 tbsp) of rum in a graduated
cylinder and pour into a shot glass (chupito). Repeat
with 30 ml (2 tbsp) of pear juice and serve.

SUGGESTED USE
Excellent after a meal.

 "Cat's Tongue" Biscuits   EASY

ingredients for 4 people
time: 1 hour

14 tbsp (7/8 cup) butter
1 2/3 cups flour
0.30 lbs (4.9 oz) dark chocolate
1 1/3 cup icing sugar
1 vanilla sachet
6 egg whites

Prepare a froth, softening the butter in a bowl and then adding the
sugar. Add the sifted flour gradually, to avoid lumps and beat the
egg whites until firm. Fill a pastry bag (made with a round sprout)
with the mixture. Grease and flour a baking sheet and carefully draw
cat tongues (about 5 cm in length), making sure to leave a good
distance between each one. Bake for 15 minutes at 356°F (180°C).
Meanwhile, melt the chocolate in a bain-marie. Pour into a bowl and
dip half of the freshly baked cat tongues. Place them on a tray and
allow to set. To serve, sprinkle with a little icing sugar.

DAIQUIRI

INGREDIENTS

WHITE RUM
LEMON OR LIME JUICE
LIQUID SUGAR

ORIGINS AND ODDITIES

Many legends revolve around the origin of this drink.
One of them tells the story of a team of engineers
who decided, one late afternoon after work in the
early 1900s, to prepare a drink by mixing the
ingredients at their disposal: rum, sugar and lime.
What they created proved so palatable it soon
became the famous cocktail we know today. It was
named in honor of the Daiquiri town that housed the
copper mine at which the engineers were working.

PREPARATION

Measure 50 ml (3 1/3 tbsp) of rum in a graduated cylinder
and pour into a shaker. Repeat with 30 ml
(2 tbsp) of lemon or lime juice and 10 ml (2 tsp) of sugar
syrup. Add a few ice cubes and shake vigorously for a few
seconds. Pour into a glass (pre-chilled in the freezer) and
serve.

SUGGESTED USE

Excellent both as an after dinner digestive or as
a refreshing drink throughout the day.

Rum Caresses   EASY

ingredients for 4 people
time: 1 hour and 30 minutes

1 oz chopped raisins
2 3/4 tbsp white rum
1/3 cup + 1 tbsp flour
3 1/2 tbsp (1/4 cup) butter at room
temperature
1/3 cup icing sugar
drops of vanilla extract
1 beaten egg
pearl sugar

Pour the rum in a bowl and let the raisins soak for 1 hour. Work the
butter and sugar in a bowl. Add the vanilla extract and egg while still
stirring the mixture, thus preventing lumps. Gradually add the sifted
flour and raisins (well drained from the rum). Mix everything to best
blend the mixture. With a pastry bag with a large spout, decorate the
sweets directly on the baking sheet, letting your imagination guide you
(the size of each caress, however, should not exceed 3 cm in diameter).
Bake for 10 minutes at 356°F (180°C) and serve, sprinkling everything
with the pearl sugar.

GROG

INGREDIENTS

DARK RUM

CANE OR WHITE SUGAR

MINERAL WATER

SMALL CUBES OF LEMON

SMALL CUBES OF ORANGE

CLOVES

CINNAMON

ORIGINS AND ODDITIES

The ancient origins of this cocktail bring us back to the eighteenth century when, during a crossing of the English Channel, admiral Edward Old Grog Vernon decided to boil the drinking water on his ship, adding, while cooking, some spices, sugar cane and rum. The result was a mixture capable of warming you up and soothing the stomach. The drink took its name from its creator, who was also famous for the Gros Grain, a waterproof fabric that he used to wear.

PREPARATION

Measure 50 ml (3 1/3 tbsp) of dark rum in a graduated cylinder and pour into a milk jug. Repeat with 50 ml (3 1/3 tbsp) of natural water. Combine 5–6 cloves, 3 lemon cubes, 3 orange cubes, 1/2 tsp of cinnamon and 1 tbsp of sugar. Bring to a boil and serve in a heat resistant mug.

SUGGESTED USE

A drink with invigorating properties when temperatures are very cold. It is also excellent as a remedy for stomach pains.

 Chocolate Truffles   EASY

ingredients for 4 people
time: 1 hour and 30 minutes

0.88 lbs (14 oz) chestnuts
3 1/2 tbsp (1/4 cup) butter
2/3 cup cream
2 tbsp rum
0.48 lbs (7.76 oz) dark chocolate
unsweetened cocoa powder

Boil the chestnuts for 20 minutes. Drain and immediately discard the skins, mixing it all in the mixer. Heat the butter and cream in a saucepan. Combine the chestnuts and rum and continue to cook for 10 minutes without stirring. Remove from heat and let cool. Melt the chocolate in a bain-marie, then add it to the chestnuts. When lukewarm, form the truffles with the help of two spoons, rolling several times in the cocoa powder just before serving.

JAMAICA'S DREAM

INGREDIENTS

LIGHT RUM	TROPICAL JUICE
DARK RUM	MANGO SYRUP
PASSION LIQUEUR	PAPAYA SYRUP

ORIGINS AND ODDITIES

This recently created drink refers to the famous Jamaican cooking pot. It is highly alcoholic and rich in tropical fruit.

PREPARATION

Measure 30 ml (2 tbsp) of dark rum in a graduated cylinder and pour into a shaker. Repeat with 30 ml (2 tbsp) of light rum, 30 ml (2 tbsp) of Passion liqueur, 50 ml (3 1/3 tbsp) of tropical juice, 10 ml (2 tsp) of papaya syrup and 10 ml (2 tsp) of mango syrup. Add some ice cubes and shake vigorously for a few seconds. Pour into a glass cup filled with ice. Cover with plenty of crushed ice and have fun in decorating as desired, alternating slices of mango, papaya, passion fruit, pineapple, banana. To serve, garnish with 2 long straws and some toothpicks.

SUGGESTED USE

This lively drink will delight your guests, and can enliven every hour of the day and evening.

Passion Cake

EASY

ingredients for 6/8 people
time: 1 hour and 30 minutes

3 passion fruit
3 eggs
1 2/3 cups flour
1/3 cup cornstarch
1/2 cup + 2 tbsp sugar
2/3 cup milk
4 1/2 tbsp plain yoghurt
1 packet baking powder
icing sugar

In a bowl mix the sugar with the eggs, until you obtain a frothy mixture. Gently combine the yogurt, mixing it with the rest. Add the milk, sifted flour and cornstarch (previously mixed with yeast). Complete, combining the dough with the pulp from 2 passion fruit. Pour the batter into a cake mold and bake at 356°F (180°C) for about 40 minutes. Meanwhile prepare the glaze by the pulp of the remaining fruit with 1 tbsp of warm water and a bit of icing sugar in a bowl. Remove from the oven and serve the cake, accompanied with the icing/glaze (which can be poured on the cake before serving, or served separately in a beautiful gravy boat).

JUS D'AMOUR BARBARA

INGREDIENTS

WHITE RUM
MARASCHINO LIQUEUR
PINEAPPLE JUICE

STRAWBERRY PUREE OR
STRAWBERRY JUICE
GRENADINE SYRUP

ORIGINS AND ODDITIES

This cocktail was created in 2007 by bartender
Gianfranco Di Niso, who won an international
competition organized by Italian magazine
Bargionale in Malaysia.

PREPARATION

Measure 30 ml (2 tbsp) of rum in a graduated
cylinder and pour in a shaker. Repeat with 20 ml
(4 tsp) of Maraschino liqueur, 70 ml (4 tbsp + 2 tsp)
of pineapple juice, 30 ml (2 tbsp) of strawberry juice
and 10 ml (2 tsp) of grenadine syrup. Add some ice
cubes and shake vigorously for a few seconds. Pour
into tall tumbler filled with ice and serve, garnished
with 1/2 a slice of pineapple, 2 cherries and
2 long straws.

SUGGESTED USE

An excellent long drink that is low in alcohol and
sweet on the palate, it is particularly loved by
women and suitable for any time of day.

 ## Strawberry Tiramisù

EASY

ingredients for 6/8 people
time: 1 hour +
cooling time (4 hours)

0.33 lbs (5.3 oz) "savoiardi" (ladyfinger)
biscuits
0.55 lbs (8.8 oz, about 2 1/2 cup) mascarpone
(original Italian cream cheese)
0.55 lbs (8.8 oz) ricotta
0.55 lbs (8.8 oz, about 1 5/8 cups) fresh
strawberries
1 orange
3 tbsp sugar
3/4 cup fresh cream
1 tbsp cognac
1/2 a vanilla stick
cocoa powder

In a large bowl, work the ricotta, the mascarpone, the juice and the
grated rind of 1 orange, 2 tbsp of sugar and 1/2 a vanilla stick. Gently
add the whipped cream. Wash the strawberries and mix them in the
mixer along with 1 tbsp of cognac and 1 tbsp of sugar. At the bottom
of a baking dish place a layer of ladyfinger biscuits, and the strawberry
and cream (mascarpone and ricotta) mixture. Let stand for at least 3
hours in the refrigerator and 30 minutes in the freezer, just before
serving tiramisù. Garnish with a light dusting of cocoa and some beautiful, fresh strawberries.

MAI TAI

INGREDIENTS

LIGHT RUM   COINTREAU
DARK RUM   GRENADINE SYRUP
LIME OR LEMON JUICE   ORGEAT SYRUP

ORIGINS AND ODDITIES

This drink sprung from the imagination of Victor J.
Bergeron in 1944. He then introduced the recipe
to the menu at Trader Vic's, a popular restaurant
chain. The name came from the Tahitian "mai tai ro
a ae" ("the end of the world and nothing better"), an
exclamation uttered by a Tahitian couple after tasting
the drink.

PREPARATION

Measure 30 ml (2 tbsp) of light rum in a graduated
cylinder and pour into a shaker. Repeat with 30 ml
(2 tbsp) of dark rum, 30 ml (2 tbsp) of Cointreau,
50 ml (3 1/3 tbsp) of lime or lemon juice, 10 ml
(2 tsp) of grenadine syrup and 10 ml (2 tsp) of
orgeat syrup. Add some ice cubes and shake
vigorously for a few seconds. Pour into a tall
tumbler filled with ice and serve, garnished
with 1/2 a slice of pineapple, 2 cherries, a nice
sprig of fresh mint and 2 long straws.

SUGGESTED USE

This long drink can be enjoyable at every moment
of your day.

Pine Nut Uglies

EASY

ingredients for 4 people
time: 1 hour and 45 minutes

1 1/4 cups sugar
0.30 lbs (4.9 oz, about 5/8 cup)
pine nuts
0.35 lbs (5.6 oz, about 1 7/8 cup)
almonds
2 egg whites
1/2 vanilla sachet
cinnamon powder

Grease well with butter in a large baking pan and lay heaps of pine
nuts. Mix the almonds in the mixer and put them in a bowl. Add sugar
and vanilla. Giving a first mix with a spoon and add the egg whites
(beaten until firm). Gently mix all the ingredients and cover every pile
of pine nuts with 1 tbsp of the mixture. Allow to stand for 1 hour and
bake at 325°F (160°C) for 10 minutes. Let cool and serve, garnished
with sliced almonds and a dusting of cinnamon.

PAPA DOBLE

INGREDIENTS

WHITE RUM

GRAPEFRUIT JUICE

LIME OR LEMON JUICE

MARASCHINO LIQUEUR

ORIGINS AND CURIOSITIES

This cocktail was created at the Floridita bar in Cuba and it counted among its greatest admirers famed novelist Ernest Hemingway, who used to have a few every day. Eventually, customers in the area gave him the friendly nickname "Papa Hemingway".

PREPARATION

Measure 40 ml (2 3/4 tbsp) of rum in a graduated cylinder and pour into a food processor. Repeat with 10 ml (2 tsp) of Maraschino liqueur, 20 ml (4 tsp) of lemon or lime juice and 20 ml (4 tsp) of grapefruit juice. Add 3 tablespoons of crushed ice and blend for about 15 seconds. Pour into a low tumbler and serve, garnished with 1 grapefruit segment and 2 short straws.

SUGGESTED USE

A drink with strong thirst-quenching properties, it is perfect for the hottest hours of the day.

 Hearts of Palm Salad   EASY

ingredients for 4 people
time: 30 minutes +
cooling time (30 minutes)

0.53 lbs (8.5 oz) canned hearts
of palm
4 avocados
2 grapefruits
8 cherry tomatoes
0.39 lbs (6.35 oz, about 41) pitted
black olives
juice of 1 lemon
salt
pepper
extra virgin olive oil
belgian endive

Drain the hearts of palm and cut into thick slices. Wash and clean the avocado, then dicing them. Repeat with grapefruit and tomatoes. In a bowl, combine the olives and pour the hearts of palm, grapefruit, avocado and tomatoes. Gently mix the ingredients, season to taste with salt, pepper, extra virgin olive oil and lemon juice. Wash the endive leaves and arrange on an appetizer serving plate, so as to create the illusion of baskets. Add the hearts of palm salad in the center of each, and, before serving, allow to cool in the refrigerator for 30 minutes.

PLANTER'S PUNCH

INGREDIENTS

DARK RUM
LEMON OR LIME JUICE
GRENADINE SYRUP

SODA WATER OR
SPARKLING WATER

ORIGINS AND ODDITIES

Imported into the United Kingdom by the sailors of the British East India Company in 1632, this drink was used in Jamaica in 1879 on the occasion of the inauguration of the Myers Rum Distillery.

PREPARATION

Measure 50 ml (3 1/3 tbsp) of rum in a graduated cylinder and pour into a shaker. Repeat with 40 ml (2 3/4 tbsp) of lemon or lime juice and 20 ml (4 tsp) of grenadine syrup. Add some ice cubes and shake vigorously for a few seconds. Pour into a tall tumbler filled with ice and fill almost to the brim with 50 ml (3 1/3 tbsp) of soda previously measured in the graduated cylinder. Mix with a long-handled spoon and serve, garnished with 1/2 an orange slice, 2 cherries and 2 long straws.

SUGGESTED USE

A pleasant long drink that you can drink freely at all hours of the day.

Pomegranate Scaloppine

EASY

ingredients for 4 people
time: 40 minutes

8 slices of veal
1 large ripe pomegranate
3/4 cup sour cream
1/2 a glass dry white wine
parsley
salt
pepper
flour
extra virgin olive oil

Wash and peel the pomegranate, collecting the seeds in a bowl. Add salt and pepper, and flour the veal slices thoroughly. Heat extra virgin olive oil in a large pan, let both sides brown for about 3 minutes. Add the white wine, letting it evaporate over high heat. Add the cream, 2/3 of the pomegranate seeds and a sprinkling of chopped parsley. Let the sauce simmer for another 5 minutes and serve, garnishing with the remaining pomegranate seeds.

RUM COLLINS

INGREDIENTS

LIGHT RUM
LEMON JUICE
SUGAR SYRUP

SODA WATER OR
SPARKLING WATER

ORIGINS AND ODDITIES

This drink owes its name to the Collins family
(of English descent). Brothers Tom, John and
Pierre created the cocktail, using an ingredient
from all the places each of them had emigrated.

PREPARATION

Measure 50 ml (3 1/3 tbsp) of rum in a graduated
cylinder and pour into a tall tumbler filled with ice.
Repeat with 20 ml (4 tsp) of lemon juice and 10 ml (2
tsp) of sugar syrup. Fill almost to the rim with soda
water or mineral water. Mix everything together
with a long-handled spoon and serve, garnished
with 1/2 a slice of lemon, 2 cherries
and 2 long straws.

SUGGESTED USE

A greatly refreshing drink suitable for all hours
of the day.

 Creamy Raspberry Boats   EASY

ingredients for 4 people
time: 2 hours

0.66 lbs (10.5 oz) pastry
0.44 lbs (7 oz) milk chocolate
1/3 cup flour
3 tbsp butter
2 eggs
1/2 cup (8 tbsp) sugar
2 lemons
1 cup water
raspberries

On a floured work surface roll out the dough to obtain a thin layer.
Grease and flour the tartlet molds and line with the pastry. Bake for
15 minutes at 356°F (180°C). After removing from the oven, allow
to cool before removing them from the molds. Melt the chocolate
in a bain-marie and spread 1/2 tsp on the bottom of each tart. In a
saucepan boil the rind of the lemon and the butter with the water.
In the meantime, work the egg yolks with sugar in a bowl until it is
creamy, smooth and frothy. Combine with the flour gradually, and
then add the lemon-flavored water (previously passed through a
sieve). Pour the mixture into a saucepan, boiling it on low heat for
10 minutes. Remove from heat and add the lemon juice and egg
whites until stiff. Gently mix everything together and let cool for
1 hour. With a pastry bag, stuff the boats and serve, decorating with
raspberries.

TURQUOISE BLUE

INGREDIENTS

LIGHT RUM	PINEAPPLE JUICE
COINTREAU	LEMON JUICE
BLUE CURAÇAO	

ORIGINS AND ODDITIES

Created in the kiosks that populate Hawaiian beaches, this drink got its name from the turquoise sea that bathes the paradise islands of the area.

PREPARATION

Measure 20 ml (4 tsp) of rum in a graduated cylinder and pour in a shaker. Repeat with 20 ml (4 tsp) of Cointreau, 20 ml (4 tsp) of Blue Curaçao, 80 ml (1/3 cup) of pineapple juice and 20 ml (4 tsp) of lemon juice. Add a few ice cubes and shake vigorously for a few seconds. Pour into a tall tumbler filled with ice and serve, garnished with 1/2 a slice of pineapple, 2 cherries and 2 long straws.

SUGGESTED USE

This long drink is perfect for every hour of the day.

Citrus Dessert   EASY

ingredients for 4 people
time: 1 hour +
cooling time (3 hours)

2 egg yolks
1/4 cup + 1 1/2 tbsp sugar
3 1/3 tbsp citron juice
3 1/3 tbsp rum
grated zest of 1 lemon
whipped cream

for the sauce:
1 cup milk
2 egg yolks
2/3 cup sugar
mint syrup and fresh mint leaves

In a small saucepan create a syrup, heating the sugar with the lime juice and lemon zest. Beat the yolks with a whisk until creamy and foamy and add it to the boiling sugar. Remove from heat, stirring occasionally, and allow to cool. Then incorporate the whipped cream and liqueur, mixing the ingredients from the bottom, so that it mixes well. Pour into four ramekins for creme caramel and leave to rest in the freezer for at least 3 hours. In the meantime you can prepare the accompanying sauce, boiling the milk in a saucepan with a hint of mint syrup and whole mint leaves. Remove from heat and let stand for 20 minutes. In a bowl, beat the egg yolks and sugar with a whisk sugar until mixture is smooth and fluffy. Combine the milk (passed through a strainer) and simmer in a saucepan over medium heat for 5 minutes, being careful that it does not stick and does not form lumps. Just before serving, unmold the citron desserts into 4 dessert bowls, drowning everything with the sauce.

ZOMBIE

INGREDIENTS

WHITE RUM

AMBER RUM

DARK RUM

APRICOT BRANDY

ORANGE JUICE

PINEAPPLE JUICE

ORIGINS AND ODDITIES

Legend has it that in Hollywood in the late 1930s, bartender Don Beach served the drink to his friend, who, pleasantly surprised by its taste, ordered two more. Several days later the man returned, telling Beach how after the last drink he had felt like a zombie throughout the plane ride back home.

PREPARATION

Measure 20 ml (4 tsp) of rum in a graduated cylinder and pour into a shaker. Repeat with 20 ml (4 tsp) of amber rum, 20 ml (4 tsp) of Apricot Brandy, 40 ml (2 3/4 tbsp) of orange juice and 40 ml (2 3/4 tbsp) of pineapple juice. Shake the ingredients for a few seconds and pour into a tumbler filled with ice. Measure 20 ml (4 tsp) of dark rum in the cylinder, and, using a spoon, gently pour in the glass, so that it remains on the surface. Serve, garnished with 2 long straws, 1/2 a slice of pineapple, 1/2 an orange slice and 2 cherries.

SUGGESTED USE

A good long drink that can enliven any evening.

Apricot-Filled Chests   EASY

ingredients for 4 people
time: 1 hour and 30 minutes

0.44 lbs (7 oz) puff pastry
4 apricots in syrup
2 tbsp brown sugar
2 tsp cinnamon powder
4 amaretti cookies
4 tsp apricot jam
1 egg

On a floured work surface, roll out the puff pastry to form a thin rectangle, and, with a knife, divide into 4 squares. Drain the apricots and cut them into cubes. At the center of each square of pastry lay an amaretto cookie and cover it with 1 tsp of jam and a dusting of cinnamon. Cover with diced apricots and wrap it in puff pastry so that it resembles a little bundle, using the beaten egg as a "glue". Brush what remains of the egg on the bundle, so that, once placed in the oven, it turns a golden color. Bake at 356°F (180°C) for about 25 minutes, making sure the pastry does not burn. Place on a serving plate and let cool. Serve, garnished with slices of apricot and a sprinkling of cinnamon.

COGNAC-BASED COCKTAILS

Cognac was created in the early seventeenth century and is a distillation of wine produced in the city of Charente, in western France. Cognac's success dates back to commercial trade, first with the Dutch and then the English, who often bought poor quality wines produced in the Charente region (which is characterized by high rainfall and limestone) to produce spirits (brandy). Soon, the inhabitants of the Charente region learned to produce their own.

In 1909, standards were drafted for the production of cognac, which set the maximum limit for distillation by March 31, in order to avoid debasing the character of the final spirits. That same year, certain select zones were specified for the production of cognac, with the regions between Charente and Charente Maritime accounting for the production of six vintages according to the quantity produced:

Grande Champagne (produces delicate spirits)
Petite Champagne (produces perfect spirits with stronger tastes)
Borderie (spirits with a softer taste that age quickly)
Fins Bois (lower quality spirits, but very tasty)
Bons Bois (spirits with a very pronounced taste)
Bois Ordinaires and Communes (ordinary spirits that are less well-regarded)

Cognac is produced from a blend of 75% Ugni Blanc (which is nothing more than Italian Trebbiano imported into France by Catherine de' Medici), Piquepoul, Juraçon, Colombard, Baco. The vineyards have rows up to 3 meters wide to allow for mechanical harvesting of grapes, which occurs when the grape harvest has reached phenological maturity.

The climate of the region, which has continental and oceanic influences, determines the characteristics of the grape, which produces wines with low alcohol content but high acidity, an excellent combination for distillation.

During the fermentation process, the temperature is not controlled. As soon as the sugars turn into alcohol, the resulting wine is distilled together with yeasts that have completed the fermentation.

The distillation takes place in copper stills called "Charantais" and involves two distinct phases: the first one allows you to get "Broullis" with graduation of 30°; the second

way separates the head and tail from the heart of the distillate. The heart is a colorless spirit of about 70% vol, and is only used for the production of cognac. This is aged in Limousin oak casks for no less than 30 months. The barrels play a key role in the aging of cognac, transforming amber cognac into a colorless spirit, rich with typical and inimitable scents.

The oak of the barrels contains a good amount of tannin which, added to the caramel, gives the taste and amber color to cognac. It is preferable to use previously used casks as they provide a softer taste than new barrels. The barrels are placed in temperature-controlled cellars, characterized by moderate light and moisture.

After the aging, the product is ready to be mixed and diluted. This operation consists of mixing cognac vintages and different vineyards in order to obtain the highest quality. It is then diluted with water to reduce the alcohol content to about 40%. The final age of the distillate is calculated by taking the arithmetic mean between the youngest and most aged cognacs.

The cognacs are classified according to aging:

Three stars, which is sold after 30 months of aging
V.S., Very special: aging from 36 to 48 months
V.O., Very old: aging from 48 to 60 months
V.S.O.P., Very special old pale: aging from 60 to 72 months
X.O., Extras old: aging from 72 months onwards

Cognac is consumed in a balloon or a sniffer, served at room temperature: these glasses help the distillate to express the various personalities of the spirit. Cognac also goes well with vermouth, champagne, fortified wines, fruit liqueurs with slight tints and with soft drinks, ice cream and yogurt.

Other spirits that have phases or production similar to cognac are:

Armagnac, a wine distillate made in France using the "Armagnacais" still.

Brandy, a wine distillate produced around the world. The most famous are the Italian brandies and Spanish calvados, which are apple distillations, produced and ranked as cognac.

ALEXANDER

INGREDIENTS

COGNAC OR BRANDY   CREAM
WHITE CHOCOLATE CREAM   NUTMEG

ORIGINS AND ODDITIES

This white-colored cocktail (like a wedding dress) was
created in London in the early twentieth century
at Ciro's Club by famous bartender Harry MacElhone
for the marriage between Princess Mary and Lord
Lascelles.

PREPARATION

Measure 30 ml (2 tbsp) of brandy or cognac in
a graduated cylinder and pour into a shaker. Repeat
with 30 ml (2 tbsp) of white chocolate cream and
30 ml (2 tbsp) of cream. Add ice cubes and shake
vigorously for a few seconds. Pour into a cup
(pre-chilled in the freezer), and garnish with a light
dusting of nutmeg.

SUGGESTED USE

A great drink that can brighten your evenings.

Star-Shaped Puff Pastry   EASY

ingredients for 4 people
time: 1 hour

2 4/5 cups flour
7/8 cup (14 tbsp) butter
salt
1 egg yolk
1 cup milk
1 sachet baking powder
1/4 cup sugar

Cut the butter into slices and let it soften at room temperature. In a
bowl, sift the flour, baking powder and a pinch of salt. Add the sugar and give a first mix. Gradually add the softened butter and mix in
thoroughly. Flour the work surface and roll out the dough with a rolling
pin until you get a thin sheet. Leave to rest for about 10 minutes. In
a saucepan, heat 3 tbsp of sugar with 3 tbsp of water, until you get a
syrupy liquid. Cut the dough with special star-shaped molds and place
them on a greased baking tray. Brush first with beaten egg yolks and
then with the sugar syrup. Bake for 10 minutes at 356°F (180°C) until the
pastry is golden. Serve cold.

APOTHEKE

INGREDIENTS

COGNAC OR BRANDY
FERNET BRANCA
CRÈME DE MENTHE VERTE (GREEN MINT)

ORIGINS AND ODDITIES

This cocktail, whose name derives from the
Greek word for "pharmacy" is a perfect symbolic
representation of the European Community, given
its alcohol-base (traditional French cognac), Fernet
Branca (Italian liqueur) and crème de menthe verte
(originally from Holland).

PREPARATION

Measure 30 ml (2 tbsp) of cognac or brandy
in a graduated cylinder and pour in a glass carafe.
Repeat with 30 ml (2 tbsp) of Fernet Branca and
30 ml (2 tbsp) of crème de menthe verte. Add some
ice cubes and stir with a long-handled spoon. Pour
into a cup (pre-chilled in the freezer), holding the ice
back with the spoon so that it does not end up in
the glass, and serve.

SUGGESTED USE

An excellent digestive cocktail, it is especially
recommended for the evenings.

Grandma Rosanna's Donut Cake

EASY

ingredients for 6/8 people
time: 2 hours

3 cups flour
2/3 cup sugar
1/2 cup butter
2 eggs
1 sachet baking powder
powdered cinnamon
1 red apple

In a bowl, whisk together egg yolks and sugar in order to obtain a
smooth and frothy cream. Incorporate sifted flour and softened
butter, stirring constantly with a wooden spoon. Beat the egg whites
until firm and add to the rest of the mixture. Stir all the ingredients
vigorously for several minutes until the mixture produces small air
bubbles. Grease and flour a standard cake mould and pour in the
prepared mixture. Bake at 356°F (180°C) for about 45 minutes. Let
cool and unmold the cake onto a platter. Garnish with slices of un-
peeled red apple and a sprinkle of cinnamon.

BANANA BLISS

INGREDIENTS

COGNAC OR BRANDY
BANANA CREAM

ORIGINS AND ODDITIES

Created in Florida in the late 1930s, this drink immediately became sought after due to its peculiar lightness. The name seems to come from the exclamation of a patron who, after tasting the new cocktails, said that it "had sent her into ecstasy".

PREPARATION

Measure 50 ml (3 1/3 tbsp) of cognac or brandy in a graduated cylinder and pour into a low tumbler filled with ice. Repeat with 40 ml (2 3/4 tbsp) of banana cream. Stir with a long-handled spoon and serve.

SUGGESTED USE

A nice digestive that is especially loved by women.

 Yogurt and Banana Cake   EASY

ingredients for 6/8 people
time: 1 hour and 30 minutes

2 4/5 cups flour
2/3 cup sugar
0.28 lbs (4.6 oz, about 1/2 cup) banana yogurt
3 eggs
1 banana (cut into thin slices)
salt
extra virgin olive oil
1 lemon
butter
icing sugar

In a bowl, whisk together sugar and egg whites in order to obtain a smooth and foamy cream. Continue mixing and combine 4 tbsp of extra virgin olive oil, sifted flour and finally the egg whites that were previously whisked into stiff peaks. Add thinly sliced bananas, a pinch of salt and the grated zest of 1 lemon. After blending everything together well, pour the batter into a greased cake mold and bake at 356°F (180°C) for about 40 minutes. Serve cake warm on a platter and sprinkle with abundant of icing sugar.

BETWEEN THE SHEETS

INGREDIENTS

BRANDY OR COGNAC
WHITE RUM

COINTREAU
DROPS OF LEMON JUICE

ORIGINS AND ODDITIES

Also known as "the couples' hotel cocktail",
this aptly-named drink was often offered
to lovers who frequented afternoon motels.

PREPARATION

Measure 30 ml (2 tbsp) of cognac or brandy in a
graduated cylinder and pour into a shaker. Repeat
with 30 ml (2 tbsp) of rum and 30 ml (2 tbsp) of
Cointreau. Add a few drops of lemon juice and some
ice cubes, shake vigorously for a few seconds. Pour
into a cup (pre-chilled in the freezer) and serve.

SUGGESTED USE

A fantastic drink for the afternoon and evening.
It is also recommended for "spicy" occasions.

Gianduja Passion (Milk Chocolate and Hazelnut Sauce)   EASY

ingredients for 4 people
time: 30 minutes

12 big fresh strawberries
0.22 lbs (3.5 oz) milk chocolate
0.13 lbs (2.1 oz) toasted hazelnuts
scant 1/3 cup butter
scant 1/2 cup (8 tbsp) sugar
2/5 cup milk

In a mixer, blend sugar, toasted hazelnuts and milk chocolate (previously
coarsely chopped). Pour ingredients into a saucepan, add butter and stir
vigorously. Add the milk and bring to a boil for 3 minutes, continuously
stirring with a small whisk. Serve the gianduja cream (hazelnut and chocolate mixture) into a beautiful sauce boat while it is still warm. Dip whole,
fresh strawberries in sauce before eating them.

BLACK FLY

INGREDIENTS

BRANDY OR COGNAC
COFFEE LIQUEUR
APRICOT LIQUEUR

ORIGINS AND ODDITIES

Created in the late 1990s at an international
competition among bartenders held on Lake Como.

PREPARATION

Measure 40 ml (2 3/4 tbsp) of brandy or cognac in
a graduated cylinder and pour into a shaker. Repeat
with 20 ml (4 tsp) of coffee liqueur and 30 ml
(2 tbsp) of apricot liqueur. Add a few ice cubes and
stir for a few seconds. Pour into a cup (pre-chilled in
the freezer) and serve.

SUGGESTED USE

An excellent digestive, it can be enjoyed at every
moment of the day.

Bavarian Coffee Dessert

EASY

ingredients for 6/8 people
time: 1 hour + cooling time
(3 hours)

2 1/8 cups whole milk
1 cup (16 tbsp) sugar
4 egg yolks
4 egg whites
1 sponge cake disc ("pan di spagna")
13 tsp (0.53 oz) instant coffee
2 cups fresh cream
5 gelatin leaves

In a bowl, whip together the egg whites and sugar in order to obtain a smooth and foamy cream. Add milk and pour into a saucepan.
Cook over medium heat until the mixture no longer leaves a film on
the spoon, without letting it reach the boiling point. Remove from
heat and add instant coffee, along with gelatine leaves that were
previously soaked in cold water for ten minutes and then drained.
Whip the whipping cream and whip the egg whites into stiff peaks.
Once the mixture has cooled, add the whipped cream first and then
the whipped egg whites, gently mixing at the bottom, so that the
ingredients do not collapse. Line a glass bowl with strips of sponge
cake and add the cream. Let it settle in the refrigerator for at least
3 hours before serving. Garnish with tufts of coffee flavoured
whipped cream.

BOMBAY

INGREDIENTS

COGNAC OR BRANDY
RED VERMOUTH
DRY VERMOUTH

COINTREAU
PERNOD OR RICARD

ORIGINS AND ODDITIES

A cocktail created in the 1920s by a bartender
in honor of a pair of Indian customers who came
to his bar and ordered the drink.

PREPARATION

Measure 20 ml (4 tsp) of cognac or brandy in a
graduated cylinder and pour into a shaker. Repeat
with 30 ml (2 tbsp) of dry vermouth, 20 ml (4 tsp)
of red vermouth, 20 ml (4 tsp) of Cointreau and
5 ml (1 tsp) of Pernod or Ricard. Add a few ice cubes
and shake vigorously for a few seconds. Pour into
a cup (pre-chilled in the freezer) and serve.

SUGGESTED USE

An excellent apéritif, it is good throughout the
evening.

Asparagus Vol-au-Vents

EASY

ingredients for 4 people
time: 1 hour

8 ready-made vol-au-vents
0.88 lbs (14 oz) asparagus heads
1 fillet of prague ham (0.33 lbs, 5.3 oz)
2 tbsp (1/8 cup) butter
2 egg yolks
zest of 1 lemon
1 glass dry white wine
3/4 cup béchamel
salt
pepper
chopped parsley

Boil the asparagus in salted water for 15 minutes. Meanwhile, dice the
ham into small cubes. Pour the egg whites in a pot and add white
wine, softened butter, grated lemon zest, salt and pepper. Drain the
asparagus, chop and add to the stuffing, and cook continuously in a
double boiler in order to obtain a soft and foamy cream. Remove from
heat and incorporate the béchamel and the diced ham. Arrange the
vol-au-vent on a baking sheet covered with baking paper, and bake
at 356°F (180°C) for about 5 minutes. With a pastry bag, stuff each
vol-au-vent with asparagus cream and serve very hot. Garnish with
chopped parsley.

CANNES

INGREDIENTS

BRANDY OR COGNAC　　CAMPARI
DRY VERMOUTH　　　　ORANGE JUICE

ORIGINS AND ODDITIES

This cocktail was served in France in the 1960s at events organized to welcome filmmakers and actors to the Cannes Film Festival.

PREPARATION

Measure 20 ml (4 tsp) of cognac or brandy in a graduated cylinder and pour into a shaker. Repeat with 30 ml (2 tbsp) of dry vermouth, 20 ml (4 tsp) of Campari and 20 ml (4 tsp) of orange juice. Add ice cubes and shake vigorously for a few seconds. Pour into a low tumbler filled with ice and serve, garnished with 1/2 an orange slice, 2 cherries and 2 short straws.

SUGGESTED USE

Perfect as an aperitif.

 Shrimp Cocktail　　　　　　　　　　　　　　　　　　　　　　　EASY

ingredients for 4 people
time: 45 minutes

1.3 lbs (21 oz, about 3 cup) shrimps
20 tbsp mayonnaise
4 tbsp ketchup
3 1/3 tbsp brandy
1 tbsp worcestershire sauce
6 lettuce leaves
6 radicchio leaves
1 lemon
pepper
chopped parsley

Thoroughly wash the shrimps and remove the black vein that runs along the belly to the head. Place them in a pan with lightly salted cold water and boil for 5 minutes. Remove from heat and let cool. Drain shrimps and carefully remove the heads and shells, making sure to leave the tail. Put the mayonnaise in a bowl and add Worcestershire sauce, brandy, ketchup and a pinch of pepper. Mix the sauce with a spoon for a couple of minutes. Wash and dry the lettuce and radicchio leaves well and thinly slice them. Take four ice-cream cups and first place in them the radicchio and then the lettuce leaves. Arrange the shrimps in a circle around the cup so that the tails protrude from the edge. Cover them with plenty of cocktail sauce and garnish with a sprinkle of chopped parsley just before serving.

COCKTAIL CHAMPAGNE

INGREDIENTS

BRANDY OR COGNAC

CHAMPAGNE OR DRY
SPARKLING WINE

SUGAR

GRAND MARNIER

ORIGINS AND ODDITIES

Created as an aperitif in the early 1920s in France,
it quickly became well known and was soon
among the most popular sparkling wine cocktails
in the world.

PREPARATION

Place 1 lump of sugar in a cup (pre-chilled
in the freezer) and add 20 ml (4 tsp) of
cognac or brandy and 20 ml (4 tsp) of Grand
Marnier (previously measured in a graduated
cylinder). Repeat with 100 ml (20 tsp) of
champagne or dry sparkling wine and mix
gently with a long-handled spoon. To serve,
garnish with 1/2 an orange slice and 1 cherry.

SUGGESTED USE

A sophisticated drink for cocktail hour,
it is nevertheless good for any time of day.

Oysters

MEDIUM

ingredients for 4 people
time: 30 minutes

16 oysters
4 lemons
white pepper

Carefully clean the outsides of oysters, but completely avoid passing
them under running water. Open the shellfish with a knife, maintaining
the concave side downwards, leveraging from the most pliable part. Split
them into two halves, remove the oyster from its shell and gentle lay
it back in its half shell. On a platter, spread a generous bed of crushed
ice and then impressively place the oysters on top. Serve immediately,
accompanied with lemon wedges and white pepper so that the oysters
can be spiced according to the personal taste of the diners.

FRENCH COFFEE

INGREDIENTS

COGNAC

WHITE OR CANE SUGAR

LONG COFFEE

CREAM

ORIGINS AND CURIOSITIES

Following the creation of Irish Coffee, the patriotism of French bartenders spurred them on to create their own hot drink, replacing the traditional Irish Whiskey with something distilled in France: Cognac.

PREPARATION

Measure 50 ml (3 1/3 tbsp) of cognac in a graduated cylinder and pour into a milk jug. Add 1 long coffee and 10 g (3 tsp) of white sugar. Bring to a boil and pour into a heat-resistant mug. Just before serving, add 40 ml (2 3/4 tbsp) of cream (previously measured in a graduated cylinder) using the edge of a teaspoon, so that it remains separate from the rest.

SUGGESTED USE

To drink during the winter season: your excursions in the mountains or on ski slopes will benefit from the powerful energy and invigorating qualities of this fine hot drink.

 Pears in Red Wine

EASY

ingredients for 4 people
time: 3 hours

4 big pears
2 1/8 cups red wine
1 cinnamon stick
6 cloves
scant 1/2 cup (8 tbsp) sugar
orange zest

Pour the wine into a deep pot combing half the sugar, the cinnamon stick and the cloves. Bring to a boil and wait for the liquid to reduce half way. Meanwhile, wash the pears, cut them into quarters and place them in a large basin. Cover them with the hot wine passed through a fine sieve. Let the fruit marinate for at least 2 hours, turning them from time to time. Ten minutes before serving, caramelize the remaining sugar and add 3 tbsp of water. Drain the pear slices and arrange them in 4 dessert bowls. Decorate with drizzles of caramelized sugar and matchstick-size strips of orange zest.

FRENCH CONNECTION

INGREDIENTS

COGNAC OR BRANDY
DISARONNO AMARETTO

ORIGINS AND ODDITIES

This drink was created in the 1950s at a national convention of French bartenders. From the late 1980s on, it would become a classic cocktail.

PREPARATION

Measure 50 ml (3 1/3 tbsp) of cognac or brandy in a graduated cylinder and pour into a tumbler filled with ice. Repeat with 40 ml (2 3/4 tbsp) of Disaronno Amaretto. Stir with a long-handled spoon and serve.

SUGGESTED USE

This excellent digestive is suitable for all hours of the evening.

French Plum Cake   EASY

ingredients for 6/8 people
time: 1 hour and 30 minutes

0.33 lbs (5.3 oz) dried prunes
1 1/5 cups flour
3 1/3 tbsp cognac
3/5 cup sugar
0.44 lbs (7 oz) dark chocolate
4 eggs
1 sachet baking powder
3 1/2 tbsp (1/4 cup) butter
fresh mint
salt

In a saucepan, drown the prunes with brandy and cook at low heat, making sure the fruit has not completely absorbed the liquid. In a bowl, work the egg yolks and sugar with a whisk, until the mixture is smooth and fluffy. Melt the chocolate in a bain-marie, add butter and some chopped mint leaves. Combine the chocolate cream with the eggs and then the sifted flour. Finally, add the prunes and egg whites, stirring continuously until stiff. Line a standard plum cake mold with baking paper and pour in the mixture. Bake at 356°F (180°C) for about 40 minutes. Serve cold, garnished with tufts of mint-flavored whipped cream and fresh mint leaves.

HORSE'S NECK

INGREDIENTS

BRANDY OR COGNAC
GINGER ALE

ORIGINS AND ODDITIES

A drink whose color recalls the mane of a horse. It was created at British race courses in the 1950s.

PREPARATION

Measure 40 ml (2 3/4 tbsp) of brandy or cognac in a graduated cylinder and pour into a tall tumbler filled with ice. Fill almost to the brim with Ginger Ale and serve, garnished with 1/2 an orange slice and 2 long straws.

SUGGESTED USE

A good long drink suitable for all hours of the day.

 Sliced Oranges in Cointreau   EASY

ingredients for 4 people
time: 30 minutes

4 oranges
1/4 cup sugar
Cointreau
icing sugar
2 1/8 cups water

Wash and peel raw oranges, making sure to separate the white skin from the peel. Cut peel into thin strips and boil for 10 minutes in a saucepan with water. In a pan, pour in the sugar and combine with the Cointreau. Add a tablespoon of water and boil on high until syrupy. Slice the oranges and gently place them in 4 salad cups. Add a teaspoon of drained orange peels and top with plenty of Cointreau syrup. Just before serving, dust with icing sugar.

SIDECAR

INGREDIENTS

COGNAC OR BRANDY
COINTREAU
LEMON JUICE

ORIGINS AND ODDITIES

This cocktail almost certainly was created in the 1920s at Harry's Bar in Paris, thanks to the creativity of a sidecar driver. The bartender of the restaurant followed this original customer's directions to the letter and named the drink in his honor.

PREPARATION

Measure 50 ml (3 1/3 tbsp) of brandy or cognac in a graduated cylinder and pour into a shaker. Repeat with 30 ml (2 tbsp) of Cointreau and 10 ml (2 tsp) of lemon juice. Add some ice cubes and shake it all for a few seconds. Pour into a cup (pre-chilled in the freezer) and serve.

SUGGESTED USE

A wonderful digestive drink, suitable for all hours of the evening.

Ricotta and Lemon Soufflé
EASY

ingredients for 4 people
time: 1 hour

4 eggs
0.22 lbs (3.5 oz) ricotta cheese
1/4 cup potato starch flour
3 tbsp sugar
butter
2 lemons

Dissolve the starch in 6 tbsp of water, and after having mixed evenly, pour into a large saucepan. Combine the egg yolks, the lemon juice and lemon zest, along with the sugar. Simmer over medium heat until it becomes smooth and creamy. Remove the saucepan from heat and add in crumbled ricotta. Mix vigorously and let everything cool. Combine the egg whites and whip into stiff peaks, then give it a final gentle mix for an even texture. Grease ramekins with butter and pour the mixture close to the edge. Place ramekins in a double boiler and cook for 25 minutes in the oven at 320°F (160°C). Serve warm.

STINGER

INGREDIENTS

COGNAC OR BRANDY
CRÈME DE MENTHE BLANCHE
(WHITE MINT)

ORIGINS AND ODDITIES

Created in Britain in the early 1910s, this particularly strong cocktail was popular at the time of Prohibition, as the mint effectively masked the alcohol.

PREPARATION

Measure 55 ml (11 tsp) of cognac or brandy in a graduated cylinder, pour into a shaker and repeat with 35 ml (2 tbsp + 1 tsp) of crème de menthe blanche. Add a few ice cubes and shake vigorously for a few seconds. Pour into a cup (pre-chilled in the freezer) and serve.

SUGGESTED USE

This is considered one of the best digestive cocktails in the world.

Delicious Mint Desserts

EASY

ingredients for 6/8 people
time: 1 hour and 30 minutes

1 7/8 cups flour
1 packet prepared mint pudding
4 tbsp sweetened cocoa
cornstarch
scant 1/2 cup (8 tbsp) sugar
1 tbsp sunflower seed oil
2 eggs
baking powder
salt
1 glass milk to soften the dough
drops of green food coloring
butter
icing sugar

In a bowl, work the eggs with a whisk, a pinch of salt and the sugar until the mixture is smooth and frothy. In another bowl, sift flour, baking powder and the prepared pudding. Stir the mixture, gradually adding the flour, oil and milk in the first bowl until the dough is fluid. Add a few drops of dye and give a final stir. Pour the batter into a buttered baking dish with a diameter of 24 cm and bake for about 30 minutes at 356°F (180°C). Remove from the oven and let rest on a serving plate. In a bowl, prepare a cream, working the cocoa with a hint of cornstarch and 4 tbsp of milk. Bring the ingredients to a boil in a saucepan and allow to cool. Fill a small pastry bag (with a fine spout) with chocolate cream and stuff the cake, injecting it into scattered points. Before serving, sprinkle with plenty of icing sugar.

SUPER VIN BRÛLÉ

INGREDIENTS

RED WINE

BRANDY OR COGNAC

WHITE OR CANE SUGAR

LEMON ZEST

ORANGE ZEST

CLOVES

CINNAMON STICKS

ORIGINS AND ODDITIES

Probably one of the oldest existing cocktails, it seems that monks in the Middle Ages served this refreshing and therapeutic drink in their monasteries.

PREPARATION

Measure 100 ml (20 tsp) of red wine in a graduated cylinder and pour into a milk jug. Repeat with 50 ml (3 1/3 tbsp) of brandy or cognac. Add 10 g (3 tsp) of sugar, 2 lemon peels, 2 orange peels, 5 cloves and 1 tsp (2.5 g) cinnamon sticks. Bring everything to a boil, stirring occasionally. Serve in a heat-resistant mug

SUGGESTED USE

A great drink to warm you up, it is recommended for when you have the flu.

Chestnut Cake

EASY

ingredients for 6/8 people
time: 1 hour

2 1/4 cups chestnut flour
0.11 lbs (1.76 oz, about 1/3 cup) raisins
0.08 lbs (1.41 oz) walnuts
0.08 lbs (1.41 oz) pine nuts
extra virgin olive oil
salt
rosemary
butter
flour

Carefully sift chestnut flour and pour into a large bowl. Add exactly 2 1/8 cups of water. Mix everything vigorously until you get a rather fluid and lump free mixture. Combine 2 tbsp of extra virgin olive oil and the raisins, which were previously soaked and softened in warm water, followed by a pinch of salt. Grease and flour a cake mould and pour in the mixture. Sprinkle with crushed walnuts, whole pine nuts, a few rosemary leaves and a drizzle of oil. Bake in the oven for about 30 minutes at 356°F (180°C). Can be served either hot or cold.

THE BEST

INGREDIENTS

BRANDY OR COGNAC
COFFEE LIQUEUR
COINTREAU

ORIGINS AND ODDITIES

This cocktail was presented at the prestigious
Hotel La Concorde in Lausanne in the mid-'80s
at a European competition between 500 bartenders.
It finished in second place.

PREPARATION

Measure 40 ml (2 3/4 tbsp) of brandy or cognac in
a graduated cylinder and pour into a shaker. Repeat
with 30 ml (2 tbsp) of coffee liqueur and 20 ml (4 tsp)
of Cointreau. Add a few ice cubes and stir for a few
seconds. Pour into a low tumbler filled with ice and
serve.

SUGGESTED USE

A perfect drink for after dinner, it is particularly
suitable as a digestive.

 Rice Pudding Cake   EASY

ingredients for 6/8 people
time: 2 hours

1/2 cup rice
0.08 lbs (1.41 oz) pine nuts) pine nuts
0.08 lbs (1.41 oz, about 1/4 cup
packed) raisins
3 1/4 cups milk
1/4 cup (4 tbsp) sugar
powdered cinnamon
1 vanilla sachet
2 cloves
salt
butter
flour

Soak raisins in warm water to soften and then drain well. Pour milk in
a saucepan and bring to a boil over medium heat. Mix together rice, a
pinch of salt, vanilla and cloves and stir continuously. After 5 minutes,
add sugar, pine nuts and the raisins, which were previously soaked and
drained. Continue to cook over medium heat for 20 minutes; remove
from heat when the rice is al dente. Grease a cake mould with butter,
coat with flour and pour mixture in until it is level to the surface. Bake
in the over at 356°F (180°C) for 30 minutes. Serve the pudding cold and
sprinkle with cinnamon.

WHISKY-BASED COCKTAILS

The history of whisky is slightly conflicted, with Scotland and Ireland both believing to be the home of this popular spirit. Scotland emphasizes the importance of its malt distillation, while Ireland focused on distillation techniques imported from the East by monks of St. Patrick's followers.

In 1172, English troops of Henry II invaded Ireland, discovering a '"fire water" that they called whisky, mangling the original Gaelic term "uisge". Irish monks and samples of this product soon landed in Scotland, along with the technologies necessary to obtain this spirit.

With advancements in distillation technology, the quality of the distillate also improved, and the demand grew, forcing an eventual law in 1579, which limited the production of whisky.

In 1707, with the political union between Scotland and England, the demand for whisky grew rapidly, and taxation soon followed. Many Scottish distilleries therefore, started producing bootleg whisky. This lasted throughout the eighteenth century, until, in 1823, King George IV promulgated the Excise Act, which put an end to illegal distilling.

In 1908, after nearly a century of technological and agronomic improvements, the Royal commission decided to apply the term "Scotch Whisky" to all the spirits that came from the Scottish region. In 1877, manufacturers of Scotch Whisky, met to found the Distillers Company Limited, which launched the distillate on world markets.

Today this spirit's production reaches the four corners of the globe, with five major producing countries (Scotland, Ireland, USA, Canada, Japan), each of which offer a wide range of qualities, characteristics and organoleptic techniques.

The production of whisky is divided into five phases: the preparation of grains, also known as malting, followed by maceration (mash) and fermentation, which includes distilling and aging. Then it's time for filtration and dilution. A key element is water, which must be pure.

SCOTCH WHISKY

The European Union defines Scotch Whisky as a distillate procued in Scotland obtained by the distillation of cereals. Scotch Whisky is essentially divided into two families: Single Malt, obtained from the distillation of a particular barley called "holistic"; Blended, obtained from the distillation of different cereals. The most meticulous and traditional processing is restricted to Single Malt. Scotland is divided into different areas of production: Highlands, Lowlands, Islay, Spay Side Cambpelltown, etc. All Single Malts have organoleptic properties that are well defined and determined by the processes and raw materials used to produce them. Strictly distilled in pot stills, they undergo two distillations: during the first you get the "low wines", with an alcohol content of 25% vol. The low wines are then properly trimmed (heads and tails) and then put in a second distillation with the tail (the heart and tail), which gives the distillate an alcohol content ranging from 72 to 75% vol. In this second phase, cuts are made to the head and tail to extract and age only the heart for a minimum of three years.

The wooden barrels used for aging Scotch Whisky varies depending on the distillery (the best is American oak), but they most usually are barrels that have already been used to age other spirits or fortified wines (port, sherry, madeira, etc). This is to ensure that the final product has its own uniqueness and peculiarities.

IRISH WHISKEY

Irish whiskey differs from Scotch through some important processes. For the production of Irish Whiskey, grains are not dried with a heat source fueled by peat, but with other materials. The distillation process in this case can be either continuous (patent-still) or discontinuous (pot-still), also, in the case of discontinuous distillation extracted from the first batch, it is not redistilled with the heart in the second batch but again distilled separately. Finally, the stills used for producing Irish Whiskey have a higher capacity than those used for the production of Scotch.

AMERICAN WHISKY

The main raw material used in the production of American Whisky is maize (corn) and grains that have not undergone the process of malting. Fermentation is achieved through the addition of selected yeasts. The distillation process used is continuous (patent-still). The aging, which can vary between 4 and 12 years, is done in wooden casks made from American oak. There are various types of American Whisky:

Bourbon whisky, made using grains, such as corn 51%, malted barley and rye. Aged in new American oak barrels.

Tennessee whisky differs from bourbon through a series of additional operations, such as Sour Mash, the recovery of the "sour mass" of exhausted yeast that triggers a new fermentation and filtration through the smoky taste of maple charcoal. It is then aged in new barrels.

Rye whisky (rye), produced as the only variant of bourbon with at least 51% rye.

Canadian Whisky, produced by a mix of grains, it is mashed and fermented with selected yeasts. Distilled twice, it is aged in oak for 3 years, and before bottling, cut with agricultural alcohol.

JAPANESE WHISKY

Japanese whisky uses the same production processes as Scotch Whisky. The only real difference is in the barley.

Whiskys are generally appreciated in short-stemmed tulip-shaped glass, which can retain the aroma as long as possible. Generally, however, they are served in old-fashioned glasses with another glass of ice water, to bring out the taste. Whiskys are often used with soft drinks or in fresh tasting long drinks, like the classic Whisky Sour. It also goes very well with creams, juices and coffee.

COCA WHISKY
(HIGH BALL)

INGREDIENTS

AMERICAN WHISKY AND COLA

ORIGINS AND ODDITIES

This drink was created in the United States around
the 1920s, after a bartender started replacing soda
with cola in order to make the then well-known
Whisky and Soda less dry. The new cocktail was
an instant hit, thanks to word of mouth among
younger drinkers.

PREPARATION

Measure 50 ml (3 1/3 tbsp) of whisky in a graduated
cylinder and pour into a tall tumbler filled with ice.
Fill to the brim with cola and stir with a long-handled
spoon. To serve, garnish with 1 lemon slice and 2 long
straws.

SUGGESTED USE

Beloved by the younger crowd, it is good at any
time of day.

 American Dessert   EASY

ingredients for 6/8 people
time: 1 hour and 30 minutes

0.46 lbs (7.4 oz) dark chocolate
3 eggs
1/2 cup butter
7/8 cup sugar
0.33 lbs (5.3 oz, about 1 5/8 cups)
ground almonds
0.11 lbs (1.76 oz, about 1/3 cup)
raisins
1/2 cup flour
3 tbsp bitter coffee
salt
2 shot glasses American whisky
icing sugar

In a bowl, soak the raisins in whisky to soften for 10 minutes. In a
double boiler, melt the chocolate along with the coffee until you
get a creamy fluid. Remove from heat and add previously softened
butter and let cool. In a bowl, whisk together the sugar and egg yolks
in order to get a smooth and fluffy mixture. Add this cream to the
coffee and mix together. To this preparation, gradually add sifted
flour, a pinch of salt, ground almonds, eggs whites that have been
whisked into stiff peaks, and stir well from the bottom to avoid col-
lapsing the mixture. Pour the batter into a buttered and floured cake
mould. Bake at 356°F (180°C) for about 40 minutes. Remove from the
oven and let settle for 10 minutes. Before serving, sprinkle the cake
with abundant icing sugar.

DAY DREAM

INGREDIENTS

AMERICAN WHISKY

CRÈME DE MENTHE VERTE
(GREEN MINT)

AN ITALIAN BITTER
(RABARBARO ZUCCA
IS RECOMMENDED)

ORIGINS AND ODDITIES

This drink debuted at the prestigious Moët & Chandon national competition in 1994 at the Hilton Hotel in Milan. It finished in first place.

PREPARATION

Measure 50 ml (3 1/3 tbsp) of whisky in a graduated cylinder and pour into a shaker. Repeat with 25 ml (5 tsp) of crème de menthe verte and 15 ml (1 tbsp) of Rabarbaro Zucca. Add some ice cubes and shake vigorously for a few seconds. Pour into a low tumbler filled with ice and serve.

SUGGESTED USE

A drink with amazing digestive properties, it is good for all hours of the evening.

Chocolate Muffins

EASY

ingredients for 6/8 people
time: 2 hours

4 cups flour
1/4 cup + 1 1/2 tbsp sugar
0.13 lbs (2.1 oz, about 1/3 cup)
chocolate chips
2 eggs
1 cup milk
extra virgin olive oil
1 sachet baking powder
salt

On a large work surface, sift some flour. Add sugar to a bowl and give it an initial mix. Add the baking powder, a pinch of salt and once again mix the ingredients; then place in a heap. Crack the eggs in a large bowl and beat with a whisk. Combine with the milk and 5 tbsp of extra virgin olive oil. Pour this preparation into the middle of the heap and mix vigorously until you get a smooth mixture. Finally, add the chocolate chips and give a final mix. Grease classic muffin moulds with butter and fill each up with 2/3 of mixture. Bake at 356°F (180°C) for about 20 minutes, until the muffins have increased in volume and become golden. Turn off the oven and let rest for 5 minutes, keeping the oven door semi-closed. Remove from the oven and let cool before serving.

GODFATHER

INGREDIENTS

WHISKY
DISARONNO AMARETTO

ORIGINS AND ODDITIES

It seems that the name of this drink, created
in the 1960s, came from the exclamation of
an enthusiastic bar patron after he had tasted it.

PREPARATION

Measure 60 ml (1/4 cup) of whisky in a graduated
cylinder and pour into a low tumbler full of ice.
Repeat with 30 ml (2 tbsp) of Disaronno Amaretto.
Stir with a long-handled spoon and serve.

SUGGESTED USE

A perfect drink for after dinner.

 Spicy Cookies   EASY

ingredients for 4 people
time: 1 hour

1 1/4 cups (20 tbsp) sugar cane
1 1/8 cups + 1 1/2 tbsp flour
1/4 cup (4 tbsp) butter
1 lemon
2 cloves
cinnamon
ginger
2 eggs
ground hazelnuts
salt

Sift the flour into a large bowl. Combine the sugar and butter and work
into a cream, then add the zest of 1 lemon, the spice to your taste, a
pinch of salt, the egg yolks and mix everything vigorously with a spoon.
Whip the egg whites into stiff peaks and add to the mixture, continuing
to stir from below so that the mixture does not collapse. Cover a baking
tray with baking paper and lay out many tablespoons of dough, trying
to get a rounded shape. Sprinkle each cookie with ground hazelnuts
and bake at 320°F (160°C) for about 10 minutes. Remove from the oven,
let cool, and then sprinkle with plenty of cinnamon.

IRISH COFFEE

INGREDIENTS

IRISH WHISKEY
LONG COFFEE

BROWN SUGAR
CREAM

ORIGINS AND ODDITIES

It has been said that already in the 1950s the Irish
served this celebrated cocktail with the intention of
warming up shivering patrons who frequented the
bar at the Shannon seaplane station. One of them,
a reporter from the *San Francisco Chronicle* asked
local bartender Joe Sheridan for the recipe, and
subsequently introduced this drink to the US.

PREPARATION

Measure 50 ml (3 1/3 tbsp) of Irish whiskey in
a graduated cylinder and pour it into a milk jug.
Add 1 long coffee and 12.5 g (3 tsp) of brown sugar.
Bring to a boil and pour into a heat-resistant mug.
Just before serving, add 40 ml (2 3/4 tbsp) of cream
previously measured in a graduated cylinder, using
the edge of a teaspoon, so that it remains separate
from the rest.

SUGGESTED USE

A invigorating and energy boosting tonic that can
help deal with the coldest periods of the year.

Scones   EASY

ingredients for 6/8 people
time: 1 hour and 15 minutes

2 cups flour
2/5 cup milk
0.17 lbs (2.8 oz) raisins
1/4 cup (4 tbsp) butter
1/2 a sachet baking powder
1 tbsp sugar
salt
1 egg
honey

Combine sugar with a pinch of salt and mix well with a spoon. Soften
butter into chunks and add into a bowl followed by raisins. Once again,
mix the ingredients. Gently combine and work in the milk with the rest
using a fork, then knead everything with bare hands in order to form a
ball. On a floured work surface, roll out the dough so that it becomes 1
cm thick. With a round and floured cookie cutter, cut out the scones,
then lay them out on a baking tray covered in baking paper. Brush
the surface of these Irish desserts with beaten egg and bake at 400°F
(200°C) for about 15 minutes. Remove from the oven and let cool before serving. Accompany the scones with honey.

MANHATTAN

INGREDIENTS

CANADIAN WHISKY
RED VERMOUTH
ANGOSTURA

ORIGINS AND ODDITIES

Legend has it that Winston Churchill's mother
was the person to suggest the recipe for this
famous drink, guiding one of the bartenders at the
Manhattan Club in New York in the 1920s.

PREPARATION

Measure 60 ml (1/4 cup) of Canadian Whisky
in a graduated cylinder and pour into a glass
carafe. Repeat with 30 ml (2 tbsp) of red vermouth.
Add a few drops of angostura and ice cubes. Mix
everything together with a long-handled spoon.
Pour into a cup (previously chilled in the freezer),
holding the ice back with the spoon so that it
does not end up in the cup. Serve, garnished
with 1 cherry.

SUGGESTED USE

One of the best apertifs, it is very good for the
entire evening.

Chef's Green Noodles

EASY

ingredients for 4 people
time: 1 hour

0.80 lbs (12.6 oz) green noodles with
basil
1 cup + 3 1/2 tbsp béchamel
3 tbsp genoese pesto
0.33 lbs (5.3 oz) shrimp tails
1 shallot
brandy
6 small tomatoes
8 basil leaves
salt
pepper
extra virgin olive oil

Wash and dry the shrimps, remove the shells and the black vein that
runs along the back. Wash the tomatoes and dice into small cubes.
Clean the shallots and slice very thinly. Clean the basil and slice into
strips. Cook the pasta in plenty of salted water. Meanwhile, sauté the
shallot in a large pan with 3 tbsp of extra virgin olive oil. When it is
golden brown, add the shrimps and cook over medium heat while
mixing continuously. Flambé everything by adding a glass of brandy.
When the fire goes out, add the béchamel sauce and half the basil.
Season with salt and pepper and finalize with pesto. Continue cooking
for 1 minute and remove from heat. Drain the pasta that was cooked
al dente and throw directly into the sauce. Serve in a beautiful dish and
garnish with remaining basil and fresh diced tomatoes.

MARY ANN

INGREDIENTS

CANADIAN WHISKY
DISARONNO AMARETTO
SOUTHERN COMFORT

ORIGINS AND ODDITIES

According to those in the know, this drink was
created specifically by a Canadian bartender for
a Mrs. Mary Ann, who, returning from an excellent
dinner, confessed to having a stomach ache.
The digestive effect of the new cocktail proved
surprising and pleasing.

PREPARATION

Measure 40 ml (2 3/4 tbsp) of Canadian whisky in a
graduated cylinder and pour into a shaker. Repeat
with 20 ml (4 tsp) of Disaronno Amaretto and 30 ml
(2 tbsp) of Southern Comfort. Add ice cubes and
shake vigorously for a few seconds. Pour into a cup
(pre-chilled in the freezer) and serve, garnished with
a cherry.

SUGGESTED USE

A wonderful digestive cocktail, it is recommended
throughout the evening.

Blanched Apples   EASY

ingredients for 4 people
time: 30 minutes

6 rennet apples
3 tbsp brown sugar
1/2 cup + 1 tsp (8 1/2 tbsp) butter
cinnamon
whipped cream
juice of 1 lemon

Wash, peel and core the apples. Cut into slices about 1.5 cm thick
and soak in a bowl of cold water and lemon juice. Melt the butter in
a saucepan and dip the apples (once you've drained and dried them
with paper towels). Arrange the apples on a hot plate, and cook for 5
minutes, turning them halfway through cooking. Arrange the apples
on a serving dish and sprinkle with brown sugar and a dusting of
cinnamon. Serve hot, garnished with whipped cream.

MINT JULEP

INGREDIENTS

AMERICAN WHISKY

SUGAR

SODA WATER OR SPARKLING
MINERAL WATER

FRESH MINT LEAVES

ORIGINS AND ODDITIES

This drink originally came to be at the beginning
of the 1900s at the Kentucky-Derby (the famed
horse race that takes place annually in early May).
The Mint Julep would soon became one of the
more commonly served cocktails in Southern United
States, before eventually conquering the rest
of the world.

PREPARATION

In a low tumbler place a few leaves of fresh mint.
Combine 10 g (3 tsp) of white sugar, 10 ml (2
tsp) of American whisky and 20 ml (4 tsp) of soda
water or mineral water (previously measured in a
graduated cylinder). Stir with a long-handled spoon,
trying to press the mint leaves against the sides of
the tumbler. Fill with crushed (preferably) ice and
finish with 50 ml (3 1/3 tbsp) of whisky previously
measured in a graduated cylinder. Stir again with
a spoon for a few seconds and serve, garnished with
2 short straws.

SUGGESTED USE

A great drink that can be enjoyed throughout the
evening.

 Mint Triangles   EASY

ingredients for 4 people
time: 1 hour

1 1/2 cups (24 tbsp + 1 tsp) of flour
1 cup butter
2/3 cup sugar
1 cup corn flour
2 eggs
0.88 oz fresh mint
mint syrup
pine nuts
icing sugar

Gently wash the mint leaves and chop them finely, or pass them
through a mixer. In a large bowl, work the butter with a spoon until
creamy. While continuously mixing, add the sugar, sifted flour, eggs
and a drop of mint syrup. Finally, add the chopped mint and mix
all the ingredients well in order to get a smooth paste. Spread the
dough with a rolling pin on a floured work surface. With a triangular
cookie cutter, or with a knife, cut out the biscuits and lay them out
on a baking tray covered with baking paper. Brush the surface with
beaten egg yolk and sprinkle with pine nuts. Bake at 356°F (180°C) for
about 20 minutes until the triangles are golden brown. Remove from
the oven and serve cold with a dusting of icing sugar.

OLD FASHIONED

INGREDIENTS

WHISKY
ANGOSTURA

SODA WATER OR SPARKLING
MINERAL WATER
SUGAR

ORIGINS AND ODDITIES

A drink created in the early 1900s, it was named after
the particular glass it was served in.
Its main advocate seems to have been Colonel
James E. Pepper.

PREPARATION

Place 1 lump of sugar in the center of a low
tumbler, moistened with a few drops of angostura.
Measure 30 ml (2 tbsp) of soda water or sparkling
mineral water in a graduated cylinder and add it
to the glass. Fill with ice and add 60 ml (1/4 cup)
of whisky (previously measured in a graduated
cylinder). Stir gently with a long handled spoon
and serve, garnished with 2 cherries, 1/2 a slice
of orange and 2 short straws.

SUGGESTED USE

This drink can be enjoyed at all hours of the day, and
is even good as an aperitif.

Parisian Scallops   EASY

ingredients for 4 people
time: 45 minutes

8 scallops
1/3 cup (5 1/2 tbsp) butter
breadcrumbs
1 glass white wine
salt
pepper
parsley

Wash the scallops in a lot of running water. Put them in a sauce pan
over medium heat with the white wine and 2 tbsp of water in order to
open them. Once open, remove the scallops from their shells, being
careful to eliminate all the guts, the black bag and all other impurities.
Once again, wash four shells and in the center of each lay out 2 scallops
cut into 4. Finely chop parsley and some peeled garlic. In a saucepan,
melt the butter and brown the chopped parsley and garlic, later adding
a tablespoon of the mixture on top of each single serving of scallop.
Cover the shells with breadcrumbs and the remaining butter shaved
into small curls. Season with salt and pepper and bake at 356°F (180°C)
until the scallops are lightly browned. Serve hot.

OLD PALE

INGREDIENTS

AMERICAN WHISKY
DRY VERMOUTH
CAMPARI

ORIGINS AND ODDITIES

An aperitif created in the 1950s by an American bartender, it quickly became popular throughout the world. Beloved by actors like Richard Burton, it was named Old Pale because of its transparent appearance, free of residues and impurities.

PREPARATION

Measure 30 ml (2 tbsp) of whisky in a graduated cylinder and pour in a transparent pitcher. Repeat with 30 ml (2 tbsp) of dry vermouth and 30 ml (2 tbsp) of Campari. Add a few ice cubes and stir with a long-handled spoon. Pour into a cup (pre-chilled in the freezer), holding the ice back so that it does not end up in the glass. To serve, garnish with 1 cherry.

SUGGESTED USE

A classic aperitif.

Carpaccio with Soybean Sprouts

EASY

ingredients for 4 people
time: 30 minutes + cooling time
(30 minutes)

24 slices of beef rump
1/2 a yellow bell pepper
1/2 a red bell pepper
4 radishes
1 zucchini
1 celery stalk
0.22 lbs (3.5 oz) canned soybean sprouts
grana padano cheese flakes
2 lemons
extra virgin olive oil
salt and pepper

Lightly grease a nice platter with extra virgin olive oil and place all the slices of Carpaccio, trying to overlap them as little as possible. Wash all the vegetables, and with a potato peeler, shave an abundance of Grana Padano flakes, being careful not to crumble the shavings. Finely chop the peppers and put them all in a bowl. Combine zucchini cut into matchstick-size strips, the radishes and celery cut into thin slices, and well drained bean sprouts. Add the lemon juice, salt and pepper and gently mix everything. Evenly sprinkle the meat with the vegetable mixture and dress everything with extra virgin olive oil. Let settle in the refrigerator for 30 minutes, and just before serving, cover the Carpaccio with plenty of Grana Padano flakes.

ROB ROY

INGREDIENTS

WHISKY
RED VERMOUTH
ANGOSTURA

ORIGINS AND ODDITIES

It's been said that a bartender (originally from Scotland) created this cocktail in the 1930s in Manhattan, naming it after a beloved Scottish patriot.

PREPARATION

Measure 60 ml (1/4 cup) of Scotch whisky in a graduated cylinder and pour into a glass carafe. Repeat with 30 ml (2 tbsp) of red vermouth. Combine a few drops of angostura and ice cubes, then mix it all with a long-handled spoon. Pour into a cocktail glass (pre-chilled in the freezer) and serve, garnished with 1 cherry.

SUGGESTED USE

Excellent as an aperitif, it is recommended for the evening.

Tuna Tartar
MEDIUM

ingredients for 4 people
time: 30 minutes + cooling time
(1 hour)

0.88 lbs (14 oz) fresh tuna filet
2 small tomatoes
4 large lettuce leaves
1 shallot
celery
juice of 1 lemon
salt
pepper
extra virgin olive oil

Finely chop the cleaned shallot, or pass it through a mixer, along with a small and washed celery stalk. On a cutting board, dice the tuna filet into very small cubes and put them in a bowl. Combine with chopped vegetables as well as salt and pepper to taste, followed by the lemon juice and 4 tbsp of extra virgin olive oil. Mix everything gently with bare hands, fill four moulds with the preparation and let settle in the refrigerator for at least 1 hour. Carefully unmold the tuna tartar onto saucers and serve as an appetizer, along with a tuft of finely chopped lettuce and a tablespoon of dice tomatoes.

RUSTY NAIL

INGREDIENTS

WHISKY

DRAMBUIE LIQUEUR

ORIGINS AND ODDITIES

According to some, this was created in the 1960s.
The Rusty Nail owes its name to the early habit
of adding a few cloves to the drink.

PREPARATION

Measure 50 ml (3 1/3 tbsp) of whisky in a graduated
cylinder and pour into a low tumbler full of ice.
Repeat with 40 ml (2 3/4 tbsp) of Drambuie liqueur.
Stir for a few seconds with a long-handled spoon
and serve.

SUGGESTED USE

An excellent digestive, this drink is most especially
recommended at the end of a big dinner.

 Margherita Cake   EASY

ingredients for 6/8 people
time: 1 hour and 30 minutes

3/4 cup + 1 tbsp flour
4 eggs
7/8 cup (14 tbsp) butter
6/9 cup sugar
2/3 cup potato starch flour
1 sachet baking powder
1 vanilla sachet
salt
icing sugar

In a bowl, whisk eggs with sugar in order to obtain a smooth and
foamy cream. Break up and lightly soften the butter and add to the
bowl. While continuously mixing, combine, little by little, the sifted flour, starch, baking powder, vanilla and a pinch of salt. Give the
dough a final mix and pour into a cake pan covered with baking
paper. Bake for 30 minutes at 356°F (180°C) and let cool. Before serving, decorate with abundant icing sugar.

SAZERAC 2012

INGREDIENTS

AMERICAN WHISKY   ANGOSTURA
ABSINTHE   SUGAR

ORIGINS AND ODDITIES

A Creole pharmacist in New Orleans came up
with this drink in 1830, sparking great enthusiasm
among the first tasters. The name of the cocktail
seems to derive from a brand of cognac that
was very well known at the time. Italian barman
Gianfranco Di Niso has proposed a modern day twist
on this classic, creating an "on the rocks" version.

PREPARATION

Place 1 lump of sugar in the center of a low
tumbler then pour in a few drops of angostura
and crush everything with a pestle. Add 75 ml
(5 tbsp) of whisky and 15 ml (1 tbsp) of absinthe
(previously measured in a graduated cylinder).
Fill the tumbler with ice and mix together with
a long-handled spoon. Garnish with a lemon peel.

SUGGESTED USE

Effective as a digestive, it is good for every moment
of the evening.

Dark Whisky Cake   EASY

ingredients for 6/8 people
time: 2 hours

1 7/8 cups flour
4/5 cup butter
4/5 cup sugar
0.61 lbs (9.87 oz, about 1 1/2 cup)
dark chocolate
1 shot glass whisky
1 tbsp vanilla extract
4 eggs
salt
icing sugar

Sift the flour into a large bowl. In a separate bowl, work the butter
into a cream with a spoon and gradually add 3/4 cup of sugar. Crack
the eggs and incorporate the yolks to the butter, mixing with a wood-
en spoon. Chop up the chocolate and melt in a double boiler until it
becomes creamy and smooth, then add whisky and vanilla. Stir the
melted chocolate into the butter and egg yolks and mix thoroughly.
Add flour to the mixture. Beat the egg whites into stiff peaks, with a
pinch of salt, along with 1/6 cup of the remaining sugar, subsequently incorporating it to the whole mixture. Pour into a greased cake
mould and bake at 356°F (180°C) for about 45 minutes, checking it
from time to time. Remove from oven and let cool. Serve on a platter
and sprinkle with plenty of icing sugar.

WHISKY COBBLER

INGREDIENTS

AMERICAN WHISKY   GINGER ALE

GRENADINE SYRUP   FRESH FRUIT
OF THE SEASON

ORIGINS AND ODDITIES

Apparently, it was a shoemaker (or a "cobbler" as
they say in England) who suggested the idea for
this to an American bartender, who then created
this drink in the 1940s.

PREPARATION

Measure 50 ml (3 1/3 tbsp) of whisky in a graduated
cylinder and pour into a high tumbler. Repeat with
20 ml (4 tsp) of grenadine syrup and
80 ml (1/3 cup) of Ginger Ale. Combine 3 tbsp of
fresh seasonal fruit, filling almost to the brim with
crushed ice. Stir with a long-handled spoon and
serve, garnished with a 1 long toothpick and
2 long straws.

SUGGESTED USE

A low alcohol and very festive long drink, it can be
enjoyed at all hours of the day.

 Almond Brittle   MEDIUM

ingredients for 4 people
time: 2 hours

1 1/3 cups sugar
0.66 lbs (10.5 oz, about 3 1/2 cup)
almonds
butter
1/2 a lemon

In a deep saucepan, parboil the almonds. Drain everything, remove
the skins and coarsely chop the almonds. In a saucepan, melt a knob
of butter and add the sugar. While continuously mixing with a spoon,
add the almonds and lemon juice. When the mixture is golden brown,
remove from heat and pour into a buttered baking pan, spreading
everything evenly with a spatula. Leave to cool completely at room
temperature. Serve the brittle cut into squares.

WHISKY SLING

INGREDIENTS

AMERICAN WHISKY

WHITE SUGAR

LEMON JUICE

SODA WATER OR SPARKLING WATER

ORIGINS AND ODDITIES

With the spread of the Singapore Sling, bartenders tried to devise a similar drink with a nationally distilled spirit. In the process they created one of the most popular long drinks in the world.

PREPARATION

Measure 50 ml (3 1/3 tbsp) of whisky in a graduated cylinder and pour into a tall tumbler filled with ice. Repeat with 30 ml (2 tbsp) of lemon juice. Combine 1 tbsp (10 g) of white sugar and fill almost to the brim of the glass with soda or sparkling mineral water. Stir for a few seconds with a long-handled spoon and serve, garnished with 2 cherries 1/2 a slice of lemon and 2 long straws.

SUGGESTED USE

A long drink suitable for any time of the day or evening.

Carrot Cake

EASY

ingredients for 6/8 people
time: 1 hour and 30 minutes

1 1/5 cups flour
1 sachet baking powder
powdered nutmeg
powdered ginger
powdered cinnamon
9/10 cup cane sugar
2/3 cup sunflower seed oil
2 eggs
0.48 lbs (7.76 oz, about 3 1/2 medium) grated carrots
1.41 oz (0.08 lbs) walnut kernels
4 tsp cointreau
butter and icing sugar

Butter and flour a classic donut cake mould. Pass the walnuts through a mixer along with the carrots. In a large bowl, sift the flour, baking powder, cinnamon, ginger, and nutmeg and give an initial mix. In another bowl, whisk together the cane sugar and eggs until the mixture is smooth. Add the sunflower seed oil, Cointreau, and little by little, add the sifted flour mixture while continuously stirring. Pour it all into the greased cake mould and bake at 356°F (180°C) for about 45 minutes. Unmold the carrot cake unto a platter, and before serving, sprinkle with abundant icing sugar.

WHISKY SOUR

INGREDIENTS

WHISKY
LEMON JUICE
SUGAR SYRUP

ORIGINS AND ODDITIES

Created in the early 1900s, this drink immediately
transformed into the sour par excellence.

PREPARATION

Measure 40 ml (2 3/4 tbsp) of whisky in a graduated
cylinder and pour into a shaker. Repeat with 30 ml (2
tbsp) of lemon juice and 20 ml (4 tsp) of sugar syrup.
Add some ice cubes and shake vigorously for a few
seconds. Pour into a cocktail glass (pre-chilled in the
freezer) and serve, garnished with 1 cherry.

SUGGESTED USE

An excellent digestive, this drink can be enjoyed
throughout the evening.

 Profiterole (Cream Puffs)   EASY

ingredients for 4 people
time: 1 hour + cooling time
(2 hours)

12 big puffs
3 1/4 cups milk
2/3 cup sugar
3/4 cup + 1 tbsp flour
4 big eggs
zest of 3 lemons
1 vanilla sachet
1 cup cream
2 shot glasses limoncello
(lemon liqueur)
fresh strawberries

Put the milk to boil with a sachet of vanilla. In a bowl, whisk the sugar
and egg yolks in order to obtain a foamy cream. Add the lemon zest
in pieces and the milk passed through a sieve, and continue to cook
everything in a double boiler while continuously stirring in order to
get a lump free and fluid cream. Remove from heat and discard the
lemon rinds. Let cool and add the limoncello and previously whipped
cream. With a box cutter or knife, pierce the base of the puffs and fill
them with cream using a pastry bag with a small, smooth beak. On a
platter, arrange the cream puffs in the form of a pyramid and cover
them abundantly with all the remaining cream filling. Let settle in the
refrigerator for at least 2 hours. Just before serving, decorate with fresh
strawberries and tufts of whipped cream.

TEQUILA-BASED COCKTAILS

Tequila has an ancestor: pulque. Its origins date back to the time of the Aztecs, who extracted a sweet drink from a tropical plant called agave. The drink was used during religious ceremonies.

The production system has been passed down from generation to generation by indigenous people in Mexico, until the arrival of Spanish Conquistadors in the middle of the sixteenth century. European colonists thought of trying to distill the agave juice's high sugar concentration.

Subjected to distillation, the result, which had a strong personality and a distinct taste, was then called "Mezcal wine". Tequila was born, with the name probably deriving from the place where it was first made.

Some sources, however, believe the name came from the Tequila volcano, which dominates the fields of blue agave in the state of Jalisco.

Don Jose Cuervo was the first to believe in this new distillate in the late eighteenth century, and his family contributed to its spread in Mexico and then the rest of the world, establishing itself as the first producer in the world.

Until the middle of last century, however, tequila was produced primarily for the domestic market: it had very high alcohol content and the flavor was very strong. With wider distribution, tequila producers began to reduce agave production, with the proportions of agave and sugar reaching nearly 50%. This blend of tequila was very popular with American consumers, and sales increased, especially in the United States.

In 1977, after many legal battles, Mexican producers were able to obtain an official recognition, certifying that the product could only be done within the Mexican border. In 1994, an agency (CRT, the Tequila Regulatory Council), was created to monitor compliance with the criteria laid down by this production specification. The rules for the production of tequila are very strict and closely monitored by this agency.

To produce tequila that the CRT views as a 100% natural product, producers have to use or produce: blue agave from only five states, a double distillation process, alcohol content of at least 35%, and a label with the words "hecho en Mexico" (made in Mexico). Tequila production is made using the *Agave Tequilana Weber Azul*, also known as blue agave, which matures in about 10 years. Once you cut the plant, this can not be reused for a new production.

The heart of the plant, called "pine cone" because of its particular form, is cooked in a steam oven and left to cool. The pine cones are reduced to a pulp, and then washed with water to extract the agave juice (called "honey water"). The juice is fermented, and you get an agave wine of about 10% vol. This wine is distilled twice to get tequila that, at this point, may be refined or aged. Aging in oak barrels gives the distillate its amber color and softness. Tequila is brought to an alcohol content of 40% vol by adding water. It is then ready to be bottled and sold.

There are two types of tequila:
100%, obtained with blue agave sugar
Blended, obtained with 51% blue agave sugar, plus other sugars

There are fivae official categories that differ according to the years of aging in barrels:
Silver, Gold, Reposado, Anejo, Extra Anejo.

Regarding the use of tequila in cocktails, you have to consider its distinct taste and pungent aroma. There are, however, many famous cocktails made with tequila, such as the Margarita, Tequila Sunrise, Tequila Boom Boom, and many others, which always tied to the Mexican territory and culture. Tequila can also be easily consumed on its own, in shot glasses with salt and lime: it is a party distillate, best enjoyed with drinking companions. The darker (and therefore older) varieties can be served, like other aged spirits, in large balloon glasses.

Mezcal is a close relative of tequila. This is a homemade agave distillate (a different species is used from the agave blue) and is produced in all of Mexico, without the legal and protective constraints of the tequila consortium. Production has a significantly lower cost than tequila, and it is has become much more prevalent in Mexico. In fact, it is regarded as the national distillate. The unique characteristic of mezcal, which led it to be known around the world, is the presence of a gusano (worm) at the bottom of each bottle.

There are also variations of aged mezcal, which are now regarded as a premium distillate. Mezcal's similarity to tequila makes it useful in numerous cocktails, like Mezcal Margarita.

BLACK EGG

INGREDIENTS

TEQUILA

COFFEE LIQUEUR

EGG YOLK

CREAM

ORIGINS AND ODDITIES

The creation of this cocktail has been attributed to a Mexican lady who used to prepare this energy-boosting drink for her four children before they went to work in the fields.

PREPARATION

Measure 30 ml (2 tbsp) in a graduated cylinder and pour into a shaker. Repeat with 20 ml (4 tsp) of coffee liqueur and 20 ml (4 tsp) of cream. Combine 1 1/2 tbsp (20 g) egg yolk and some ice cubes, then shake for a few seconds. Pour into a cup (pre-chilled in the freezer) and garnish with coffee beans.

SUGGESTED USE

An excellent energy-boosting drink, it is recommended for particularly challenging days.

 Mocha Cake   EASY

ingredients for 6/8 people
time: 1 hour and 30 minutes

1 7/8 cups flour
2 4/5 cups icing sugar
0.26 lbs (4.2 oz) dark chocolate
1 sachet baking powder
salt
6 eggs
1/2 cup water
1/2 cup vegetable oil
2/5 cup coffee

Melt the chocolate in a double boiler. Remove from heat, and while mixing, add water and coffee. Combine the egg yolks and mix everything well with a whisk. In a bowl, sift the flour and add sugar, baking powder, and a pinch of salt, stirring well until you get a smooth mixture. Combine this last mixture to the first chocolate-based one, and while continuously stirring from below, add stiffened egg whites. Pour the batter into a mocha or donut cake mould without buttering. Bake in the oven at 356°F (180°C) for about 45 minutes. Remove from oven and let cool completely. Unmold the mocha cake on a platter and sprinkle with abundant icing sugar before serving.

BLOODY MARIA

INGREDIENTS

TEQUILA
TOMATO JUICE
LEMON JUICE

SPICES (SALT, PEPPER,
WORCESTERSHIRE SAUCE,
TABASCO, JAPALEÑO
PEPPERS)

ORIGINS AND ODDITIES

A cocktail that pays homage to the more famous
Bloody Mary, this Mexican variation makes two
changes from the British mainstay: tequila in place
of vodka and the addition of jalapeño peppers.

PREPARATION

Measure 50 ml (3 1/3 tbsp) of tequila in a graduated
cylinder and pour into a high tumbler. Repeat with
20 ml (4 tsp) of lemon juice and 90 ml (6 tbsp) of
tomato juice. Add salt, pepper, a few sprinkles of
Tabasco, Worcestershire sauce, jalapeño peppers
and some ice cubes. Mix the ingredients thoroughly
with a long-handled spoon and serve, garnished
with 1 slice of avocado, 1 celery stick (optional)
and 2 long straws.

SUGGESTED USE

Perfect for any cocktail hour, this drink is good
throughout the evening.

Jalapeños   EASY

ingredients for 4 people
time: 45 minutes

8 jalapeños
0.13 lbs (2.1 oz) cream cheese
0.13 lbs (2.1 oz) mexican cheese
8 slices spicy salami
1 medium onion
2 cloves garlic
chopped coriander
juice of 1 lime
salt
butter
extra virgin olive oil

Wash and open the hot peppers lengthwise, removing the seeds. Bake
on a lightly buttered baking pan for 10 minutes on maximum heat
and let cool. In a small frying pan, sauté the chopped onion in 1 tbsp of
extra virgin olive oil, then add the chopped sausages. Pour into a large
bowl and add the minced garlic, coriander, lime juice, cheese, salt and
pepper, mixing everything well in order to get a smooth filling. Stuff
the jalapeños and bake once again on high until the cheese begins to
appear golden. Serve the jalapeños very hot.

BLUE MARGARITA

INGREDIENTS

TEQUILA

BLUE CURAÇAO

COINTREAU

LEMON JUICE OR

LIME JUICE

SALT

ORIGINS AND ODDITIES

A drink created in the wake of the Margarita's success. Its color pays homage to the beautiful sea that bathes Acapulco.

PREPARATION

Measure 40 ml (2 3/4 tbsp) of tequila in a graduated cylinder and pour into a shaker. Repeat with 20 ml (4 tsp) of Blue Curaçao, 10 ml (2 tsp) of Cointreau, 20 ml (4 tsp) of lemon or lime juice. Add ice cubes and stir for a few seconds. Remove a cup from the freezer and moisten the rim with half the lemon and dip into a plate of salt. Pour the drink into the cup to serve.

SUGGESTED USE

A drink suitable for all hours of the evening, it has become increasingly popular as an aperitif.

Acapulco-Style Fusilli

EASY

ingredients for 4 people
time: 1 hour

0.80 lbs (12.6 oz) fusilli pasta

2 yellow bell peppers

0.44 lbs (7 oz, about 1 cup) black beans

1 clove garlic

lemon juice

salt

pepper

extra virgin olive oil

sage

At least 10 hours prior to the preparation, leave the black beans to soften in plenty of cold water. Then, boil beans in a pot for about 40 minutes and add crushed garlic and coarsely chopped sage. Drain and put aside, removing the spices. Meanwhile, wash the peppers and cut into small cubes. Cook the pasta in plenty of salted water. Drain pasta when it is al dente and cool immediately under running water. Pour the pasta into a bowl and combine the peppers and beans. Season with 4 tbsp of extra virgin olive oil, salt, pepper, and lemon juice. Mix gently until everything is evenly distributed and serve.

CAIPIRITA

INGREDIENTS

TEQUILA WHITE
WHITE SUGAR OR CANE SUGAR
LIME

ORIGINS AND ODDITIES

A drink recently created in Mexico in the wake of the Brazilian Caipirinha's success, it immediately aroused the enthusiasm of younger drinkers, who greatly contributed to its spread around the world.

PREPARATION

Place 1/2 a lime, cut into small cubes, in a low tumbler and add 10 g (3 tsp) of sugar. With a pestle, pound the whole until it's a pulp. Combine 50–60 ml (10 tsp–12tsp) of tequila previously measured in the graduated cylinder and fill almost to the brim with crushed ice. Stir vigorously for a few seconds with a long-handled spoon and serve, garnished with 2 short straws.

SUGGESTED USE

A great drink for any time of day.

Burritos   EASY

ingredients for 4 people
time: 1 hour

8 readymade mexican tortillas
0.11 lbs (1.76 oz) sliced bacon
1 onion
1 roast chicken
0.88 lbs (14 oz) readymade taco sauce
0.15 lbs (2.46 oz) mushrooms
0.26 lbs (4.2 oz) grated edam cheese
salt
pepper
extra virgin olive oil

Preheat oven at 356°F (180°C). Debone and skin the chicken, then cut the meat into frayed strips. Wash mushrooms and cut them into thin slices. Peel and finely chop the onion, then sauté in a large pan with extra virgin olive oil. Add the bacon strips, and after 1 minute, add the mushrooms. After 5 minutes, add the chicken and taco sauce, stirring everything together and cooking for another 5 minutes. Meanwhile, heat the tortillas, covered with foil, in the oven. Once they are hot, remove from the oven and fill with the chicken mixture. Sprinkle with grated cheese and close the tortillas. Serve very hot, accompanied by taco sauce at room temperature.

CAIPIRITA ANEJO

INGREDIENTS

AGED TEQUILA
BROWN OR CANE SUGAR
LIME OR ORANGE

ORIGINS AND ODDITIES

Recently created in the wake of the enormous succes of the "crushed" cocktail family, the Caipira Anejo has now spread throughout the world. It is most especially popular with women.

PREPARATION

Place 1/2 a lime, cut into small cubes, in a low tumbler and add 10 g (3 tsp) of cane sugar. Grind everything with the help of a pestle until it's a pulp. Measure 50–60 ml (10 tsp–12 tsp) of tequila in a graduated cylinder and pour into the glass, filling almost to the brim with crushed ice. Stir with a long-handled spoon, to best mix all the ingredients, and serve, garnished with 2 short straws.

SUGGESTED USE

A drink that can be enjoyed throughout the evening.

Olives and Orange

EASY

ingredients for 4 people
time: 30 minutes

5 oranges
24 black olives
24 green olives
extra virgin olive oil
salt pepper
sesame seeds

Peel 600 g (21.16 oz) raw oranges and cut the pulp into large cubes. Peel and thinly slice the remaining two. Put the oranges along with the washed and pitted olives in a bowl. Gently mix everything together and add 1 tbsp of extra virgin olive oil, as well as salt and pepper to taste. Line 4 single-serving salad cups, which were previously chilled in the freezer, with the orange slices, then deposit 1 tbsp of the olives and orange salad in the center of each. Sprinkle with the sesame seeds and serve.

GRAN MARGARITA

INGREDIENTS

AGED TEQUILA
GRAND MARNIER
LEMON OR LIME JUICE

ORIGINS AND ODDITIES

Following the creation of the Margarita cocktail, some Mexican bartenders tried to create a more delicate version. The excellent result was the Gran Margarita, a drink that is especially loved by women.

PREPARATION

Measure 40 ml (2 3/4 tbsp) of aged tequila in a graduated cylinder and pour into a shaker. Repeat with 30 ml (2 tbsp) of Grand Marnier and 20 ml (4 tsp) of lemon juice. Add ice cubes and shake vigorously for a few seconds. Remove a cup from the freezer and moisten the rim with half the lemon. Dip the cup onto a plate of salt. Pour the drink into the cup to serve.

SUGGESTED USE

A drink that can be enjoyed throughout the evening.

Baked Mixed Fruit   EASY

ingredients for 4 people
time: 1 hour

0.66 lbs (10.5 oz) apricots
0.66 lbs (10.5 oz) cherries
4 egg yolks
2 1/8 cups milk
1/3 cup potato starch flour
1 cup (20 tbsp) sugar
2 tbsp grand marnier
0.15 lbs (2.46 oz, about 7/8 cup) flaked almonds

In a large bowl, whisk together the egg yolks with 7/8 cup (40 tsp) of sugar, in order to get a frothy cream. Gradually add sifted potato starch, and while continuously mixing, add the milk. Pour the mixture into a saucepan and cook over medium heat, but do not allow the cream to curdle. Remove from heat and add the liqueur, then transfer the cream into a pan to cool. Wash the apricots, open them vertically and remove the pits. Pit the cherries after they have been washed under running water. Pour the remaining sugar into a large bowl along with 2/3 cup of water and cook until the syrup does not leave a film on a spoon. Combine apricots and cherries and continue cooking for 5 minutes on high heat. Drain the fruit through a skimmer spoon and place it decoratively on top of the cream in the pan, making sure that the convex part of the fruit remains upward. Allow the syrup to reduce longer and distribute it abundantly over the fruit. Top it off by sprinkling with flaked almonds. Bake at 356°F (180°C) for a few minutes, laying the pan just under the grill until the surface of the dessert begins to brown.

MERCEDES

INGREDIENTS

TEQUILA

APEROL

STRAWBERRY JUICE

GRAPEFRUIT JUICE

ORIGINS AND ODDITIES

A drink created by a bartender in Acapulco in honor of Mercedes, a beautiful Mexican girl who frequented the beaches in the area.

PREPARATION

Measure 20 ml (4 tsp) of tequila in a graduated cylinder and pour into a tall tumbler filled with ice. Repeat with 70 ml (4 tbsp + 2 tsp) of Aperol, 40 ml (2 3/4 tbsp) of grapefruit juice and 30 ml (2 tbsp) of pureed strawberries or strawberry juice. Stir for a few seconds with a long-handled spoon and serve, garnished with 1/2 a slice of orange, 2 strawberries and 2 long straws.

SUGGESTED USE

An excellent long drink, it is recommended as an aperitif before a Mexican meal.

 Mexican Paella   MEDIUM

ingredients for 4 people
time: 1 hour

2 cups rice
2 chicken breasts
0.33 lbs (5.3 oz) pork meat
0.33 lbs (5.3 oz) boiled shrimps
0.44 lbs (7 oz) spicy sausage
3 bell peppers (1 red/1 green/1 yellow)
0.33 lbs (5.3 oz, about 1 cup) fresh peas
0.22 lbs (3.5 oz) onion
2 cloves garlic and extra virgin olive oil
2 hot chili peppers
2 sachets saffron
4 1/4 cups vegetable broth
salt and pepper

Boil 4 1/4 cups of vegetable broth, so that it is always on hand throughout the preparation. In a saucepan, heat 2 tbsp of extra virgin olive oil and brown the two crushed garlic cloves as well as thinly chopped onion slices. Add diced chicken and thinly shredded pork. Cook everything at medium heat. In a large pan, fry the rice with extra virgin olive oil. Combine the chicken, pork and chunks of sausage. While continuously stirring with a wooden spoon, add the peas, as well as the sweet and spicy peppers that have been cleaned and cut into strips. Dissolve saffron in a cup of water, combine to the rest and continue cooking. Gradually add the hot vegetable broth. When the rice is almost ready, add the peeled shrimps, and before serving in a nice earthenware dish, allow it to cool for a couple of minutes.

MEXICAN COFFEE

INGREDIENTS

TEQUILA

COFFEE LIQUEUR

LONG COFFEE

WHITE OR CANE SUGAR

CREAM

ORIGINS AND ODDITIES

A Mexican variation of the most famous hot drink
in the world: Irish Coffee.

PREPARATION

Measure 40 ml (2 3/4 tbsp) of tequila in a graduated
cylinder and pour into a milk jug. Repeat with
20 ml (4 tsp) of coffee liqueur. Add 1 long coffee
and 10 g (3 tsp) of white sugar. Bring to a boil,
stirring frequently. Pour into a heat-resistant mug
and, just before serving, add 40ml (8 tsp) of cream
(previously measured in a graduated cylinder) using
the edge of a teaspoon, so that it remains separated
from the rest.

SUGGESTED USE

A decidely flavorful hot drink, it is perfect on the
coldest days of the year.

Chocolate and Pear Cake   EASY

ingredients for 6/8 people
time: 1 hour and 15 minutes

1 7/8 cups flour
1/2 cup (9 tbsp) sugar
1/2 cup butter
3 eggs
3 medium pears
1 sachet baking powder
0.17 lbs (2.8 oz) dark chocolate
powdered cinnamon

In a large bowl, whisk together the sugar and eggs until the mixture
is smooth and foamy. Soften pieces of butter and add to the bowl
while continuously mixing. Gradually add the sifted flour and baking
powder. When the dough is smooth and well blended, add the finely
chopped chocolate, and the previously washed and diced pears. Stir
well one last time and pour into a previously buttered and floured cake
mould. Bake at 320°F (160°C) for about 30 minutes. Serve the cake either warm or cold, and decorate with fan-shaped slices of pear and a
sprinkle of cinnamon.

MEZCALIBUR

INGREDIENTS

MEZCAL
SPEARMINT LIQUEUR
MARASCHINO LIQUEUR
PINEAPPLE JUICE

ORIGINS AND ODDITIES

A cocktail created in the 1950s by a barman
in Acapulco.

PREPARATION

Measure 40 ml (2 3/4 tbsp) of mezcal in a graduated
cylinder and pour into a transparent shaker. Repeat
with 20 ml (4 tsp) of green mint liqueur, 10 ml (2 tsp)
of Maraschino liqueur and 90 ml (6 tbsp) of pineapple
juice. Add some ice cubes and shake vigorously for
a few seconds. Pour into a highball filled with ice
and serve, garnished with 1/2 a slice of pineapple,
1/2 an orange slice, 1 nice sprig of fresh mint and
2 long straws.

SUGGESTED USE

A long drink that is particularly recommended
during the hottest days of summer.

 Avocado and Pineapple Specialty   EASY

ingredients for 4 people
time: 30 minutes

1 big avocado
0.33 lbs (5.3 oz, about 1 cup) corn
0.44 lbs (7 oz) pineapple
1/2 a red bell pepper
chopped parsley
3 tbsp extra virgin olive oil
1 tbsp vinegar
1 tbsp mustard
1 tbsp sugar
juice of 1 lemon
salt
pepper
curly endive salad

Wash and open the avocado. Remove the pit and peel it carefully, then
dice the flesh into large cubes. Set it down in a bowl, bathing it well in
lemon juice, in order for it not to turn brown. Cover it with aluminum
foil and store in the refrigerator. Wash and dry the lettuce and cut
into large chunks. Wash the bell pepper, and then cut into matchstick sized strips. Clean the pineapple and cut into small wedges. With
a fork and in a bowl, mix the vinegar, mustard, 1/2 tbsp of sugar,
and salt and pepper to taste, in order to obtain a dense and smooth
dressing. Combine the extra virgin olive oil, the remaining sugar and
parsley. On a platter, arrange a bed of salad. Add the pineapples and
well drained corn. Add the drained avocado, and just before serving
sprinkle everything well with the dressing. Decorate with strips of
red pepper.

ORANGE JAM CAIPIRITA

INGREDIENTS

TEQUILA
WHITE OR CANE SUGAR
LIME

ORANGE MARMALADE
LIQUID SUGAR

ORIGINS AND ODDITIES

A drink recently created in Milan by Dario Comini, one of the best bartenders in the world. It has become very popular with younger drinkers.

PREPARATION

Put 1/2 a diced lime in a glass jar and add 10 g (3 tsp) of white sugar. Grind everything with the help of a pestle until it's a pulp. Combine 15 ml (0.50 oz) of orange marmalade, 50–60 ml (10 tsp–12 tsp) of tequila and 20 ml (4 tsp) of sugar syrup (previously measured in a graduated cylinder). Fill the jar with the crushed ice and stir vigorously for a few seconds with a long-handled spoon. Serve, garnished with 2 short straws.

SUGGESTED USE

A young drink that can be enjoyed at all hours of the evening.

Lollipops

MEDIUM

ingredients for 4 people
time: 2 hours

1 cup (16 tbsp) sugar
0.17 lbs (2.8 oz) fruit syrup
2/5 cups water
almond oil

In a saucepan, combine all the cold ingredients and mix vigorously with a whisk. Cook on low heat until the sugar dissolves completely. Stop stirring and let the sugar start to solidify again. Grease a baking sheet with almond oil and, with a spoon, deposit the mixture in order to get lollipops with a diameter of about 4 cm. Before the mixture begins to solidify, put a popsicle stick at the center of each disk. Allow to cool and, just before serving, gently remove the lollipops from the baking sheet with the help of a knife.

PEPITO COLLINS

INGREDIENTS

TEQUILA   SUGAR SYRUP

LEMON JUICE   SODA WATER OR SPARKLING WATER

ORIGINS AND ODDITIES

A drink created in California in the 1950s from the mixture known by the name "Reuben." As tequila's fame increased, the Pepito Collins was consequently spread throughout the world.

PREPARATION

Measure 50 ml (3 1/3 tbsp) of tequila in a graduated cylinder and pour into a tall tumbler filled with ice. Repeat with 30 ml (2 tbsp) of lemon juice, 20 ml (4 tsp) of sugar syrup and 60 ml (1/4 cup) of soda water or sparkling water. Stir gently for a few seconds with a long-handled spoon and serve, garnished with 1/2 a slice of lemon, 2 cherries and 2 long straws.

SUGGESTED USE

An excellent refreshing long drink that can be served at all hours of the day.

 Drunken Apricots   EASY

ingredients for 4 people
time: 30 minutes

0.88 lbs (14 oz) apricots in syrup
2 eggs
scant 1/2 cup (8 tbsp) sugar
2 tbsp tequila
0.08 lbs (1.41 oz) candied cherries
4 tbsp whipped cream

In a bowl, whisk whole eggs and sugar until the mixture is smooth and fluffy. Add the tequila and unsweetened whipped cream. In 4 dessert bowls, which were previously chilled in the freezer, create a bed of cream and then place the half-drained apricots on top. Add a teaspoon of cherries to each bowl and finish off with a teaspoon of cream. Serve immediately.

TEQUILA BUM BUM

INGREDIENTS

TEQUILA
CLEAR SODA POP
(SPARKLING WATER, TONIC, CLUB SODA, ETC.)

ORIGINS AND ODDITIES
This cocktail was created around the mid-'80s
as a last drink for the evening. It was also called
the "goodnight drink."

PREPARATION
Measure 30 ml (2 tbsp) of tequila in a graduated
cylinder and pour into a shot glass with a thick
bottom. Repeat with a 30 ml (2 tbsp) of transparent
soda. Cover the glass with a paper towel and slam
(quite forcefully) 2–3 times on a hard surface. Serve.

SUGGESTED USE
A great drink for after dinner or the late evening.

Bizcochitos de Grasa (Lard Biscuits)   EASY

ingredients for 4 people
time: 1 hour and 30 minutes

4 cups flour
salt
5 1/4 cups warm water
0.53 oz (2 tsp) fresh yeast
0.53 oz (1 3/5 tbsp) fresh yeast
0.27 lbs (4.4 oz) lard

Sift flour into a heap on a work surface, add a pinch of salt, lard and
fresh yeast that was previously mixed with warm water. Knead the ingredients with bare hands in order to obtain a homogeneous ball with
a smooth surface. Flour a work surface and roll out the dough with a
rolling pin, forming a rectangle, and then fold it on itself a couple of
times. Roll out one last time and with a round cookie cutter, about the
width of a glass, cut out biscuits. Prick the surface of each biscuit with
a fork and space them out on a baking tray covered with baking paper.
Bake at 356°F (180°C) for 15 minutes. Remove from the oven once the
biscuits become golden around the edges, so that, once cooled, they
maintain their softness.

TEQUILA PUERTO VALLARTA

INGREDIENTS

TEQUILA
ORANGE JUICE

LIME JUICE
GRENADINE SYRUP

ORIGINS AND ODDITIES

When Hollywood producers discovered the paradise of Mismaloya Bay, they decided to "invade" the little nearby Mexican village of fishermen, building a real and proper cinema city. It was a local bartender who came up with this drink, in honor of the movie stars who began to frequent their premises, naming the new cocktail after the town that hosted them.

PREPARATION

Measure 50 ml (3 1/3 tbsp) of tequila in a graduated cylinder and pour into a tall tumbler. Repeat with 80 ml (1/3 cup) of orange juice, 20 ml (4 tsp) of lime juice and 10 ml (2 tsp) of grenadine syrup. Stir with a long-handled spoon and serve, garnished with 1/2 a slice of lime, 2 cherries and 2 short straws.

SUGGESTED USE

This refreshing drink is recommended for all hours of the day.

Guacamole

EASY

ingredients for 4 people
time: 30 minutes

1 ripe avocado
juice of 1 lime
extra virgin olive oil
salt and black pepper

Peel and open the avocado and remove the pit. Once cut into cubes, put into a mortar and crush with a pestle along with lime juice. Add a drizzle of extra olive virgin oil and a generous sprinkle of salt and black pepper (preferably freshly ground). Give it a final mix and cover with plastic wrap up until serving time, so as to delay oxidation of the sauce as much as possible. Perfect to accompany with nachos, tortillas, or grilled meat and fish.

TEQUILA SUNRISE

INGREDIENTS

TEQUILA
ORANGE JUICE
GRENADINE SYRUP

ORIGINS AND ODDITIES

Created in Mexico in the 1950s, this "welcome cocktail" was served to tourists arriving in the then nascent Cancún and Acapulco.

PREPARATION

Measure 50 ml (3 1/3 tbsp) of tequila in a graduated cylinder and pour into a tall tumbler filled with ice. Repeat with 90 ml (6 tbsp) of orange juice. Stir with a long-handled spoon. Pour 20 ml (4 tsp) of grenadine syrup (previously measured in a graduated cylinder), letting it slide slowly through the drink until it reaches the bottom of the tumbler, thus obtaining the rising sun effect. To serve, garnish with 1/2 an orange slice and 2 long straws.

SUGGESTED USE

One of the most visual and highly recommended long drinks in times of great heat.

Vanilla Flan

EASY

ingredients for 4 people
time: 1 hour + cooling time
(3 hours)

2 1/8 cups whole milk
2/3 cup sugar
2 egg yolks
1 sachet vanilla
zest of 1 lemon
zest of 1 orange
1 tbsp cornstarch
1 stick cinnamon
caramel syrup
white chocolate flakes or chips

In a large bowl, whisk the egg yolks, sugar, vanilla, cornstarch and 2/5 cup of milk until the mixture is smooth. In a saucepan, pour the remaining milk, the cinnamon stick, orange and lemon zest; then bring everything to a boil. Remove from heat and gradually pour the flavored milk through a sieve into the egg and sugar mixture while continuously stirring. Return this mixture to heat and continue to cook while constantly stirring in order to avoid sticking or lumps. A second before reaching the boiling point, remove from heat and pour into 4 large pudding moulds. Put the flan in the refrigerator and let settle for at least 3 hours. Unmold, serve and garnish with a drizzle of caramel syrup and white chocolate flakes.

TORO LOCO

INGREDIENTS

MEZCAL
COFFEE LIQUEUR

ORIGINS AND ODDITIES
A classic South American drink enjoyed after dinner, it is especially popular in France, a nation that holds two European records: the highest consumption of mezcal and the most Mexican establishments.

PREPARATION
Measure 40 ml (2 3/4 tbsp) of mezcal in a graduated cylinder and pour into a low tumbler full of ice. Repeat with 50 ml (3 1/3 tbsp) of coffee liqueur. Stir with a long-handled spoon and serve, garnished with 2 short straws.

SUGGESTED USE
An excellent digestive that is especially appreciated by male drinkers.

End of September Pudding

EASY

ingredients for 6/8 people
time: 1 hour + cooling time
(2 hours)

0.28 lbs (4.6 oz, about 32) walnut kernels
1/2 cup flour
butter
2 tbsp breadcrumbs
5 eggs
scant 1/2 cup (8 tbsp) sugar
caramel syrup

In a large bowl, whisk the egg whites into stiff peaks along with 1/4 cup (4 tbsp) of sugar. In another bowl, whisk together the egg yolks with the remaining sugar, until you get a smooth and fluffy mixture. Gradually add sifted flour while continuously mixing. Combine the walnuts that were previously passed through a mixer, and finally, the whisked egg whites. Gently give a final mix, starting from the bottom, so that the egg whites don't collapse. Pour the mixture into 4 large ramekins that have been buttered and dusted evenly with bread crumbs. Cover with aluminum foil and bake in a double boiler in the oven for about 35 minutes at 356°F (180°C). Remove from the oven and let cool. Just before serving, unmold the pudding and decorate with caramel syrup.

GRAPPA- AND PISCO-BASED COCKTAILS

Grappa, according to one of the many legends about its origin, was invented by a Roman legionnaire who stole a distiller in Egypt and, once back in Italy, distilled wine from his vineyard in Friuli. Another version links the first production of grappa to the Burgundians, a Germanic tribe that distilled pomace.

Either way, grappa, as is often the case for distillates, was first used medically before becoming a beverage. From the seventeenth century on, production and consumption of spirits soared, thanks to the appearance of the first dephlegmate rectifier. This new technology greatly helped the development of alembic stills, making spirits purer. At that time, grappa was actually a distillation of wine, as the distillation of pomace was still very territorial and reserved for the lower classes. From grapes, farmers could get a strong and refreshing drink, though it was the only liquor, in those days, obtained directly from a solid material, making it something of a crude alcoholic product.

The true birth of grappa as we know it, is dated between the late eighteenth and early nineteenth century. At that time there was shortage in the supply of wine, so a "waste" product from wine production was used to create a spirit that could somewhat make up the demand for wine.

While distillates had something of an "underground" period, by the nineteenth century the first liqueurs and well-known distillates were being created. Today, grappa is very popular around the world, with new technologies and native grapes helping it find admirers.

The grappa made in Italy is a direct distillation of grape marc with the addition of natural wine sediment (lees). The distillation takes place after a careful selection of raw material. The grapes are then fermented and distilled in discontinous alembic stills (steamed or bain-marie), with the heads and tails removed.

Grappa usually matures in wood for at least 6 months and in some cases for years. As by law, the alcohol content of grappa can not be higher than 86% vol, even if it's generally accepted that the best grappas are extracted at about 75% vol. In any case, alcohol content can be reduced by adding water.

In Italy, grappa is produced in the following regions: Piedmont, Lombardy, Trentino, Alto Adige, Veneto, Friuli, Tuscany, and Sicily. In France, the Marc de Champagne – a grappa made from the pomace (or marc) used to make champagne – is produced.

Grappa is served after dinner in tulip glasses, but every vine has a corresponding glass that can enhance its fragrance and taste. Grappa also works very well with hot drinks and coffee, while less intense, low-grade grappa can form an excellent base for cocktails and long drinks.

PISCO

Pisco is the South American equivalent of brandy. The distillate is made from fermented grape juice and is produced in large quantities in Chile, Peru and Mexico. Chile and Peru, in fact, have

been disputing the origins of this spirit for years, with both claiming paternity, much the same way that Ireland and Scotland both lay claim to whisky.

Even the word "pisco" is the subject of debate: it could be derived from the Quechua language, once common in Peru, with the meaning being "little bird"; or it might have emanated from the traditional indios clay container, called "piskos", in which the distillate was sold by the Spaniards. Pisco is also the name of a river and the coastal town near the town of Ica (Peru), where you have the first evidence of the distillate.

The vine arrived in South America in the mid-sixteenth century. The first written attestation of the distillate is the will, dated 1613, of Pedro Manuel, a citizen of Ica, who bequeathed a portion of pisco and the stills needed to produce it. The latter certainly came from Spain and were presumably discontinuous.

The Spanish Crown, under the pressure of European wine producers, increased taxes on Peruvian wine to prevent the import and the lowering of prices on the market, causing a backlog of wine from the South American colony. The only solution was to divert the wine to other markets and add incentives to distillation, which lead to the widespread distribution of pisco among the population.

The distillate would become the product of choice for workers and sailors, and thanks to its low cost, its fame quickly spread.

Today almost all manufacturers own vineyards and most are equipped with modern machines for the production of wine. In some cases, though, the habit of pressing grapes (in a low, walled-in, pool) with feet continue. The wine obtained is stored in tinajas (large clay pots with a variable capacity of 300/400 liters) for the start of fermentation, after which we proceed to distillation.

According to regulations, pisco is aged a minimum of three months in stainless steel or glass containers, giving the distillate time to rest, mix and properly blend its edgy characteristics. High quality products are aged in wood, with the lenght of time dependent on the manufacturer's preference. In some countries, the addition of caramel is allowed, as this softens the distillate and increases the visual effect of aging (though this is not reflected on the palate).

With Chilean pisco, the grape used differs, with almost all varieties of Muscat, from Canelli to Frontignan. As well, for industrial distillation, alembic column stills are used. The classification of pisco in Chile is based on the volume of the product.

It is rare to hear someone ordering pisco in a European bar, unless the clientele are South American. Nevertheless, it serves as a base for a number of famous cocktials, including the Pisco Sour, which is made with lemon juice and sugar. This cocktail was invented by American bartender Victor Morris at a bar in Lima.

ALBA ALPINA

INGREDIENTS

WHITE GRAPPA
WHITE MINT LIQUEUR
LEMON JUICE

ORIGINS AND ODDITIES

According to legend, the creation of this drink
occurred in the Aosta Valley in a Courmayeur hotel,
where one night, a guest asked for something
that would help him digest and get to sleep.
When the bartender served the drink, it was getting
light outside. Hence the name (Alba means "dawn"
in Italian), which helped introduce the new cocktail
to the rest of the world.

PREPARATION

Measure 40 ml (2 3/4 tbsp) of grappa in a graduated
cylinder and pour into a shaker. Repeat with 40 ml
(2 3/4 tbsp) of mint liqueur and 10 ml (2 tsp) of lemon
juice. Add a few ice cubes and shake vigorously for
a few seconds. Pour into a cup (pre-chilled in the
freezer) and serve, garnished with 4–5 cloves.

SUGGESTED USE

An excellent digestive cocktail.

Fragrant Fir-Shaped Cookies   EASY

ingredients for 4 people
time: 2 hours

2 1/2 cups flour
1 cup (16 tbsp) sugar
3 eggs
salt
2 tsp (1/2 tbsp) butter
3/4 tsp baking powder
2 sprigs rosemary
2 sprigs thyme
icing sugar

Sift the flour and place it in a heap on a work surface. Break the eggs
into the center of the heap then add the yeast and butter that was
previously cut into cubes and softened at room temperature. Mix
everything quickly with bare hands until the dough is soft and smooth
to the touch. Form a large ball and lay it on a plate, cover with a damp
cloth and let it rest in the refrigerator for 1 hour. Meanwhile, remove
the rosemary and thyme leaves, wash them quickly and gently pat
them dry with paper towel. Then, finely chop the spices. Spread the
mixture onto the work surface and knead the dough thoroughly, until
the rosemary and thyme are well incorporated. With a rolling pin, roll
out the dough on the floured work surface to reach a thickness of
1 cm. With a cookie cutter in the shape of a pine tree, cut out the
cookies from the dough and lay them, with the help of a spatula, on a
baking sheet coated with baking paper. Bake at 356°F (180°C) for about
20 minutes. Serve hot and sprinkle with icing sugar to your taste.

CAIPIGRAPPA

INGREDIENTS

WHITE GRAPPA
LIME
WHITE OR CANE SUGAR

ORIGINS AND ODDITIES

It's been said that this innovative variation of
the famous Caipirinha was created by a bartender
from the Trentino-Alto Adige region area in
Northern Italy in the late 1990s.

PREPARATION

Put 1/2 a lime, cut into cubes, in a low tumbler and
add 10 g (3 tsp) of white sugar. Grind everything
with a pestle until it's a pulp. Fill the tumbler with
crushed ice and add 50–60 ml (10 tsp–12 tsp) of
grappa (previously measured in a graduated cylinder).
Mix thoroughly with a long-handled spoon and serve,
garnished with 2 short straws.

SUGGESTED USE

Good as a digestive, it can be enjoyed throughout
the evening.

Bergamaschi (Bergamo-Style Biscuits)   EASY

ingredients for 4 people
time: 45 minutes

1 1/5 cups (19 tbsp) corn flour
1 shot glass bergamo grappa
7 tbsp butter
0.08 lbs (1.41 oz) roasted hazelnuts
1/4 cup + 1 1/2 tbsp sugar
2 egg yolks

In a bowl, soften the butter and the sugar with a tablespoon until you
get a smooth paste. While continuously stirring, add the flour and egg
yolks. Combine the finely chopped hazelnuts and grappa. With bare
hands, form balls with the dough and lay them on a baking sheet
covered with baking paper. Then squash the balls with a fork to get flat
cookies with grooves on the surface. Bake at 356°F (180°C) and serve.

GASOLINA

INGREDIENTS

PISCO   SUGAR SYRUP
BLUE CURAÇAO   STRAWBERRY PUREE
LEMON JUICE

ORIGINS AND ODDITIES

It is said that this bizarre drink was created in the 1960s by a Peruvian bartender who worked at a gas station. One day he decided to invent a cocktail that was the same color as oil. The cocktail would prove to be very popular throughout Lima.

PREPARATION

Measure 30 ml (2 tbsp) of pisco in a graduated cylinder and pour into a shaker. Repeat with 30 ml (2 tbsp) of Blue Curaçao, 20 ml (4 tsp) of lemon juice, 10 ml (2 tsp) of sugar syrup and 70 ml (4 1/2 tbsp) of the strawberry puree. Add a few ice cubes and shake vigorously for a few seconds. Pour into a tall tumbler filled with ice and serve, garnished with 2 long straws.

SUGGESTED USE

A drink recommended for all hours of the evening.

Pastry Baskets with Strawberries   MEDIUM

ingredients for 4 people
time: 1 hour + cooling time
(30 minutes)

0.48 lbs (7.76 oz) ready-made puff pastry
0.35 lbs (5.6 oz, about 1 cup) fresh strawberries
1 2/3 cup fresh cream
0.08 lbs (1.41 oz, about 1/4 cup) dark chocolate chips
flour
icing sugar
powdered cocoa

Flour a work surface and roll out the pastry dough to form a sort of square. Cut the dough into four and with the excess shape the squares into baskets, using the reverse of a classic soup ladle as a "mould". Put the baskets onto a pan covered with baking paper and bake for 10 minutes at 356°F (180°C). Whip the cream with 2 tbsp of icing sugar. Add the chocolate chips to the cream and fill the baskets, almost to the edge, with the chocolate-cream mixture. Wash the strawberries then cut them in half. Put a large tablespoon of strawberries on top of the cream and let settle in the refrigerator for 30 minutes before serving. Decorate with a light sprinkle of cocoa powder.

GRIGIO-VERDE

INGREDIENTS

WHITE GRAPPA
MINT GREEN LIQUEUR

ORIGINS AND ODDITIES

This drink was originally drunk by the Alpini, the elite mountain warfare soldiers of the Italian Army, during the First World War. The gray-green (Grigio-Verde in Italian) uniformed soldiers used to mix grappa with mint-flavored liqueur, creating a fantastic union of flavors.

PREPARATION

Measure 50 ml (3 1/3 tbsp) of grappa in a graduated cylinder and pour into a low tumbler full of ice. Repeat with 40 ml (2 3/4 tbsp) of mint green liqueur. Mix with a long-handled spoon and serve, garnished with a nice sprig of fresh mint and 2 short straws.

SUGGESTED USE

A great digestive, it can be enjoyed throughout the evening.

Grappa Sweet Fritters   MEDIUM

ingredients for 4 people
time: 2 hours

3 1/5 cups flour
scant 1/2 cup (8 tbsp) sugar
3 tbsp butter
3 eggs
2 big tbsp white grappa
zest of 1 lemon
salt
icing sugar
frying oil

Sift the flour and place in a heap onto a work surface. In the center, add previously chopped and softened butter, sugar, eggs, grappa, lemon zest and a pinch of salt. With bare hands, thoroughly knead the ingredients until the dough is smooth and somewhat elastic. Form a large ball, lay it on a plate, cover it with a damp cloth and leave in the refrigerator for at least 30 minutes. Flour the work surface thoroughly and finely roll out the dough. With a knife, draw strips of about 10 cm in width and then cut into regular rectangles, with parallel small cuts in the center. Fry the sweet fritters in plenty of hot frying oil, and once golden, drain them with a skimmer spoon and place on a tray covered with paper towel. Allow to cool, and just before serving, sprinkle with a generous shower of icing sugar.

GROLLA VALDOSTANA

INGREDIENTS

WHITE GRAPPA
GENEPY LIQUEUR (OPTIONAL)
RED WINE

COFFEE
WHITE OR CANE SUGAR
CLOVES

LEMON PEEL AND ORANGE PEEL
JUNIPER BERRIES
ORANGE PUNCH OR COINTREAU

ORIGINS AND ODDITIES

The origins of this cocktail are ancient. It seems that the Grolla Valdostana was already highly appreciated during the Middle Ages, when its ingredients were served in a traditional wooden vessel with different nozzles called "grolla", from which gatherings of people would drink, passing it from hand to hand.

PREPARATION

Measure 20 ml (4 tsp) of grappa in a graduated cylinder in a milk jug. Repeat with 30 ml (2 tbsp) of red wine, 20 ml (4 tsp) of Genepy liqueur and 20 ml (4 tsp) of orange punch or Cointreau. Add 1 coffee, 10 g (3 tsp) of white sugar, 4–5 cloves, 2–3 lemon and orange peels and 5–6 juniper berries. Bring to a boil. Pour into a heat-resistant mug and serve.

SUGGESTED USE

A very suitable drink for winter evenings in the company of friends and family.

Sbrisolona (Almond Shortbread)   MEDIUM

ingredients for 6/8 people
time: 2 hours and 30 minutes

1 2/3 cups white flour
1 1/3 cups sifted corn flour
0.44 lbs (7 oz, about 2 1/3 cup) chopped almonds
1 cup (16 tbsp) sugar
0.22 lbs (3.5 oz) lard
scant 1 cup (7 tbsp) butter
3 egg yolks
grated zest of 1 lemon
2 tbsp mandarin liqueur

In a large bowl, sift the white flour, add the corn flour, sugar and chopped almonds and mix everything well with a wooden spoon. Add the lemon zest and egg yolks to the center of the mixture. While continuously stirring, add the lard and butter that were both previously left to soften at room temperature. Mix all ingedients quickly, intentionally avoiding that the mixture become too smooth, but allow small lumps of up to 2 cm in diameter. Then drop the batter onto a buttered baking sheet to form an irregular layer about 2 cm thick. Bake at 356°F (180°C) for about 50 minutes. Sprinkle with white sugar just before serving.

ITALIA-CILE

INGREDIENTS

APEROL

CAMPARI

PISCO

PINEAPPLE JUICE

ORIGINS AND ODDITIES

A drink created in 1998 in a South American bar in France (the country that hosted the 16th FIFA World Cup) to celebrate the match between the Italian and Chilean national teams. In a room crowded with fans of both teams, the bartender invented the Italia-Cile in honor of their enthusiasm.

PREPARATION

Measure 20 ml (4 tsp) of pisco in a graduated cylinder and pour into a shaker. Repeat with 30 ml (2 tbsp) of Aperol, 30 ml (2 tbsp) of Campari, 30 ml (2 tbsp) of pineapple juice. Add some ice cubes and shake vigorously for a few seconds. Pour into a low tumbler filled with ice and serve, garnished with 1/2 an orange slice, 1/2 a slice of pineapple, 2 cherries and 2 short straws.

SUGGESTED USE

Excellent as an aperitif, it is good at all hours of the day.

Citrus Chicken Stew

EASY

ingredients for 4 people
time: 45 minutes

4 chicken breasts
1 glass white wine
3 glasses orange juice
2 glasses mandarine juice
1 glass lemon juice
flour
butter
salt
pepper
2 cups basmati rice

Squeeze all the citrus juices and add to a jug, removing, if necessary, any seeds or impurities. Clean the chicken breasts and cut into cubes (like for a classic stew). Salt and pepper the chicken and pass it through plenty of white flour. In the meantime, cook the rice in moderately salted water. In a large pan, heat a little butter and fry the chicken while turning constantly, so that it develops an even and golden crust. Sprinkle with white wine and when it has evaporated, add in the jug of citrus juices that have been passed through a sieve. Complete the cooking on high heat, so that the juices reduce and become a moderately thick sauce. Drain the rice and arrange on a serving dish. On top of the rice, lay the chicken with citrus sauce and serve hot. Finally, garnish with curls of orange, tangerine and lemon peel.

ITALIAN COFFEE

INGREDIENTS

WHITE GRAPPA

WHITE OR CANE SUGAR

LONG COFFEE

CREAM

ORIGINS AND ODDITIES

Yet another variation of the most famous hot cocktail in the world, the Irish Coffee, this drink seems to have been created in the 1970s in Trentino-Alto Adige, when bartenders in the area began to replace distilled Irish whiskey with an Italian speciality: grappa.

PREPARATION

Measure 40 ml (2 3/4 tbsp) of grappa in a graduated cylinder and pour into a milk jug. Add 10 g (3 tsp) of white sugar and 1 long coffee and bring to a boil, stirring occasionally.
Pour into a heat-resistant mug, and just before serving, add 40 ml (8 tsp) of cream (previously measured in a graduated cylinder) with the use of a teaspoon, so that it remains separate from the rest.

SUGGESTED USE

A refreshingly cool drink, it is recommended for days when the outside temperatures are very cold.

 Messed-up Panettone

EASY

ingredients for 4 people
time: 3 hours

1 panettone
3 eggs
0.66 lbs (10.5 oz) mascarpone (original Italian cream cheese)
2 tbsp grappa
3 tbsp sugar
mixed berries
whipped cream
icing sugar

In a large bowl, whisk together the egg yolks and sugar in order to get a smooth cream. While continuously stirring with a wooden spoon, add the grappa and, little by little, add the mascarpone cheese. Let this cream settle in the refrigerator for 2 hours. Cut the panettone horizontally into three parts of the same thickness and stuff it with plenty of mascarpone cream. Once again, let it settle in the refrigerator for 1 hour, and just before serving, decorate the cake with fresh berries and whipped cream as desired. Finally, sprinkle with icing sugar.

ITALIAN ICE TEA

INGREDIENTS

WHITE GRAPPA

VODKA

DRY WHITE RUM

GIN

LEMON OR LIME JUICE

COLA

ORIGINS AND ODDITIES

A late 1990s Italian response to the legendary Long Island Ice Tea.

PREPARATION

Measure 20 ml (4 tsp) of grappa in a graduated cylinder and pour into a shaker. Repeat with 20 ml (4 tsp) of vodka, 20 ml (4 tsp) of rum, 20 ml (4 tsp) of gin and 20 ml (4 tsp) of lemon juice. Shake vigorously for a few seconds and pour into a tall tumbler filled with ice. Fill almost to the brim with cola and serve, garnished with 1 lemon slice, 2 cherries and 2 long straws.

SUGGESTED USE

A long drink loved by young people, and one to drink in moderation at all hours of the evening.

Chocolate Salami

EASY

ingredients for 6/8 people
time: 1 hour + cooling time
(3 hours)

0.33 lbs (5.3 oz) hard biscuits
1/3 cup butter
0.22 lbs (3.5 oz) dark chocolate
1 tbsp rum
1 egg
1/4 cup (4 tbsp) sugar

Before starting, let the butter soften at room temperature. In a large bowl, crumble the biscuits with your hands. In a saucepan, melt the chocolate in a bain-marie, stirring with a wooden spoon to remove any lumps. Remove from heat and let the chocolate cool down. Place the butter in a large bowl, working it into a cream with a spatula. Add sugar, egg, rum and the chocolate, which by now should be cold. Mix the ingredients well in a bowl and combine with the biscuits. Stir gently until the dough is smooth. Slowly lay the mixture on a sheet of baking paper, distributing the mixture horizontally from the center. Roll everything up in the paper, in order to create the classic elongated cylindrical salami shape. Wrap everything in a sheet of aluminum foil, which will add further pressure on the "salami". Let stand in refrigerator for about 3 hours before slicing the chocolate salami. Serve.

MOJITO DIGESTIVO

INGREDIENTS

WHITE GRAPPA
AMARO BRAULIO
AMARO RAMAZZOTTI
(OR OTHER ITALIAN BITTERS)
LIME

FRESH MINT
WHITE SUGAR
OR CANE SUGAR
SODA WATER
OR SPARKLING WATER

ORIGINS AND ODDITIES

The Mojito Digestivo (Digestive Mojito), a revisiting
of the classic Mojito, was presented for the first
time in 2007 at the "Metamorfosi Mojito" (Mojito
Metamorphosis), an international competition
in Rimini organized by the Italian magazine
Bargiornale.

PREPARATION

Put 1/2 a lime, cut into small cubes, in a tall tumbler
and add 10 g (3 tsp) of white sugar. Grind everything
with a pestle until it is a pulp. Add a few leaves of fresh
mint, gently pressing each one down. Fill the tumbler
with crushed ice and add 20 ml (4 tsp) of Amaro
Braulio, 20 ml (4 tsp) of white grappa and
20 ml (4 tsp) of Amaro Ramazzotti (previously
measured in a graduated cylinder). Fill to the brim
with soda water or sparkling mineral water and
mix with a long-handled spoon, to best blend the
ingredients. Serve, garnished with 1 beautiful sprig
of mint and 2 long straws.

SUGGESTED USE

An excellent digestive drink.

Poppy Diamonds

EASY

ingredients for 4 people
time: 2 hours

1/8 cup (2 tbsp) butter
2/3 cup flour
1/4 cup potato starch
1/4 cup (4 tbsp) sugar
1 tsp baking powder
zest of 1 lemon
1 tbsp poppy seeds
1 egg
1 tbsp honey
icing sugar

Sift the flour, the starch and the baking powder in a bowl. Stir in the poppy seeds and lemon zest. In a second bowl, soften the butter and whisk it together with the egg and sugar until it becomes creamy and frothy. Add honey and stir thoroughly until the mixture is smooth. Combine the cream into the first bowl and mix vigorously with a large fork. Pour everything on a floured work surface and knead for a few minutes with bare hands. Roll out the dough in order to get a sheet of about 1.5 cm thick. Cut out biscuits with a diamond-shaped cookie cutter, and then lay them down on a baking tray covered with baking paper. Bake for 356°F (180°C) for about 15 minutes. Remove from heat and let cool. Just before serving, dust the diamonds with icing sugar and some poppy seeds.

ITALIAN MOJITO

INGREDIENTS

WHITE GRAPPA
LIME
FRESH MINT

WHITE OR CANE SUGAR
SODA WATER OR
SPARKLING WATER

ORIGINS AND ODDITIES

This all-Italian version of the traditional Cuban cocktail was presented in 2007 during the same competition that saw the debut of the Mojito Digestivo.

PREPARATION

Put 1/2 a lime, cut into small cubes in a tall tumbler and add 10 g (3 tsp) of white sugar. Grind everything with a pestle until it is a pulp. Add a few leaves of fresh mint, gently pressing them down. Fill the tumbler with crushed ice and add 50 ml (3 1/3 tbsp) of grappa (previously measured in a graduated cylinder). Fill almost to the brim with soda water or sparkling mineral water and stir with a long-handled spoon, so as to best blend the ingredients. Serve, garnished with a nice sprig of mint and 2 long straws.

SUGGESTED USE

A great drink that can be enjoyed throughout the evening.

Struffoli (Neapolitan Donuts)   MEDIUM

ingredients for 4 people
time: 2 hours and 30 minutes

2 1/2 cups flour
2 eggs
1 egg yolk
1 tbsp sugar
3 tbsp butter
1 tbsp limoncello (lemon liqueur)
salt
grated zest of 1/2 a lemon
frying oil
0.39 lbs (6.35 oz) honey
0.11 lbs (1.76 oz) colored sprinkles
0.11 lbs (1.76 oz) candied fruit

Sift the flour on a work surface and place into a heap. In the center, add the eggs, sugar, softened butter, lemon zest, lemon liqueur and a pinch of salt. Knead thoroughly with bare hands until the dough is smooth and firm. Form a ball, cover it with a damp cloth, and let it settle in the refrigerator for 45 minutes. Knead the dough again for a few minutes and divide it into small balls. Spread them out in order to form rods to be cut into small pieces and, without overlapping, lay on a floured sheet. In plenty of hot oil, fry a small amount of the struffoli at a time. When they become puffed and golden, drain them with a skimmer spoon and place on a tray covered with paper towels. In a saucepan, heat the honey and add the struffoli, stirring until the honey is absorbed well. Add 2/3 of the sprinkles along with 2/3 of finely chopped candied fruit and give a final mixture. Remove from heat and place onto a platter, cover with the remaining sprinkles and candied fruit. Let cool and serve.

PISCOLA

INGREDIENTS

PISCO
COLA

ORIGINS AND ODDITIES

Chile's response to the classic Cuba Libre, with
the rum replaced with Chile's national drink: pisco.

PREPARATION

Measure 110 ml (7 1/4 tbsp) of cola in a graduated
cylinder and pour into a tall tumbler filled with ice.
Combine 50 ml (3 1/3 tbsp) of pisco with the edge
of the spoon so that it gives the appearance that it is
floating, and serve, garnished with 2 long straws.

SUGGESTED USE

Drinks recommended for very hot days.

 Pastel de Choclo   EASY

ingredients for 4 people
time: 1 hour

0.66 lbs (10.5 oz) ground beef
2 cloves garlic
12 pitted black olives
2 hard-boiled eggs
1 tbsp sultana raisins
0.44 lbs (7 oz) corn
4 boiled chicken legs
1 tsp powdered cumin
4 basil leaves
1 onion
extra virgin olive oil and butter
salt and pepper

In a saucepan, sauté the minced garlic and chopped onion in 2 tbsp
of extra virgin olive oil. Add the ground beef, salt and pepper and
cook on low heat. When the meat is almost cooked, add the cumin.
Mix the corn with the basil and cook for 10 minutes in a pan with
1 tbsp of extra virgin olive oil. Grease a large baking pan with high
edges and spread out the meat, the chicken legs, raisins (previously
soaked in warm water), olives and wedges of hard-boiled eggs. Cover
everything with corn and bake at 430°F (220°C) until the surface becomes a golden brown crust.

PISCO COLLINS

INGREDIENTS

PISCO
LIQUID SUGAR
LEMON JUICE

SODA WATER OR
SPARKLING WATER

ORIGINS AND ODDITIES

The family of the Collins' Cocktails could not
refrain from including in its list of ingredients
a Chilean-Peruvian classic: pisco.

PREPARATION

Measure 50 ml (3 1/3 tbsp) of pisco in a graduated
cylinder and pour into a shaker. Repeat with 30 ml
(2 tbsp) of lemon juice and 20 ml (4 tsp) sugar syrup.
Add a few ice cubes and shake vigorously for a few
seconds. Pour into a tall tumbler filled with ice and
fill almost to the brim with soda water or sparkling
mineral water. Stir with a long-handled spoon and
serve, garnished with 1/2 a slice of lemon, 2 cherries
and 2 long straws.

SUGGESTED USE

A drink with marked thirst-quenching properties.

Peruvian-Style Rice With Milk

EASY

ingredients for 4 people
time: 1 hour

2 1/2 cups whole milk
scant 1 1/3 cups condensed milk
1 1/4 cups water
scant 1 cup rice
about 2/3 cup (packed) raisins
salt
2 cinnamon sticks
vanilla
butter

In a large saucepan, pour the whole milk and water and bring to a boil
on low heat. Add the rice and cinnamon, cook for about 25 minutes
and stir occasionally until the rice becomes soft. With a spoon, remove
the cinnamon from the saucepan and add the condensed milk, a pinch
of salt, a dash of vanilla and the raisins that were previously soaked in a
basin of warm water. While continuously stirring, cook on low heat for
about 10 minutes, until most of the broth has been absorbed and the rice
becomes creamy and consistent, similar to that of a pudding. Remove
from heat and stir in 2 knobs of butter and a sprinkle of cinnamon. Serve
very hot.

PISCO PASSION

INGREDIENTS

PISCO
LEMON JUICE

MARACUJÁ SYRUP OR
PASSION FRUIT SYRUP
PASSION FRUIT

ORIGINS AND ODDITIES

South American passion fruit has always been
appreciated by bartenders. Barmen in London
(home of the Vodka Sour and numerous South
American establishments) decided around the 1990s
to combine this fruit (considered an aphrodisiac)
to the still little-known pisco, creating one of the
world's most sensual cocktails.

PREPARATION

Measure 40 ml (2 3/4 tbsp) of pisco in a graduated
cylinder and pour into a shaker. Repeat with
30 ml (2 tbsp) of lemon juice and 20 ml (4 tsp) of
either maracujá or passion fruit syrup. Add a few
ice cubes and the pulp from 1/2 a passion fruit,
then shake it all for a few seconds. Pour into a pre-
chilled cocktail glass and serve, garnished with the
remaining passion fruit.

SUGGESTED USE

A drink best enjoyed among good company, it can
also be recommended as a digestive.

Maracujá Mousse

EASY

ingredients for 4 people
time: 30 minutes + cooling time
(10 hours)

7/8 cup condensed milk
7/8 cup concentrated maracujá juice
gelatin
7/8 cup cooking cream
0.22 lbs (3.5 oz) maracujá pulp
1 basket fresh currants

In a bowl, mix the fruit juice and pulp with 1 tbsp of gelatin that was previously dissolved in 3 tbsp of water in a double boiler. In a second bowl,
vigorously whip the cream with a whisk. Add the condensed milk to the
maracujá mixture, continuously and gently mixing everything. When the
mixture is smooth, pour it into 4 dessert cups. Let the dessert cool in
the refrigerator for at least 10 hours. Serve cold and garnish with sprigs
of currant.

PISCO SOUR

INGREDIENTS

PISCO
LEMON JUICE
SUGAR SYRUP

ORIGINS AND ODDITIES

Chile and Peru both claim the authorship of this
cocktail, with the two nations stating its creation
occured in the 1920s. Drinkers in both countries
religiously celebrate Pisco Sour Day on the first
Saturday of every February.

PREPARATION

Measure 50 ml (3 1/3 tbsp) of pisco in a graduated
cylinder and pour into a shaker. Repeat with
25 ml (5 tsp) of lemon juice and 15 ml (1 tbsp)
of sugar syrup. Add a few ice cubes and shake
vigorously for a few seconds. Pour into a cup
(pre chilled in the freezer) and serve.

SUGGESTED USE

An excellent digestive, it can be enjoyed throughout
the evening.

Suspiro a la Limena   EASY

ingredients for 4 people
time: 1 hour

2/3 cup + 1 tsp sweetened condensed
milk
2/3 cup + 1 tsp unsweetened condensed
milk
4 egg yolks
1 tsp powdered cinnamon
1/2 cup + 2 tbsp sugar
1 shot glass pisco

In a large bowl, pour in all the condensed milk. Add the cinnamon and
cook on low heat in order to get a slightly think puree. Remove from
heat and add the egg yolks, mixing everything well with a whisk. Let
the mixture cool completletly and then pour into 4 dessert bowls. Top
off each portion with a spoonful of syrup made by heating sugar and
pisco in a saucepan.

PISCO SUNRISE

INGREDIENTS

PISCO
ORANGE JUICE
GRENADINE SYRUP

ORIGINS AND ODDITIES

Peruvian bartenders were inspired by the Tequila
Sunrise for this drink, replacing the tequila, obvious-
ly, with pisco.

PREPARATION

Measure 50 ml (3 1/3 tbsp) of pisco in a graduated
cylinder and pour into a tall tumbler filled with ice.
Repeat with 90 ml (6 tbsp) of orange juice, stirring
for a few seconds with a long-handled spoon. Measure
20 ml (4 tsp) of grenadine syrup in the cylinder and
pour it slowly into the tumbler, using the edge of the
spoon until it reaches the bottom, thus obtaining the
rising sun effect. Serve, garnished with 2 orange slices
and 2 cherries.

SUGGESTED USE

A great drink for the whole day, especially
when it's hot.

Chilean Peasants' Salad   EASY

ingredients for 4 people
time: 30 minutes + cooling time
(30 minutes)

0.44 lbs (7 oz, about 1 cup) canned
chickpeas
2 red onions
2 hard-boiled eggs
0.66 lbs (10.5 oz) mozzarella
1 lemon
extra virgin olive oil
salt
pepper
chopped lettuce
chopped parsley

Peel and cut off the ends of the onions, slice them thinly, and put
into a beautiful salad bowl. Add mozzarella that has been drained,
squeezed, and diced into medium cubes. Cut the hardboiled eggs
into wedges and set aside. Drain the chickpeas well and combine
them to the salad. Dress with lemon juice, salt, pepper and plenty
of extra virgin olive oil. Gently mix all the ingredients and serve on a
platter that was previously covered with a bed of washed, dried, and
finely chopped lettuce. Let settle in refrigerator for 30 minutes and
before serving garnish with egg wedges and chopped parsley.

BLENDED COCKTAILS

The blender used professionally in a bar has different technological characteristics than a household blender, and with a little effort and some little tricks, you can get great frozen cocktails, batidas, milkshakes, smoothies and excellent pre-mixes.

Frozen Cocktails

Frozen drinks are usually served in large, imaginative and decorative glasses with fresh fruit and straws. Many popular cocktail recipes can be transformed into frozen drinks. This has become an increasingly fashionable thing to do, especially in the summer.

Generally, frozen cocktails have a creamy density and are prepared in the blender. Frozen cocktail should have the texture of fine snow with the straws driven in vertically.

In order for frozen cocktails not to be watered-down, you have to pay attention to the quality and quantity of ice used.

A little trick to determine how much ice to put in the blender is to fill the serving glass with crushed ice and use it as a measurement cup.

Another good tip is to remember that you can get good results using the same blender to prepare multiple drinks.

The most famous frozen cocktails are: Piña Colada, Daiquiri, Banana Daiquiri and Strawberry Margarita, but as the world of frozen cocktails is still in its infancy, there will no doubt be a much greater variety with time.

To make a good frozen cocktail, you must put ingredients in the blender using the following order: solid elements, soft drinks, liqueurs and spirits, then crushed ice:

1. Use the blender's first speed (low) to mix the solid and liquid ingredients and ice / 3 seconds
2. Increase the speed (high) to chop the ice and combine it with other ingredients / 3 seconds
3. Go back to the first speed (low) to perfectly blend the mixture / 3 seconds

Batidas

Batidas are colada-styled cocktails that are simply prepared: fresh and light, they have to be made with fresh (and not frozen) fruit and they must maintain a certain creaminess, which differentiates it from Margarita or Daiquiri drinks.

The magical combination of cachaça, fresh fruit, ice and sometimes a small amount of condensed milk, gives rise to a sweet drink that perfectly balances the power of cachaça, creating a pleasant and surprisingly tasty combination.

The batida originates from the streets and beaches of Brazil, where the most popular

cultural trends from the outlying neighborhoods transfer over to the city at large in a wave of contrasting colors and styles. In the *carrinhos de batidas*, which are commonplace today, veritable cocktail artists transform the mixing of simple and typical tropical fruit smoothies into something new and original.

Bartenders at these types of streetside parlors have created numerous popular recipes by combining fresh fruit and a touch of exotic cachaça. Colorful and aromatic batidas were an instant success and they quickly overran the streets of Brazil, from Rio to São Paulo to Bahia.

In the 1950s, in Rio de Janeiro alone, there were about 1,000 roaming batida sellers. The state of cachaça and batidas in Brazil is the main concern of the "Academia da Cachaça" in Rio de Janeiro, where more than 2000 different brands can be sampled, as well as many drinks that use this oft-overlooked ingredient as a base.

Milkshake (Frappé)

Milkshakes are made from milk (which must always be semi-skimmed and well chilled), sugar, flavoring and a little ice.

To make a classic milkshake you need to pour 70 cl of semi-skimmed milk, 20 cl of your choice of syrup (for example, black cherry or mint) sugar and crushed ice into a blender. Blend at maximum speed for 1-2 minutes until the mixture is visibly blended and thick, then pour into a tall glass with long straws. Remove all residual ice and serve.

Smoothies

Fresh fruit is the basic required ingredient for smoothies.

Smoothies are made with a high concentration of aqueous fruit, such as watermelon, melon, pineapple, peach, etc. It is prepared with crushed ice, sugar and water: all these elements are put into the container of the blender and the mixture is served in large glasses with a straw (and without decoration).

Smoothies made from fresh fruit pulp, such as bananas, apples, pears, etc., are prepared by blending crushed ice, fruit, sugar and a little milk with water (1 to 1 proportion). This kind of smoothie is served in glasses with big fancy straws.

The increasingly popular concept of wellness has led some to even introduce vegetables (rich in vitamins and fiber) to the smoothie ingredient arsenal.

Pre-Mixes

Pre-mixes are compounds that facilitate the preparation of blender-dependent cocktails. They help speed up the work and maintain the quality of the cocktails.

An example of a pre-mix is the strawberry mix: a unique strawberry smoothie that, used in small quantities, gives balanced color and flavor to cocktails, such as the Strawberry Caipiroska.

AMARETTO COLADA

INGREDIENTS

DISARONNO AMARETTO

PINEAPPLE JUICE

WHITE RUM

COCONUT SYRUP OR MILK

ORIGINS AND ODDITIES

A drink that is particularly prevalent in Central America. It was named after the Italian liqueur Disaronno Amaretto, which gives the cocktail a pleasant taste.

PREPARATION

Measure 20 ml (4 tsp) of rum in a graduated cylinder and transfer it to a blender. Repeat with 40 ml (2 3/4 tbsp) of Disaronno Amaretto, 70 ml (4 tbsp + 2 tsp) of pineapple juice and 30 ml (2 tbsp) of coconut syrup or milk. Add 1/2 a low tumbler of crushed ice and blend for 15–20 seconds. Pour into a tall tumbler and serve, garnished with half a slice of pineapple, 2 cherries and 2 long straws.

SUGGESTED USE

This long drink is particularly suitable for afternoons.

 Peach Melba   EASY

ingredients for 4 people
time: 2 hour and 30 minutes

4 peaches
0.88 lbs (14 oz) raspberries
1 1/3 cups sugar
1 tbsp potato starch
juice of 1 lemon
1 vial vanilla flavoring
plain ice cream

Wash the raspberries and mix them in the mixer and then drain in a colander, so as to permanently remove all impurities. Pour into a saucepan with 3 tbsp of sugar and cook over low heat. Add the potato starch and lemon juice, stirring vigorously with a spoon. When the raspberry sauce has thickened, remove from the stove. Heat 4 1/4 cups of water in a pot. Combine the remaining sugar and a few drops of vanilla essence. When the water has evaporated to half, dip the peaches (which have been washed, and cut in half, their cores removed) and simmer for 8 minutes over medium heat. Remove from heat and let the peaches cool directly in the syrup. Just before serving, lay half a peach in each cup, with the concave side up. Fill it in with a nice scoop of ice cream and close with the remaining peach half. Finally, drown everything in raspberry sauce.

FROZEN BANANA DAIQUIRI

INGREDIENTS

WHITE RUM

LEMON JUICE

LIQUID SUGAR

FRESH BANANA

ORIGINS AND ODDITIES

A drink created in Cuba in the 1950s, enriching the classic Daiquiri with endless varieties of fresh fruit. Together with strawberry, banana flavor seems to be the most appreciated by the general public.

PREPARATION

Measure 50 ml (3 1/3 tbsp) of rum in a graduated cylinder and pour in blender. Repeat with 25 ml (5 tsp) of liquid sugar and 15 ml (1 tbsp) of lemon juice. Add 1/2 a fresh sliced banana, 1 tall tumbler of crushed ice and blend for 15–20 seconds. Pour into a low tumbler and serve, garnishing with the other 1/2 banana and 2 short straws.

SUGGESTED USE

A refreshing drink that can brighten up any summer day.

Banana Flambé   EASY

ingredients for 4 people
time: 30 minutes

4 bananas
4 tbsp sugar
1 shot glass rum
1 1/2 tbsp butter

Peel the bananas, being careful not to break them. Dip in a buttered pan for 2 minutes and sprinkle evenly with 3 tbsp of sugar. When the bananas are caramelized, add the rum (previously mixed with the remaining sugar). Immediately remove from heat and carefully lay the bananas on a serving plate, lighting them on fire with a match before serving.

BATIDA DE CAFÉ

INGREDIENTS

CACHAÇA
COFFEE LIQUEUR
LONG COFFEE

LIQUID SUGAR
SUGAR CANE

ORIGINS AND ODDITIES

It was, of course, Brazilian barmen who launched the
union between their two national drinks:
coffee and cachaça. The popularity of the new
drink is such that ready-made bottles are sold
in supermarkets across Europe.

PREPARATION

Measure 40 ml (2 3/4 tbsp) of cachaça in a graduated
cylinder and pour in a blender. Repeat with 20 ml
(4 tsp) of coffee liqueur, and 20 ml (4 tsp)
of liquid sugar. Add 1 long room temperature
coffee, 12.5 g (3 tsp) of brown sugar, 1/2 a tall
tumbler of crushed ice and blend for 15–20
seconds. Pour everything into the tumbler and
serve, garnished with 2 long straws and a dusting
of ground coffee.

SUGGESTED USE

Recommended for those who want to stay
up all night.

 Brazilian Pudding

EASY

ingredients for 4 people
time: 45 minutes + cooling time
(3 hours)

4 tbsp butter
1/4 cup (4 tbsp) flour
1/3 cup (5 tbsp) sugar
1 cup fresh cream
2/5 cup milk
2/5 cup coffee
2 tbsp kahlúa (coffee liqueur)

Melt the butter in a saucepan and, stirring continuously, add the
sugar, letting it caramelize. Remove from heat and dilute with coffee
and liqueur. In a bowl, work the flour with the milk. Combine the
mixture of sugar and coffee and stir vigorously with a whisk. Finally,
slowly add the cream and give it a final mix. On low heat, let the
cream reduce. Remove from heat and continue stirring for a couple
of minutes. Pour the cream into 4 bowls and let rest in refrigerator
for at least 3 hours. Serve, garnished with small shots of whipped
cream flavored with coffee.

BATIDA DE COCO

INGREDIENTS

CACHAÇA
BROWN SUGAR
LIQUID SUGAR

COCONUT SYRUP OR CREAM
FRESH COCONUT

ORIGINS AND ODDITIES

Among the family of batidas, this drink has proven to be so popular that ready-made bottles are sold in supermarkets across Europe. In its native Brazil, however, it is strictly prepared fresh.

PREPARATION

Measure 40 ml (2 3/4 tbsp) of cachaça in a graduated cylinder and pour in a blender. Repeat with 20 ml (4 tsp) of liquid sugar and 30 ml (2 tbsp) of coconut syrup or cream. Add 12.5 g (3 tsp) of brown sugar, 1/2 a low tumbler of crushed ice and blend for 15–20 seconds. Pour into a tall tumbler and serve, garnished with a touch of fresh coconut and 2 long straws.

SUGGESTED USE

A delicious drink that can be enjoyed at all hours.

Cuddly Coconut   EASY

ingredients for 4 people
time: 45 minutes

1 cup coconut flour
1/2 cup sugar
2 egg whites
0.08 lbs (1.41 oz) dark chocolate flakes or chips
chopped coconut

Work the egg whites and sugar in a large bowl with a whisk until the mixture is creamy and smooth. Stirring continuously, gradually add the coconut flour. Combine chocolate chips and then knead it so that everything is evenly blended. With your bare hands, create balls of dough and place them on a baking sheet covered with baking paper. Bake for 15 minutes at 400°F (200°C). Serve warm and sprinkle with the chopped coconut.

BATIDA DE LIMAO

INGREDIENTS

CACHAÇA   LIQUID SUGAR
LIME JUICE   WHITE OR CANE SUGAR

ORIGINS AND ODDITIES

Young Brazilians were the first to mix the cachaça
with fresh fruit, creating very refreshing drinks,
like this lime-based one.

PREPARATION

Measure in a graduated cylinder and pour 40 ml
(2 3/4 tbsp) of cachaça in a food processor. Repeat
with 40 ml (2 3/4 tbsp) of lime juice and 20 ml
(4 tsp) of liquid sugar. Add 12.5 g (3 tsp) of brown
sugar and 1/2 a tall tumbler of crushed ice. Blend
for 15–20 seconds and pour into tumblers. To serve,
garnish with 1 lime slice and 2 long straws.

SUGGESTED USE

A particularly fresh and refreshing drink.

 Mint Omelets   EASY

ingredients for 4 people
time: 1 hour

6 eggs
1 1/2 cup + 1 1/2 tbsp grated
Parmigiano Reggiano cheese
12 fresh mint leaves
salt and pepper
extra virgin olive oil
1 lime

In a large bowl, beat the eggs with a whisk. Combine the salt, pepper
and grated cheese. Mix well until the mixture is smooth and without
lumps. Wash and finely chop the mint leaves. Add the mint and stir
the eggs further. Heat a drizzle of extra virgin olive oil in a pan. When
it is very hot, pour a ladle of the mixture, scattering in such a way that
it completely covers the bottom of the pan. Cook over low heat and,
when the eggs begin to solidify, flip the frittata with a spatula. Finish
cooking over very low heat, laying the omelette on sheets of blotting
paper. Repeat all the steps to make 3 more omelettes. Serve hot,
accompanied with small wedges of lime.

BATIDA
DE MORANGO

INGREDIENTS

CACHAÇA
WHITE OR CANE SUGAR

FRESH STRAWBERRIES
OR STRAWBERRY SYRUP
LIQUID SUGAR

ORIGINS AND ODDITIES

The origin of this batida (*batida* means "to beat"
in Brazilian portuguese) seems to be related to
traditional Brazilian festivals, during which older
drinkers drank the Caipirinha, while younger crowds
thought to combine cachaça with sugar cane, fresh
fruit and ice, "beating" the ingredients until it was
a pulp. The recent use of a blender achieves the
same result.

PREPARATION

Measure 40–50 ml (8–10 tsp) of cachaça in a
graduated cylinder and pour in a blender. Repeat
with 30 ml (2 tbsp) of liquid sugar. Add 12.5 g (3 tsp)
of brown sugar, 5 fresh strawberries and 1/2 a tall
tumbler of crushed ice. Blend for 15–20 seconds
and pour into tumblers. Serve, garnished with
fresh strawberries and 2 long straws.

SUGGESTED USE

A great drink suitable for any time of day.

Garganelli Sweet Salad   EASY

ingredients for 4 people
time: 1 hour

0.88 lbs (14 oz) garganelli pasta
0.17 lbs (2.8 oz, about 1/2 cup +
1 tsp) strawberries
0.17 lbs (2.8 oz) diced melon
juice of 1 lemon
3 tbsp liquid sugar
0.22 lbs (3.5 oz) palm hearts
0.22 lbs (3.5 oz) crab meat
walnut kernels
4 figs
blueberries

Cook the garganelli in abundant, unsalted water. Drain when al dente and cool immediately under running cold water. In a large bowl,
pour the lemon juice and sugar solution. Combine all the ingredients
gradually: the whole walnuts, hearts of palm and crab meat (drained
and cut into similar sized rounds), the diced melon and strawberries (cleaned and cut into pieces). Pour the seasoned garganelli into
the salad, stirring gently until the ingredients are evenly distributed.
Serve the salad in 4 rectangular bowls, garnishing each one with
1 open fig heart and a few blueberries.

BLUE HAWAIAN COLADA

INGREDIENTS

WHITE RUM
BLUE CURAÇAO

PINEAPPLE JUICE
COCONUT SYRUP OR MILK

ORIGINS AND ODDITIES

It's been said that this reinterpretation of the famous Piña Colada was created in the 1950s by the bartender of a restaurant overlooking the blue ocean blue (hence the name) at a Hawaiian beach paradise.

PREPARATION

Measure 30 ml (2 tbsp) of rum and 30 ml (2 tbsp) of Blue Curaçao in a graduated cylinder and transfer it to a blender. Repeat with 60 ml (1/4 cup) of pineapple juice and 30 ml (2 tbsp) of coconut syrup or milk. Add 1/2 a low tumbler of crushed ice and blend for 15–20 seconds, then pour it all into a tall tumbler. Serve, garnished with half a slice of pineapple, 2 cherries and 2 long straws.

SUGGESTED USE

A delicious drink perfect for the afternoon and evening.

 Fresh Coconut Balls

EASY

ingredients for 4 people
time: 45 minutes

0.55 lbs (8.8 oz) ricotta cheese
1/4 cup (4 tbsp) sugar
1/4 cup (4 tbsp) grated coconut
0.17 lbs (2.8 oz) pine nuts
icing sugar

Preheat oven to 356°F (180°C) and toast the pine nuts on a baking tray covered with baking paper. Set them aside. In a large bowl, work the grated coconut pulp, sugar and ricotta with a spoon to obtain a homogeneous mixture. With your hands, use the dough to form small balls the size of walnuts and dip them abundantly in toasted pine nuts (previously mixed in a mixer). Place the balls on a plate and let them rest for 2 hours in the refrigerator. Before serving, sprinkle everything with plenty of icing sugar.

BRAZIL COLADA

INGREDIENTS

CACHAÇA
PINEAPPLE JUICE

COCONUT SYRUP OR MILK
LIQUID SUGAR

ORIGINS AND ODDITIES

One of the most appreciated variations of the classic
Caribbean Piña Colada. In this case the leading role is
played by cachaça.

PREPARATION

Measure 50 ml (3 1/3 tbsp) of cachaça in a graduated
cylinder and pour in a blender or food processor.
Repeat with 30 ml (2 tbsp) of coconut syrup or milk,
20 ml (4 tsp) of liquid sugar and 60 ml (1/4 cup)
of pineapple juice. Add 1/2 a tall tumbler of crushed
ice and blend for 15–20 seconds. Pour into tumblers
and serve, garnished with half a slice of pineapple, 2
cherries and 2 long straws.

SUGGESTED USE

A perfect drink to liven up any time of day.

Cocada   EASY

ingredients for 4 people
time: 1 hour and 15 minutes

1 small coconut
1 cup whole milk
1/2 cup + 1 tbsp sugar
0.06 lbs (1 oz, about 3/8 cup) sliced
almonds
1 tbsp batida de coco
2 tbsp fresh cream
2 egg yolks
butter
cinnamon powder

Puncture holes in the coconut, in order to drain the milk. Split and
wash the pulp (removing the brown layer) under running water.
Blend the coconut and pour into a large pot. Combine milk, cream
and coconut liqueur. Mix all the ingredients and cook over low
heat for 20 minutes. In a bowl, work the egg yolks with sugar until
creamy, frothy and smooth. Pour the mixture into the saucepan and
continue to cook until it has thickened, stirring vigorously. Grease a
baking dish with butter and pour in the mixture. Sprinkle with sliced
almonds and cinnamon. Bake at 400°F (200°C) for 15 minutes. Serve
warm.

FROZEN DAIQUIRI

INGREDIENTS

WHITE RUM
LEMON JUICE

LEMON SYRUP
LIQUID SUGAR

ORIGINS AND ODDITIES

This drink is the frozen version of the classic Daiquiri.
Born at the Floridita in Havana, it was one of Ernest
Hemingway's favorite cocktails and was even cited in
"Suddenly Last Summer," the 1959 film directed by
Joseph L. Mankiewicz starring
the late Montgomery Clift.

PREPARATION

Measure 30 ml (2 tbsp) of rum in a graduated
cylinder and pour in a blender. Repeat with 30 ml
(2 tbsp) of lemon juice, 20 ml (4 tsp) of lemon syrup
and 10 ml (2 tsp) of liquid sugar. Add 1 tall tumbler
with crushed ice and blend for 15–20 seconds.
Pour into a tumbler bottom, and garnish with 1 slice
of lemon and 2 short straws.

SUGGESTED USE

A great refreshing and digestive drink.

 Lemon Cream   EASY

ingredients for 4 people
time: 45 minutes + cooling time
(2 hours)

6 lemons
4 eggs
7/8 cup + 1 1/4 tbsp butter
2 cups sugar
currants

Chop the butter, letting it soften at room temperature. Lay it in a
bowl and work in cream with the sugar until the mixture is homogeneous. Add the eggs and mix the ingredients again. Add the juice from
6 lemons and the grated rind of 2. Pour everything in a saucepan and
cook over low heat, until the mixture has thickened. Remove from
heat and blend well. Pour the cream into 4 cocktail cups and leave to
cool in the refrigerator for at least 2 hours before serving. Garnish with
a few currants.

FROZEN PICK ME UP

INGREDIENTS

EGG LIQUEUR
CHOCOLATE LIQUEUR
COFFEE LIQUEUR

ORIGINS AND ODDITIES

A newer drink recently created by bartender
Gianfranco Di Niso to reinterpret the tiramisù
dessert with the use of alcoholic liquors.

PREPARATION

Measure 30 ml (2 tbsp) of egg liqueur in a graduated
cylinder and then pour it in a food processor. Repeat
with 30 ml (2 tbsp) of chocolate liquor and 30 ml
(2 tbsp) of coffee liqueur. Add 1 tall tumbler of
crushed ice and blend for 15–20 seconds. Pour
into a low tumbler down and serve, garnished
with 2 short straws and a dusting of cocoa.

SUGGESTED USE

Perfect as an after dinner drink. Good as a digestive.

Dry Fruit Loaf   EASY

ingredients for 6/8 people
time: 1 hour + cooling time (3 hours)

3 slices of sponge cake
0.44 lbs (7 oz, about 3/4 cup)
mascarpone
(original Italian cream cheese)
2 eggs
1/4 cup + 2 1/2 tbsp sugar
0.13 lbs (2.1 oz) dried fruit
1 long coffee
whipped cream
powdered cocoa

In a bowl, work the egg yolks and sugar with a whisk until creamy, frothy
and smooth. Mix the dried fruit and mascarpone in a mixer and stir all
the ingredients. Beat the egg whites until they're stiff and give them
another mix, so that they do not rise. On the work station, place the
slices of sponge cake, soaking them up with coffee with the aid of a
brush. Spread 1/3 of the cream on first slice and repeat two more times,
resulting in a tile with three layers. Let the dessert cool in the refrigerator
for at least 3 hours before serving. Sprinkle with cocoa powder and decorate as desired with dried fruits.

PIÑA COLADA

INGREDIENTS

WHITE RUM
PINEAPPLE JUICE

COCONUT MILK
OR SYRUP

ORIGINS AND ODDITIES

A fusion of coconut, pineapple and rum, the Piña Colada was most probably created in the 1950s in South America, spreading first to the United States and later becoming one of the most popular long drinks in the world.

PREPARATION

Measure 50 ml (3 1/3 tbsp) of rum in a graduated cylinder and transfer it into in a blender.
Repeat with 80 ml (1/3 cup) of pineapple juice and 30 ml (2 tbsp) of coconut milk or syrup.
Add 1/2 a tall tumbler of crushed ice and mix together for 15–20 seconds. Pour into tumblers and serve, garnished with half a slice of pineapple, 2 cherries and 2 long straws.

SUGGESTED USE

A heavy long drink, it is recommended for all hours of the day.

 Puerto Rico Pie   EASY

ingredients for 6/8 people
time: 2 hours

0.88 lbs (14 oz) short pastry
0.22 lbs (3.5 oz, about 1/2 cup) pastry cream
1 ripe pineapple
1/3 cup (5 tbsp) cane sugar
4 tbsp margarine
1 shot glass rum
1 egg
0.08 lbs (1.41 oz) white chocolate flakes or chips

Wash and clean the pineapple, removing the central core and skin. Cut into slices with about 1 cm thickness. In a low, wide casserole, melt the margarine with the sugar. When the syrup begins to brown, dip the slices of pineapple, letting them caramelize over high heat for about 8 minutes, and turning them frequently with a fork. Sprinkle with rum and let it flame until the fire subsides. Remove from the heat and let it rest. On a floured work station, roll out the pastry and line a low baking sheet (previously brushed with margarine) for tarts and pies. Curl the edges and prick the bottom with a fork. Bake at 356°F (180°C) for 15 minutes. Remove the base from the oven and fill with pastry cream. Halve the pineapple slices and lay them in a concentric manner on the cream to cover it completely. Brush edges of pie with beaten egg and return to the oven. Cook for 15 minutes at the same temperature. Remove the tart from the oven and allow to cool. Shortly before serving, sprinkle with white chocolate flakes.

PINK COLADA

INGREDIENTS

CLEAR RUM

PINEAPPLE JUICE

COCONUT SYRUP OR MILK

GRENADINE SYRUP

ORIGINS AND ODDITIES

The Pink Colada (so named in honor of younger adult drinkers) is the United States response to coladas of South American origin. Consisting, at its base, of various rums, a good amount of milk (used in many American cocktails) was added.

PREPARATION

Measure 40 ml (2 3/4 tbsp) of white rum in a graduated cylinder and pour into a blender. Repeat with 80 ml (1/3 cup) of pineapple juice, 20 ml (4 tsp) of coconut syrup or milk and 20 ml (4 tsp) of grenadine syrup. Add 1/2 a tall tumbler of crushed ice and blend for 15–20 seconds. Pour into tumblers and serve, garnished with 1/2 a slice of pineapple, 2 cherries and 2 long straws.

SUGGESTED USE

A drink with strong energy-boosting properties.

Catalan Cream
MEDIUM

ingredients for 4 people
time: 45 minutes + cooling time
(3 hours)

2 1/8 cups milk
1/5 cup cornstarch
scant 1/2 cup (8 tbsp) sugar
5 egg yolks
nutmeg
1 lemon
brown sugar
1/2 a cinnamon stick

In a bowl, dissolve the cornstarch in 1 glass of cold milk, stirring with a whisk. In a saucepan, pour the remaining milk along with half the sugar, cinnamon and the grated zest of 1 lemon. Bring to a boil without stirring and remove from the heat. In a bowl, work the remaining sugar and egg yolks with a whisk until the mixture is frothy. Add the dissolved cornstarch and mix all ingredients. Add the hot milk (passed through a sieve) and give a final mix. Pour the mixture into a saucepan and bring to boil. Continue to cook for 1 minute over medium heat for a soft and smooth cream. Remove from the heat and pour the cream into the appropriate ovenware for Catalan Cream. Let cool and refrigerate for at least 3 hours. Just before serving, sprinkle with a dusting of brown sugar and bake in the oven, making sure that the sugar does not completely caramelize.

FROZEN STRAWBERRY DAIQUIRI

INGREDIENTS

WHITE RUM
LIME JUICE
OR LEMON JUICE

LIQUID SUGAR
FRESH STRAWBERRIES
STRAWBERRY SYRUP

ORIGINS AND ODDITIES

When the classic Daiquiri consolidated its worldwide success in the 1950s, some Americans bartenders thought up ways to lighten and freshen up the drink, adding fresh fruit (strawberry flavor is much loved by women drinkers).

PREPARATION

Measure 40 ml (2 3/4 tbsp) of rum in a graduated cylinder and transfer it to a blender. Repeat with 10 ml (2 tsp) of liquid sugar, 20 ml (4 tsp) of lemon or lime juice and 20 ml (4 tsp) of strawberry syrup. Add 1 tall tumbler of crushed ice and 4–5 fresh strawberries. Blend for 15–20 seconds and pour into tumblers. Serve, garnished with 1/2 a strawberry and 2 short straws.

SUGGESTED USE

A very refreshing drink that can be enjoyed at any time of day.

 Blackberry Puffs   EASY

ingredients for 4 people
time: 30 minutes

12 puffs (average size)
0.30 lbs (4.9 oz) fresh blackberries
1 cup fresh cream
3 tbsp icing sugar
mint leaves
strawberry syrup

In a bowl, work the cream and 2 tbsp of icing sugar with a whisk. Remove the covers of the puffs with the help of a serrated boxcutter. Fill a pastry bag with whipped cream and fill them halfway. Place 1 tbsp of the blackberry filling and finish with the cream all the way to the edge. Delicately put the puff cover back on and lay them on dessert plates. Leave in the refrigerator and just before serving, decorate each serving with fresh mint leaves, 1 tbsp of strawberry syrup (in a zig zag formation) and a dusting of powdered sugar.

FROZEN STRAWBERRY MARGARITA

INGREDIENTS

CLEAR TEQUILA
COINTREAU
LEMON JUICE

STRAWBERRY SYRUP
FRESH STRAWBERRIES

ORIGINS AND ODDITIES

When the Margarita consolidated its worldwide fame in the 1950s, some American bartenders had the idea of adding fruit, which resulted in a drink that was and continues to be a bit hit with women.

PREPARATION

Measure 30 ml (2 tbsp) of tequila in a graduated cylinder and pour it in a blender or food processor. Repeat with 20 ml (4 tsp) of Cointreau, 20 ml (4 tsp) of lemon juice and 20 ml (4 tsp) of strawberry syrup. Add 4–5 fresh strawberries and 1 tall tumbler of crushed ice, blending it all for 15–20 seconds. Pour into a low tumbler, and garnish with a few strawberries and 2 short straws.

SUGGESTED USE

A great refreshing drink, recommended for all times of the day.

Strawberry Salad

EASY

ingredients for 4 people
time: 1 hour

0.66 lbs (10.5 oz) asparagus
0.44 lbs (7 oz, about 1 1/3 cups) strawberries
1 bunch of arugula (rocket)
1 pink grapefruit
juice of 1 lemon
4 tbsp extra virgin olive oil
salt

Wash and clean the asparagus, and boil in plenty of lightly salted water. Meanwhile, wash and clean the strawberries, then cut them into pieces. Wash the arugula, leaving the leaves whole. Peel the grapefruit and cut into cubes. Drain the asparagus and cut them in half lengthwise. In a small bowl, mix the olive oil, lemon juice and a pinch of salt with a fork, in order to get a smooth sauce. Pour into a bowl and add large strawberries, asparagus, grapefruit and arugula. Stir gently and serve.

VIRGIN COLADA

INGREDIENTS

PINEAPPLE JUICE
COCONUT MILK OR SYRUP
CREAM

ORIGINS AND ODDITIES

A non-alcoholic (and much beloved)
version of the famous Piña Colada.

PREPARATION

Measure 100 ml (1/3 cup + 4 tsp) of pineapple
juice in a graduated cylinder and pour into a blender.
Repeat with 20 ml (4 tsp) of cream
and 40 ml (2 3/4 tbsp) of coconut milk or syrup.
Add 1/2 a tall tumbler of crushed ice and blend
for 15–20 seconds. Pour into a tumbler and serve,
garnished with 1/2 a slice of pineapple, 2 cherries
and 2 long straws.

SUGGESTED USE

A delicious, non-alcoholic drink that is also
recommended in the morning for breakfast.

 Tropical Sorbet   MEDIUM

ingredients for 4 people
time: 3 hour and 30 minutes

1 2/3 cups pineapple juice
1 2/3 cups passion fruit juice
2 pureed bananas
2 4/5 cups icing sugar
2 egg whites
1 passion fruit

In a bowl, mash the banana with the sugar. Gradually add the fruit
juice, mixing gently until you get a smooth creamy paste. Pour into
a low rimmed rectangular bowl and let rest in the freezer for about
60 minutes. Remove from freezer and add the egg whites (which
have to be beaten until stiff). Mix well and store in the freezer again
for at least 2 hours. Serve the sorbet in a glass and garnish with
slices of passion fruit.

MOJITOS OF THE WORLD

Legend has it that the first mix of mint and alcohol had been used by pirates in the Caribbean.

"El Drake," so named in honor of the famous pirate, was a mixture of tafia (early cane brandy), lime and hierba buena, a particular mint with a relatively big and juicy stem, considered a remedy for some ailments.

The invention of the Mojito has been ascribed to Cuban bartender Angel Martinez, manager of the historical Havana establishment "La Bodeguita del Medio", which was frequented by Ernest Hemingway, a great admirer of this cocktail.

There are several theories to explain the origin of the word "mojito". One of these would be connected to *mojo*, a typical Cuban condiment made of garlic and citrus fruit used as a marinade. Another theory links it to the translation of the Spanish word *mojado*, which means "wet". A final hypothesis traces the etymology of the word to voodoo, where *mojo* means "spell".

The Original Mojito is never too alcoholic: Cubans love to drink it at any time of day and the tropical heat does not favor high alcohol content. The cocktail is then more like a refreshing drink made with simple, indigenous ingredients.

The original recipe includes: lime, refined cane sugar (i.e. white), sparkling water, white rum and of course the hierba buena that you can safely replace with fresh, sweet mint.

Place the mint leaves (usually 10/12 leaves) in a tall tumbler, squeeze lime over them, and add 1 tbsp of white cane sugar. With a pestle, you exert a little pressure to mix everything well, being careful not to tear the mint leaves (tearing the mint leads to the emergence of slightly stronger oils, which would turn this into a julep). Fill the glass with shaved ice (not crushed) and then add the white rum (4 cl), topping it with soda

or carbonated water. The ice is shaved, because even today many local Cubans keep a large block of ice near the counter, which they break off with a chisel. With the straw, lightly mix the drink.

As decoration you can add to the ice a slice of lime and mint.

A small variation is to mix two types of rum, the first a clear rum aged from one to three years and the second an amber aged up to seven years. This version takes on a more pronounced taste, but the alcohol is the same as the normal Mojito, since a more aged rum becomes softer, and not stronger.

Outside of Cuba, the Mojito has become widespread through a "European version". It is prepared by placing slices of lime at the bottom of the glass with brown sugar. Everything is then mixed well, with bartenders vigorously crushing the ingredients with a pestle and then adding the mint (gently pressed against the sides), crushed ice, and white rum. Using this method, the resulting cocktail is technically Mint Caipirissima and not Mojito. Nevertheless, this version has become so popular outside of Cuba, that the vigorous use of a pestle, not called for by the original recipe, has become the very symbol of the Mojito. Similarly, the Mojito can also be easily confused with the Mint Julep, an American cocktail that uses mint and whisky as a base.

There is also a non-alcoholic version of the Mojito, which is generally called "Virgin Mojito." It is prepared in the same way as the European Mojito, with rum replaced by soda or Ginger Ale.

The International Bartenders Association (IBA) recently selected the Mojito for use in the annual World Cocktail Competition. It is in the "Popular" category, in recognition of its status and popularity around the world.

APPLE MOJITO

INGREDIENTS

GREEN APPLE LIQUEUR
FRESH MINT
LIME

WHITE SUGAR OR CANE SUGAR
SODA WATER
OR SPARKLING WATER

ORIGINS AND ODDITIES

A revisiting of the classic Mojito, it was first presented in 2007 at "Metamorfosi Mojito" (Mojito Metamorphosis), a major international competition organized in Rimini by the Italian magazine *Bargiornale*.

PREPARATION

Cut 1/2 a lime into cubes. Put the lime cubes in a tall tumbler and add 10 g (3 tsp) of white sugar. Grind everything with a pestle until it's a pulp. Add fresh mint leaves and press lightly against the sides of the tumbler. Fill the glass with crushed ice and add 50 ml (3 1/3 tbsp) of green apple liqueur (measured in a graduated cylinder). Fill almost to the brim with soda or sparkling water and mix with a long-handled spoon, so that the ingredients blend well.
To serve, garnish with 1 nice sprig of fresh mint and 2 long straws.

SUGGESTED USE

A drink that can be enjoyed throughout the evening.

 Green Apple Parfait   EASY

ingredients for 4 people
time: 45 minutes + cooling time
(3 hours)

1 cup + 1 1/2 tbsp fresh cream
3 green apples
7/8 cup sugar
2 egg whites
1 glass of brut sparkling wine
1 vanilla stick
whipped cream

Wash, peel and core the apples, then mix in the mixer. Pour into a saucepan and add the vanilla, sugar and sparkling wine. Cover with a lid and simmer for 20 minutes. Remove from heat and let cool. Meanwhile, whip the cream and egg whites until they stiffen. Add both to the apples and mix from the bottom. Pour the mousse into 4 molds (preferably rectangular) and let stand in the freezer for at least 3 hours. Unmold the parfait and decorate with grated green apple and tufts of whipped cream.

ABSINTHE MOJITO

INGREDIENTS

ABSINTHE
LIME
FRESH MINT

WHITE SUGAR OR CANE SUGAR
SODA WATER
OR SPARKLING WATER

ORIGINS AND ODDITIES

This popular drink was created in 2000 to celebrate
the return of absinthe to the American market (after
a century long absence).

PREPARATION

Cut 1/2 a lime into cubes and put in a tall tumbler
with 10 g (3 tsp) of white sugar. Grind everything
with a pestle until it's a pulp. Add fresh mint leaves
and press lightly against the glass. Fill with crushed
ice and add 40 ml (2 3/4 tbsp) of absinthe (measured
in a graduated cylinder). Fill almost to the brim of
the tumbler with soda water or sparkling water.
Mix everything with a long-handled spoon, so that
the ingredients blend well. To serve, garnish
with 1 sprig of fresh mint and 2 long straws.

SUGGESTED USE

An excellent drink for all hours of the evening.
It is now also popular as an aperitif.

Aniseed Matchsticks

EASY

ingredients for 4 people
time: 1 hour

1 cup (16 tbsp) sugar
1 2/3 cups flour
0.44 lbs (7 oz) anise seeds
butter
salt
3 eggs
1/2 tbsp baking powder
honey

Work the eggs and sugar In a bowl with a whisk until the mixture is
smooth and frothy. Add the sifted flour, baking powder and a pinch
of salt and mix well, achieving a smooth dough. Butter a baking sheet
and spread the dough, then sprinkle the whole with the anise seeds.
Bake for 30 minutes at 356°F (180°C). Remove from oven and cut the
dough into strips with a thickness of 1 cm and a length of about 7–8
cm. Serve, accompanied with honey.

BITTER MOJITO

INGREDIENTS

CAMPARI

FRESH ORANGE

WHITE SUGAR OR CANE SUGAR

BRUT SPARKLING WINE

FRESH MINT

ORIGINS AND ODDITIES

This variation on the classic Mojito was also presented for the first time in 2007 during the "Metamorfosi Mojito" competition in Rimini. It proved to be very successful.

PREPARATION

Cut 1/2 an orange into cubes. Put the orange cubes in a tall tumbler and add 10 g (3 tsp) of white sugar. Grind everything with a pestle until it's a pulp. Add fresh mint leaves and press lightly against the sides of the tumbler. Fill the glass with crushed ice and add 40 ml (2 3/4 tbsp) of Campari (measured in a graduated cylinder). Fill almost to the brim with fresh brut sparkling wine and mix everything with a long-handled spoon, so that the ingredients blend well. To serve, garnish with 1 nice sprig of fresh mint and 2 long straws.

SUGGESTED USE

Excellent as an aperitif.

Carbonara Nests

DIFFICULT

ingredients for 4 people
time: 1 hour and 30 minutes

0.80 lbs (12.6 oz) spaghetti

0.33 lbs (5.3 oz) diced pork guanciale (lard from the pig's cheek) or pancetta (pork underbelly)

1 cup (16 tbsp) grated Parmigiano Reggiano cheese

1 cup (16 tbsp) grated pecorino cheese

black pepper

3 egg yolks

2 whole eggs

extra virgin olive oil

butter

First prepare the 4 nests of Parmigiano Reggiano, in which the spaghetti will be served. In a small pan, heat a little extra virgin olive oil. Evenly distribute 1/4 cup (4 tbsp) of grated Parmigiano Reggiano and let it melt for 2 minutes. When the cheese has browned, slide the cheese wafer (with the help of a spatula) upside down on a small glass bowl brushed with sunflower seed oil. Allow to cool and shape the cheese to your taste, until you get "baskets" or "nests" with rough edges. Boil the spaghetti in lightly salted water. Meanwhile, fry the pancetta in a sauce pan along with 2 knobs of butter. When the guanciale or pancetta is crisp, remove from heat and let stand. In a large bowl pour the eggs. Add cheese and pepper to taste, mixing everything with a small whisk. Drain the spaghetti (when it is al dente) and pour into the bowl, immediately combining with the bacon and butter. Mix everything quickly, so that the egg does not curdle. Serve piping hot in the Parmigiano Reggiano baskets.

BLACK MOJITO

INGREDIENTS

LICORICE LIQUEUR
LIME
FRESH MINT

WHITE SUGAR OR CANE SUGAR
SODA WATER
OR SPARKLING WATER

ORIGINS AND ODDITIES

This version of the classic Mojito was also made
public for the first time during Rimini's "Metamorfosi
Mojito" in 2006, a competition that proved to be
a real source of innovative ideas.

PREPARATION

Cut 1/2 a lime into cubes. Put the lime cubes in
a tall tumbler and add 10 g (3 tsp) of white sugar.
Grind everything with a pestle until it's a pulp.
Add fresh mint leaves and press lightly against the
tumbler. Fill the glass with crushed ice and add
50 ml (3 1/3 tbsp) of licorice liquor (measured in
a graduated cylinder). Fill almost to the brim with
soda water or sparkling water and mix with a long-
handled spoon, so that the ingredients blend well.
Serve, garnished with 1 wheel of licorice, 1 nice
sprig of fresh mint and 2 long straws.

SUGGESTED USE

A drink recommended for all hours of the evening.

Sage Biscuits   EASY

ingredients for 4 people
time: 2 hours

1 1/5 cups white flour
4/5 cup buckwheat flour
1/5 cup + 2 1/2 tbsp milk
1/3 cup margarine
salt
1/2 a sachet baking powder
fresh sage

Wash the 8 sage leaves and either mix them in the mixer or chop very
finely. On a work station, sift the flour and add a pinch of salt and
baking powder. Place everything in a heap and lay softened margarine
in the center. Finally, add the sage and milk, mixing everything with your
bare hands, starting from the center, until you get a smooth paste.
Form a ball of dough and let rest in the refrigerator for 1 hour, covering
it with a damp cloth. Flour the work surface, and, with a rolling pin, roll
out the dough until it reaches an even thickness of 1 cm. Cut the biscuits
according to your preferred form and lay them on a dish coated with
baking paper. Bake at 356°F (180°C) for 15 minutes. Serve lukewarm.

JAMAICAN MOJITO

INGREDIENTS

DARK RUM
LIME
WHITE SUGAR OR CANE
SUGAR

FRESH MINT
FRESH FRUIT SALAD
LIME OR LEMON JUICE
SODA WATER OR SPARKLING WATER

ORIGINS AND ODDITIES

It seems that this drink was created in a Jamaican establishment in Milan in the late 1990s. The classic Mojito ingredients were added to fruit unique to the famous Jamaican cooking pot.

PREPARATION

Put 1/2 a lime, cut into cubes, in a tall tumbler and add 10 g (3 tsp) of white sugar. Grind everything with a pestle until it's a pulp. Add fresh mint leaves and press lightly against the glass. Combine 1 tbsp of fresh fruit salad, 40 ml (2 3/4 tbsp) of rum and 20 ml (4 tsp) of lime or lemon juice. Fill the glass with crushed ice and fill almost to the brim with soda water or sparkling mineral water. Mix everything with a long-handled spoon, so that the ingredients blend well. To serve, garnish with 2 cherries and 1/2 a slice of pineapple on a long toothpick that can also be used to taste the fruit.

SUGGESTED USE

A happy and visually stimulating drink that can be enjoyed at all hours of the day.

 Jamaican Cake   EASY

ingredients for 6/8 people
time: 1 hour and 30 minutes +
freezing time (5 hours)

0.88 lbs (14 oz) sponge cake
("pan di spagna")

0.88 lbs (14 oz) pineapple in syrup

1 1/3 cups sugar

2 cups whipped cream

1 vanilla sachet

3 egg yolks

1 whole egg

0.17 lbs (2.8 oz, about 1 cup) toasted almonds

2 tbsp blue curaçao

icing sugar

Drain and dice the pineapple, pouring the syrup into a bowl along with 15 ml (1 tbsp) of Blue Curaçao. Put the diced pineapple in a bowl, leaving it to steep for 45 minutes with another spoonful of liquor and 1/4 cup (4 tbsp) of added sugar. Cut the sponge cake into 1 cm thick slices and line the bottom of the mold with pineapple syrup using a brush. In a bowl, work the eggs and the remaining sugar with a whisk, until creamy and frothy. Add the whipped cream, vanilla, diced pineapple and a few tablespoons of pineapple syrup. Mix the ingredients well and pour the mixture into the mold. Level and cover with slices of sponge cake. Cover the mold with the aluminum foil and let it rest in the freezer for at least 5 hours. Invert the mold onto a serving plate (previously chilled in the freezer), and sprinkle with abundant toasted almonds. Serve, sprinkling with icing sugar.

MOJITO
BASITO

INGREDIENTS

LIGHT RUM
LIME
FRESH BASIL LEAVES

WHITE SUGAR
OR CANE SUGAR
SODA WATER OR
SPARKLING WATER

ORIGINS AND ODDITIES

This variation on the Mojito was presented, along
with many others, at Rimini's 2007 "Metamorfosi
Mojito" competition. Certainly, it was an original idea
to replace the classic mint with another herb: basil.

PREPARATION

Put 1/2 a lime, cut into cubes, in a tall tumbler and
add 10 g (3 tsp) of white sugar. Grind everything
with a pestle until it's a pulp. Add the fresh basil
leaves and press lightly against the glass. Fill with
crushed ice and add 40 ml (2 3/4 tbsp) of rum
(previously measured in a graduated cylinder). Fill
almost to the brim with soda or sparkling water. Mix
everything with a long-handled spoon, so that the
ingredients are well blended. Serve, garnished with 1
good sprig of fresh basil and 2 long straws.

SUGGESTED USE

An aromatic drink for all hours.

Genovese Canapés

EASY

ingredients for 4 people
time: 45 minutes

1 loaf bread
0.66 lbs (10.5 oz) fresh shrimp tails
6 tbsp pesto
salt and pepper
extra virgin olive oil
1 clove of garlic
brandy
4 small tomatoes
basil

Cut 8 slices (with a thickness of 3 cm) from the loaf of bread. Grill
both sides (or toast) and set aside. Clean and chop the garlic finely.
Shell the shrimps and remove the black thread that runs along their
back. In a saucepan, saute the garlic in 2 tbsp of extra virgin olive oil.
Combine the shrimp tails and cook for 3 minutes over medium heat.
Flambé with 1 shot glass of brandy. When the flame diminishes, add
the pesto, salt and pepper. Cook for 5 minutes and remove from
heat. On the grill of the oven lay 8 slices of bread and cover 2/3
with pesto. Bake at 212°F (100°C) for 5 minutes and serve piping hot,
garnishing with beautiful leaves of basil and diced tomatoes.

MOJITO FIDEL

INGREDIENTS

LIGHT RUM
LIME
FRESH MINT
WHITE SUGAR OR

CANE SUGAR
LAGER

ORIGINS AND ODDITIES

On July 26 1953, a group of Cuban rebels led by
Fidel Castro attacked the Moncada Barracks. The
night before, the revolutionaries celebrated the
imminent attack with Mojitos prepared by a soldier
(acting as a de-facto barman). When they ran out
of soda, the man decided to replace it with lager.
Fidel Castro liked the new drink and gave it his name.

PREPARATION

Measure 40 ml (2 3/4 tbsp) of rum in a graduated
cylinder and pour in a tall tumbler. Repeating 30 ml
(2 tbsp) of freshly squeezed lime juice. Combine
10 g (3 tsp) of white sugar, some fresh mint leaves
and mix together with a long-handled spoon. Fill
the glass with ice and fill almost to the brim with
the lager. Give a final mix and serve, garnished
with 1 sprig of fresh mint and 2 long straws.

SUGGESTED USE

A drink that can be enjoyed throughout the evening,
it is also recommended as an aperitif.

Barbecue Chicken Wings

EASY

ingredients for 4 people
time: 45 minutes

8 chicken wings
breadcrumbs
2 eggs
white flour
salt and pepper
peanut seed oil
paprika powder
barbecue sauce

With poultry shears, cut the wings in half along the joint, removing
the skin. In a bowl, beat the eggs with a pinch of salt, pepper and
paprika. Sift the flour into a soup bowl and pour in the breadcrumbs.
Dip, one wing at a time, first in the flour, then the egg and then the
breadcrumbs, being careful to remove any excess breading. Half fill a
large skillet with peanut oil. When hot, fry the breaded wings a few at a
time, turning them over every 2 minutes, for a total 10 minute cook
time. Drain with a skimming spoon and lay the wings on two sheets of
blotting paper. Serve hot, accompanied with barbecue sauce.

ROYAL MOJITO

INGREDIENTS

LIGHT RUM
LIME
FRESH MINT

BRUT SPARKLING WINE
WHITE SUGAR OR
CANE SUGAR

ORIGINS AND ODDITIES

Also presented for the first time in 2007 at the
"Metamorfosi Mojito" competition in Rimini, the Royal
has become one of the most popular variations on the
Mojito.

PREPARATION

Put 1/2 lime, cut into cubes, in a tall tumbler and add
10 g (3 tsp) of white sugar. Grind everything with a pestle
until it's a pulp. Add fresh mint leaves and press lightly
against the glass. Fill with crushed ice and add 40 ml
(2 3/4 tbsp) of rum (previously measured in a graduated
cylinder). Fill almost to the brim with brut sparkling wine
and mix together with a long-handled spoon, so that
the ingredients blend well. To serve, garnish with 1 sprig
of fresh mint, 1/2 an orange slice and 2 long straws.

SUGGESTED USE

A drink that can be enjoyed throughout the evening,
it has become fashionable as an aperitif.

Green Tyrolean Spätzle   EASY

ingredients for 4 people
time: 45 minutes

0.80 lbs (12.6 oz) green spätzle
0.17 lbs (2.8 oz) thick sliced bacon
1 tbsp extra virgin olive oil
1 shot glass white grappa
3/4 cup cooking cream
rosemary
salt and pepper
grated Parmigiano Reggiano cheese

Cut the bacon into strips and sauté in a large pan with 1 tbsp of extra
virgin olive oil. Cover with brandy and allow to boil, cooking everything on low heat for 3 minutes. Add the cream and let the sauce
reduce over medium heat for 5 minutes. Combine finely chopped
rosemary, salt and pepper, away from the stove. Cook the pasta in
abundant salted water. Drain and toss directly in the sauce, and season with a good handful of grated Parmigiano Reggiano. Serve, garnished with sprigs of rosemary.

VIRGIN MOJITO

INGREDIENTS

LIME
FRESH MINT

WHITE SUGAR OR CANE SUGAR
LEMON SOFT DRINK OR GINGER ALE

ORIGINS AND ODDITIES

This non-alcoholic version of the classic Mojito was presented for the first time in 2006 at "L'altra faccia del Mojito" (The other side of the Mojito), a major national competition in Rimini organized by the Italian magazine *Bargiornale*.

PREPARATION

Put 1/2 a lime, cut into cubes, in a tall tumbler and add 10 g (3 tsp) of white sugar. Grind everything with a pestle until it's a pulp. Add fresh mint leaves and press lightly against the glass. Fill with crushed ice and fill to the brim with a lemon soft drink or Ginger Ale. Mix everything together with a long-handled spoon, so that the ingredients blend well. To serve, garnish with 1 sprig of fresh mint and 2 long straws.

SUGGESTED USE

A refreshing drink that can be enjoyed throughout the evening, it is also suitable for the very young.

 Ginger Panna Cotta

EASY

ingredients for 4 people
time: 1 hour + cooling time (2 hours)

1 1/4 cups milk
1 1/4 cups fresh cream
3/5 cup sugar
0.22 lbs (3.5 oz, about 3/8 cup) candied ginger
4 egg yolks
2 whole eggs
2 vanilla beans (pods)
powdered cocoa

Finely chop 0.15 lbs (2.46 oz, about 1/4 cup) of crystallized ginger and place in a saucepan with the open vanilla beans (pods) and milk. Bring to a boil and add the cream, stirring vigorously. Meanwhile, work the eggs and the sugar in a bowl until the mixture is creamy and frothy. Pour the milk into the eggs and give one last stir, letting it cool. With a spoon, remove the vanilla pods and pour the mixture into 4 large panna cotta molds. Place them gently in a high-sided pan and cook in a bain-marie at 356°F (180°C) for about 40 minutes. Remove from oven and let cool. Place the ramekins in the refrigerator for at least 2 hours. Just before serving, unmold the panna cotta, garnish with the remaining diced ginger, sprinkling everything with cocoa powder.

ORANGE MOJITO

INGREDIENTS

LIGHT RUM
ORANGE JUICE
WHITE SUGAR OR CANE SUGAR

FRESH GINGER
GINGER ALE
FRESH MINT

ORIGINS AND ODDITIES

Yet another variation of the Cuban cocktail, the
Orange Mojito was also presented for the first time
in 2006 at "L'altra faccia del Mojito" competition in
Rimini

PREPARATION

Cut 1/4 of an orange into cubes, put in a tall
tumbler and add 10 g (3 tsp) of white sugar. Grind
everything with a pestle until it's a pulp. Add a few
slices of ginger and mint leaves, pressing gently
against the glass all over. Fill with crushed ice and
add 40 ml (2 3/4 tbsp) of rum (previously measured
in a graduated cylinder). Fill almost to the brim with
Ginger Ale and mix with a long-handled spoon, so
that the ingredients blend well. To serve, garnish
with 1 nice sprig of fresh mint and 2 long straws.

SUGGESTED USE

An excellent drink that can be enjoyed throughout
the evening. Recently, it has even become
a popular aperitif.

Orange Octopus

EASY

ingredients for 4 people
time: 1 hour and 30 minutes

2.2 lbs octopus
3 tbsp extra virgin olive oil
2 cloves of garlic
juice of 4 blood oranges
salt and pepper
2 tomatoes (not too ripe)
fish broth
polenta
chopped parsley

Clean and wash the octopus in water, preferably salted. In a large pan
heat the olive oil and brown the garlic (chopped very finely). Add the
octopus and cook over medium heat for about 40 minutes, adding
fish broth from time to time. When almost cooked, add salt, pepper
and orange juice, leaving the sauce to reduce for 10 minutes. Remove
from heat and add the tomatoes (cut into thin strips). Give a final stir
and serve over a bed of soft polenta, sprinkling with chopped parsley.

ORIGINAL CUBAN MOJITO

INGREDIENTS

LIME
FRESH MINT*
WHITE SUGAR**

WHITE RUM
SODA WATER
OR SPARKLING WATER

ORIGINS AND ODDITIES

Here finally the recipe for the original Cuban Mojito is revealed (it may be well known, but many bartenders around the world still prepare it the wrong way). In Cuba, it is served to tourists in clubs as a welcoming drink.

PREPARATION

Measure 40 ml (2 3/4 tbsp) of rum in a graduated cylinder and pour into a tall tumbler. Repeat with 30 ml (2 tbsp) of freshly squeezed lime juice. Combine 10 g (3 tsp) of white sugar, some fresh mint leaves and mix everything with a long-handled spoon. Fill the glass with ice and fill almost to the brim with soda water or sparkling mineral water. Give a final stir and serve, garnishing with 1 sprig of fresh mint and 2 long straws.

SUGGESTED USE

The Mojito is the best known "aperitif" in the world.

*   IN CUBA IT'S PREPARED WITH HIERBA BUENA
** IN CUBA IT'S PREPARED WITH WHITE CANE SUGAR

 Cuban-Style Hash

EASY

ingredients for 4 people
time: 1 hour

1.1 lbs (17.6 oz) ground lean pork
3 tomatoes
0.22 lbs (3.5 oz) tomato puree
1 onion
1 yellow bell pepper
2 cloves garlic
0.13 lbs (2.1 oz) raisins
0.08 lbs (1.41 oz) green olives
oregano
cumin
white wine
salt and pepper – extra virgin olive oil

In a large pan, fry 2 tbsp of extra virgin olive oil, crushed garlic cloves and a finely chopped onion. Add the peppers (previously cleaned and cut into very small cubes) and continue cooking over medium heat for 3 minutes. Add the meat and roast for 5 minutes, stirring continuously. Add the tomatoes (washed and cut into wedges) and the tomato puree. Cook for another 10 minutes. Combine the raisins, olives (previously pitted), 1 tsp of cumin, 1 tsp of oregano, 1 glass of white wine, salt and pepper to taste. Cover with a lid and cook for another 20 minutes. Remove from heat and serve immediately.

PASSION MOJITO

INGREDIENTS

PASSOA LIQUEUR	FRESH MINT
LIME	SODA WATER
WHITE SUGAR	OR SPARKLING WATER
OR CANE SUGAR	FRUIT PASSION (AS A GARNISH)

ORIGINS AND ODDITIES

Also presented in 2007 at the "Metamorfosi Mojito" competition in Rimini, this version of the classic recipe adds a prodigious amount of passion fruit for sensational results.

PREPARATION

Cut 1/2 a lime into cubes. Put the lime in a tall tumbler and add 10 g (3 tsp) of white sugar. Grind everything with a pestle until it's a pulp. Add fresh mint leaves and press lightly against the tumbler. Fill the glass with crushed ice and pour 50 ml (3 1/3 tbsp) of Passoa liquor (measured in a graduated cylinder). Fill almost to the brim with soda water or sparkling water and mix with a long-handled spoon, so that the ingredients blend well. Serve, garnished with 1/2 a passion fruit, 1 nice sprig of fresh mint and 2 long straws.

SUGGESTED USE

A delicious drink that can be enjoyed throughout the evening. It is especially popular with female drinkers.

El Verdadero Amor (True Love)   DIFFICULT

ingredients for 6/8 people
time: 3 hour and 30 minutes +
freezing time (4 hours)

1.1 lbs (17.6 oz) strawberry ice cream
1.1 lbs (17.6 oz) peach ice cream
1 sponge cake disc ("pan di spagna")
2 cups sweetened whipped cream
2 peaches in syrup
1 basket fresh strawberries
cointreau
white chocolate flakes or chips

Line a deep round cake pan with plastic wrap, letting it poke out from the edges. Brush the slice of sponge cake with Cointreau and lay it gently into the mold. Cover with a layer of sweetened whipped cream and let it stand in the freezer for 90 minutes. When the cream has hardened, add a layer of peach ice cream and let it harden again in the freezer for 90 minutes. Repeat with strawberry ice cream, ending with a final layer of whipped cream. Immediately return everything to the freezer for 4 hours. Twenty minutes before serving, take the cake out of the freezer and remove it from the mold. Garnish with diced strawberries and peaches, whipped cream and white chocolate flakes.

SPRITZ MOJITO

INGREDIENTS

APEROL

ORANGE JUICE

WHITE SUGAR OR
CAN SUGAR

BRUT SPARKLING WINE

FRESH MINT

SODA WATER
OR SPARKLING WATER

ORIGINS AND ODDITIES

This fresh and very current version of the Mojito was
presented in 2007 during the "Metamorfosi Mojito"
competition in Rimini.

PREPARATION

Put 1/4 of an orange, cut into cubes, in a tall tumbler
and add 10 g (3 tsp) of white or cane sugar. Grind
everything with a pestle until it's a pulp.
Add a few fresh mint leaves and press lightly against
the sides. Fill the glass with crushed ice and add
40 ml (2 3/4 tbsp) of Aperol (previously measured in
a graduated cylinder). Repeat with 40 ml (2 3/4 tbsp)
of brut sparkling wine and 40 ml (2 3/4 tbsp) of soda
or sparkling water. Mix everything with a long-handled
spoon, so that the ingredients blend well. To serve,
garnish with 1 sprig of fresh mint and 2 long straws.

SUGGESTED USE

An excellent aperitif that can be enjoyed throughout
the evening.

 Vegetable Dip

EASY

ingredients for 4 people
time: 30 minutes

0.22 lbs (3.5 oz) carrots
1 zucchini
1 red bell pepper
1 yellow bell pepper
1 fennel
2 stalks of celery
8 radishes
1 Trevisan radicchio
salt and pepper
juice of 2 lemons
extra virgin olive oil
vinegar

Clean and wash the vegetables thoroughly. Cut the zucchini, the carrots and the peppers into long strips. Slice the radishes, celery and
fennel. Remove the radicchio leaves. On a serving platter, lay out the
vegetables, alternating colors and shapes. At the center position of the
platter, place 4 small bowls with the oil dip (e.g. extra virgin olive oil,
lemon juice, vinegar, salt and pepper) for the vegetables.

VETERINARIAN MOJITO

INGREDIENTS

AMARO MONTENEGRO
LIME
FRESH MINT

WHITE SUGAR OR CANE SUGAR
SODA WATER
OR SPARKLING WATER

ORIGINS AND ODDITIES

This revisiting of the original Mojito was created
by bartender Gianfranco Di Niso. It debuted in
2007 at the "Metamorfosi Mojito" competition
in Rimini, and has since then become one of the
most popular and well-liked variations of the Mojito.

PREPARATION

Cut 1/2 a lime into cubes. Put the lime cubes in
a tall tumbler and add 10 g (3 tsp) of white sugar.
Grind everything with a pestle until it's a pulp. Add
fresh mint leaves and press lightly against the sides
of the tumbler. Fill the glass with crushed
ice and add 60 ml (1/4 cup) of Amaro Montenegro
(measured in a graduated cylinder). Fill almost
to the brim with soda or sparkling water and mix
with a long-handled spoon, so that the ingredients
blend well. To serve, garnish with 1 nice sprig
of fresh mint and 2 long straws.

SUGGESTED USE

An excellent digestive, it is suitable for the entire
evening.

Rhubarb Pie   EASY

ingredients for 6/8 people
time: 4 hours

0.66 lbs (10.5 oz) rhubarb
8 4/5 tbsp butter
3 eggs
1/2 cup + 2 tbsp sugar
7/8 cup (14 tbsp + 2 tsp) flour
brown sugar
4 tbsp fresh cream

Clean the rhubarb and chop coarsely. Combine everything in a bowl
along with 2 tbsp of sugar and let stand for 2 hours. In a large bowl,
work the cream, butter and remaining sugar. Add the eggs and give a
good mix. Add the chopped rhubarb and the sifted flour, until a thick
paste forms. Finally, pour the cream into the bowl, mixing all the ingredients one last time. Pour into a baking pan (greased with butter) and
bake at 356°F (180°C) for 40 minutes. Remove from oven and sprinkle
with sugar cane. Let cool and serve.

VICTORIAN MOJITO

INGREDIENTS

GIN
LIME
WHITE SUGAR

FRESH MINT
SPARKLING BRUT

ORIGINS AND ODDITIES

A perfect and sophisticated blend of the traditional Cuban Mojito and English tradition, with the use of gin instead of rum and brut sparkling wine in place of soda, the Victorian was also presented for the first time in 2007 at the "Metamorfosi Mojito" competition in Rimini.

PREPARATION

Cut 1/2 a lime into cubes. Put the lime cubes in a tall tumbler and add 10 g (3 tsp) of white sugar. Grind everything with a pestle until it's a pulp. Add fresh mint leaves and press lightly against the sides of the tumbler. Fill the glass with crushed ice and add 40 ml (2 3/4 tbsp) of gin (measured in a graduated cylinder). Fill almost to the brim with fresh brut sparkling wine and mix with a long-handled spoon, so that the ingredients blend well. To serve, garnish with 1 nice sprig of fresh mint and 2 long straws.

SUGGESTED USE

An excellent aperitif that can be enjoyed throughout the evening.

 Windsor Roast Beef   MEDIUM

ingredients for 4 people
time: 2 hour and 30 minutes

1.76 lbs (28.2 oz) sirloin beef
1/8 cup (2 tbsp) butter
flour
salt
black pepper
mustard powder
white wine
green pepper
chopped chervil
extra virgin olive oil
1–2 lemons

Preheat the oven to maximum heat. Tie the piece of meat with resistant string, in order to achieve the classic roast beef shape. In a pan, pour 2 tbsp of flour, 1 tbsp of mustard and black pepper to taste and roast everything, being careful that it does not stick. Melt the butter in a saucepan and brown the meat (previously sprinkled with mustard powder) for 10 minutes. Drench with white wine and remove from heat. Put the meat on the grill of the oven, placing a large baking pan with high edges underneath it in order to collect all the juices released from the slow cooking roast beef. Salt the meat to taste and cook for 40 minutes at 400°F (200°C), brushing occasionally with the roast beef juice collected in the pan. Remove from heat and let stand for 20 minutes. Slice the meat as finely as possible and arrange on a serving dish, seasoned with extra virgin olive oil, salt, green pepper spray and a sprinkle of chervil, chopped finely. Serve with some lemon wedges.

COCKTAILS WITH ICE CREAM

The origins of ice cream can be traced back to ancient times: references to the refrigeration of fruits, milk and honey is encountered both in written chronicles and in the most famous archaeological discoveries.

Tradition has it that King Solomon was a major consumer of frozen drinks and that Alexander the Great demanded a continuous supply of snow mixed with honey and fruit during his campaigns in India.

Some scholars date the invention of ice cream to around 3000 BC, placing it in the Far East, among the Chinese. With the Mongol invasions, however, ice cream would then land in Greece and Turkey, expanding to other countries of the Mediterranean basin. Meanwhile, the ancient Egyptian pharaohs enjoyed primitive forms of granita between their courses. It's been said, in fact, that Cleopatra offered Caesar and Antony fruit blended with ice.

In the Middle Ages, in the East, a method was developped to freeze fruit juices by placing them in containers surrounded by crushed ice. The word sorbet, in fact, is derived from Arabic. The Crusaders, returning from the Holy Land, brought these products to the tables of European nobles.

With the discovery of the New World and the introduction of exotic fruits, herbs, spices, and cocoa to European cuisine, cold desserts enjoyed a veritable golden age at the European banquets.

In the Italian Renaissance, the Medici court in Florence was known for the production of fine sorbets and mounted ice creams. The idea of a true and proper ice cream, as we know it, came from a man named Ruggieri, a seller of chickens. He decided to whisk his sorbet in containers surrounded by snow for several minutes, twisting and turning them. At the same time, another Florentine, Bernardo Buontalenti, an architect, engineer and artist, created a cream flavored with bergamot, lemon and orange, and chilled it with his own invention: an innovative method of conserving snow collected during the winter and then storing it in cellars lined with straw.

At the end of the seventeenth century, a Sicilian chef named Francesco Procopio dei Coltelli founded the first cafe in Paris (Le Procope, which later became one of the most famous literary cafes of Europe) that also served ice cream, an item that was very appreciated by the Sun King.

The monarch would eventually grant exclusivity to the Sicilian for the production of such items as "icy waters", the "fruit ice cream", the "flowers of anise and cinnamon", the "lemon juice ice cream," "orange juice ice cream", "ice cream" and the "strawberry sorbet."

With the eighteenth century, cold desserts had spread to all courts and European capitals, with the standard formula based on milk, eggs and sugar.

Italian Giovanni Bosio opened his first ice cream parlor in New York in 1770 and this product became an instant success in America.

The idea of putting ice cream in a biscuit (later to become the ice cream cone) came to Italian Giovanni Torre from Bussana, who in the early twentieth century also invented the ice cream cart

with the classic three-pedal wheels, which soon spread outside of Italy. In 1927, Bologna-native Otello Cattabriga built the first automatic ice cream machine for the production of ice cream, which became popular across the world.

The production of ice cream made on an industrial scale, however, started in the United States, where the first machines were designed for the mass production of ice cream. Unlike Europeans, Americans also preferred to use cream instead of eggs as a base, and this remains one of the main differences between American and European ice cream.

After suffering a decline in the 1950s and 1960s, ice cream is now experiencing a widespread rebirth, with a range of ice cream shops and commercial products. Ice cream is not only for summer days, though, as with a little creativity, it can be used for exceptional after-dinner cocktails, served in place of dessert, and fresh drinks that can be enjoyed at all hours.

Just think, for example, how easy it is to create a variation on the Piña Colada: just by adding some chocolate ice cream, you have a Choco-colada. To make a cocktail with ice cream, though, you have to use a blender. Still, with just a few scoops of your favorite ice cream, you can get a delicious cocktail.

Here are some examples:

ICE CREAM ALEXANDER
Brandy
White cocoa cream
Cream
Vanilla ice cream
Nutmeg (top)

BURNT ARNOLD
Disaronno Original
Kalhúa liqueur
Cream
Vanilla ice cream

GRASSHOPPER ICE CREAM
Crème de menthe verte
White cocoa cream
Cream
Mint ice cream

ICE STRAWBERRY MARGARITA
Tequila
Triple sec
Lemon juice
Strawberry ice cream

ICE BANANA DAIQUIRI
White rum
Crème de banane
Lemon juice
Banana ice cream

BOMBARDINO
Scotch whisky
Disaronno Original
Plain ice cream
Cocoa (top)

AFTER EIGHT

INGREDIENTS

CRÈME DE MENTHE
BLANCHE (WHITE MINT)
OR MINT LIQUEUR

CHOCOLATE LIQUEUR
MINT ICE CREAM
CHOCOLATE ICE CREAM

ORIGINS AND ODDITIES

A successful drink created in Berlin in the late 1990s.
It was inspired by the famous chocolate mint and
has become especially popular with women.

PREPARATION

Measure 50 ml (3 1/3 tbsp) of crème de menthe
blanche or mint liqueur and pour into a blender.
Repeat with 50 ml (3 1/3 tbsp) of chocolate liqueur.
Add 1 tbsp of mint ice cream, 1 tbsp of chocolate ice
cream and 1/2 a low tumbler of crushed ice. Blend
for 15–20 seconds and pour into a tall tumbler. To
serve, garnish with 1 nice sprig of
fresh mint and 2 long straws.

SUGGESTED USE

A gourmet drink that can be enjoyed throughout
the evening. It is also good as a digestive.

 Mint Cappuccino

ingredients for 4 people
time: 30 minutes + cooling time
(3 hours)

6 egg yolks
4 egg whites
6 tbsp sugar
3 tbsp mint syrup
dark chocolate flakes or chips
whipped cream
powdered cocoa

In a bowl, work the egg yolks and sugar with a whisk until the mixture
is smooth and fluffy. Drizzle the mint syrup, stirring continuously. Beat
the egg whites until they're stiff and gradually add them and the dark
chocolate flakes. Giving a final mix, always starting from the bottom,
pour the mixture into 4 beautiful cappuccino cups. Let them stand in
the refrigerator for at least 3 hours. Just before serving, garnish with a
dash of whipped cream and a dusting of cocoa powder.

BITTER SWEET

INGREDIENTS

APEROL
CAMPARI
PEACH VODKA

SANBITTÈR
PEACH FLAVORED
ICE CREAM

ORIGINS AND ODDITIES

This drink was created in the late 1990s in an ice cream shop in Berlin. It soon became a popular drink throughout Central Europe.

PREPARATION

Measure 30 ml (2 tbsp) of Aperol in a graduated cylinder and pour in a blender. Repeat with 10 ml (2 tsp) of Campari, 30 ml (2 tbsp) of vodka and 30 ml (2 tbsp) of Sanbittèr. Add 2 tbsp of peach ice cream and 1/2 a low tumbler of crushed ice. Blend for 15–20 seconds and pour into a tall tumbler. Serve, garnished with an orange segment or fresh peach and 2 long straws.

SUGGESTED USE

A very enjoyable aperitif.

Sliced Tuna

MEDIUM

ingredients for 4 people
time: 45 minutes

4 slices of tuna [0.33 lbs (5.3 oz) each]
arugula (rocket)
2 tbsp pink peppercorn (baies rose berries)
salt and pepper
1 lemon
extra virgin olive oil

Carefully clean the slices of tuna, and season with salt and pepper to taste. Heat 2 generous tbsp of extra virgin olive oil in a large nonstick skillet. Cook the slices of tuna on high heat for no more than 3 minutes per side. Meanwhile in a sauce boat, emulsify 2 tbsp of extra virgin olive oil with the juice of 1 lemon, salt and pink peppercorn. On a platter, arrange a bed of arugula (washed and chopped coarsely). On a cutting board, slice the slices of tuna and lay on the arugula. Season the sauce with plenty of pink peppercorn and serve immediately.

BLUE ANGEL ICE

INGREDIENTS

DRY VODKA

COINTREAU

BLUE CURAÇAO

LEMON JUICE

LEMON ICE CREAM

ORIGINS AND ODDITIES

An iced version of the famous Blue Angel, which, thanks to the addition of lemon ice cream, tastes less aggressive. It has appealed to the more delicate tastes of women drinkers.

PREPARATION

Measure 30 ml (2 tbsp) of vodka in a graduated cylinder and pour into a blender. Repeat with 20 ml (4 tsp) of Cointreau, 30 ml (2 tbsp) of Blue Curaçao and 20 ml (4 tsp) of lemon juice. Add 2 tbsp of lemon ice cream and 1/2 a low tumbler of crushed ice. Blend for 15–20 seconds and pour into a tall tumbler. Serve, garnished with 1/2 a slice of orange, 2 cherries and 2 long straws.

SUGGESTED USE

A particularly thirst-quenching drink, it is a good digestive.

 ## Citrus Velvet Cream

ingredients for 4 people
time: 1 hour

3/4 cup + 1 1/2 tbsp citrus juice to taste
3 eggs
grated zest of 1 lemon
1/4 cup (4 tbsp) sugar
4 tbsp potato starch
1 basket raspberries

In a large bowl, work the egg yolks and sugar with a whisk until creamy, smooth and frothy. Stirring continuously, add the sifted potato starch, the grated zest of 1 lemon and, gradually, the citrus juice. Pour the mixture into a saucepan and bring to a boil over medium heat. Remove from heat and let cool, then blend in the blender. Transfer the mixture back into a bowl and add the egg whites (previously beaten until stiff), mixing from the bottom, so that the eggs do not rise. Allow it to rest until you serve it in 4 dessert bowls, decorating as desired with fresh raspberries.

COSMOPOLITAN ICE

INGREDIENTS

DRY VODKA
COINTREAU
LEMON ICE CREAM

CRANBERRY JUICE
OR SYRUP

ORIGINS AND ODDITIES

This cocktail was created in the mid-'90s by female bartenders in New York who wanted to enrich the classic Cosmopolitan with ice cream.

PREPARATION

Measure 50 ml (3 1/3 tbsp) of vodka in a graduated cylinder and pour into a blender. Repeat with 20 ml (4 tsp) of Cointreau and 20 ml (4 tsp) of cranberry juice or syrup. Add 2 tbsp of lemon ice cream and 1/2 a low tumbler of crushed ice. Blend for 15–20 seconds and pour into a tall tumbler. Serve, garnished with cherries and 2 long straws.

SUGGESTED USE

An excellent drink for the evening, it is especially loved by women.

Cherry Pie   EASY

ingredients for 6/8 people
time: 2 hours

0.66 lbs (10.5 oz) black cherry jam
2 1/2 cups flour
3/5 cup cane sugar
scant 1/2 cup (7 tbsp) butter
1 egg yolk
1 whole egg
salt
1 sachet baking powder
grated zest of 1 lemon

Sift the flour and place it in a bowl. Add softened butter and start to mix everything quickly with your fingertips. Place in another bowl and to the center, add salt, baking powder, lemon zest, eggs and sugar. Start to mix the ingredients quickly, in order to fully incorporate the flour and obtain smooth and homogeneous dough. Shape into a ball and cover with a damp cloth. Let it rest in the refrigerator for 45 minutes. Flour your work station and the rolling pin and roll out the dough. Line a greased baking pan. Prick the bottom of the tart with a fork and fill the base with black cherry jam. Work the scraps of dough until you have strips that cross over the top of the jam, to create the classic pie grille. Bake at 400°F (200°C) for about 30 minutes and let cool before serving.

FRENCH KISS

INGREDIENTS

APEROL

CAMPARI

GRAND MARNIER

A.C.E. (ORANGE/
CARROT/LEMON) ICE
CREAM

ORIGINS AND ODDITIES

A drink created in the 1990s by a Parisian
barlady who was hopelessly in love with
a Spanish painter who used to come
to her ice cream shop in Montmartre.

PREPARATION

Measure 60 ml (1/4 cup) of Aperol in a graduated
cylinder and pour into a blender. Repeat with 20 ml
(4 tsp) of Grand Marnier and 10 ml (2 tsp) of Campari.
Add 2 tbsp of A.C.E ice cream and 1/2 a low tumbler
of crushed ice. Blend for 15–20 seconds and pour
into a tall tumbler. Serve, garnished with 1/2 a slice
of pineapple, 2 cherries and 2 long straws.

SUGGESTED USE

A delicious aperitif.

Niçoise Salad

EASY

ingredients for 4 people
time: 30 minutes

0.66 lbs (10.5 oz, about 2 small or
about 1 1/2 medium) boiled potatoes

0.55 lbs (8.8 oz, 1 1/4 cup) steamed
green beans

8 cherry tomatoes

0.44 lbs (7 oz) tuna in oil

8 anchovy fillets

2 boiled eggs

black olives

capers

basil

salt

extra virgin olive oil

Cut the potatoes in 2 cm thick slices and halve the tomatoes. Drain
the tuna and anchovies. Drain the olives. Place all the ingredients in
4 salad bowls, alternating between forms and colors. In another bowl,
pour 4 tbsp of extra virgin olive oil and add a handful of capers and a
pinch of salt. Mix thoroughly with a spoon and sprinkle on each dish.
Garnish with beautiful basil leaves.

LIQUAICE

INGREDIENTS

LICORICE LIQUEUR
LIGHT RUM
"FIORDILATTE" (WHOLE DAIRY MILK)
ICE CREAM OR PLAIN ICE CREAM

ORIGINS AND ODDITIES

This drink was created in the mid-'90s in an ice cream shop in Italy, in honor of a young client who loved licorice.

PREPARATION

Measure 60 ml (1/4 cup) of licorice liqueur in a graduated cylinder and pour into a blender. Repeat with 40 ml (2 3/4 tbsp) of rum. Add 2 tbsp of ice cream and 1/2 a low tumbler of crushed ice. Blend for 15–20 seconds and pour into a tall tumbler up. To serve, garnish with 2 slices of licorice and 2 long straws.

SUGGESTED USE

An excellent after dinner drink, also recommended as a digestive.

Licorice Semifreddo   EASY

ingredients for 4 people
time: 45 minutes + freezing time
(2 hours)

0.7 oz (1/8 cup) licorice
scant 1/2 cup (8 tbsp) sugar
1 egg yolk
4 tbsp whole milk
2 cup + 2 1/2 tbsp whipped cream

Work the egg yolk and sugar with a whisk until frothy. In a saucepan, warm the milk at low heat, combining the licorice (previously mixed in a mixer). Continue cooking, stirring continuously, until the licorice has dissolved completely. Remove from heat before it boils and then add eggs and sugar, working vigorously with a whisk. Gradually add the whipped cream and mix all the ingredients to obtain a homogeneous mixture. Pour into 4 semifreddo molds and, before serving, let stand in the freezer for at least 2 hours.

LULÙ ICE

INGREDIENTS

APEROL

CAMPARI

MANDARINETTO ISOLABELLA

A.C.E. (ORANGE/CARROT/LEMON) ICE CREAM

ORIGINS AND ODDITIES

At the turn of the century, a lady in Freiburg loved drinking Aperol as an aperitif, followed by an A.C.E. (orange/carrot/lemon) ice cream as a dessert: a barman at one of her favorite bars decided to create a new cocktail in her honor, combining Aperol with A.C.E. ice cream.

PREPARATION

Measure 50 ml (3 1/3 tbsp) of Aperol in a graduated cylinder and pour in a blender. Repeat with 30 ml (2 tbsp) of Mandarinetto Isolabella and 20 ml (4 tsp) of Campari. Add 2 tbsp of A.C.E. ice cream and 1/2 a tumbler of crushed ice below. Blend for 15–20 seconds and pour into a tall tumbler. Serve, garnished with 1/2 a slice of orange, 1 cherry and 2 long straws.

SUGGESTED USE

An excellent aperitif.

Camembert Polenta Bites

MEDIUM

ingredients for 4 people
time: 4 hours

3 1/2 cups water
2 1/3 cups cornmeal
0.17 lbs (8 oz) camembert
grated cheese
butter
salt
0.33 lbs (5.3 oz) boiled asparagus
8 tbsp béchamel

In a copper kettle, heat water with 1 tbsp of salt. When it starts boiling, remove from heat and pour in the flour, stirring vigorously with a whisk. Put it back on the stove and continue cooking for 50 minutes after the polenta comes to boil again, stirring constantly with a large wooden spoon. When the polenta falls from the side of the pot, pour into 8 pudding molds and allow to cool. Refrigerate for at least 2 hours. Knock the polenta out and cut horizontally into 3 shapes of roughly the same thickness. Fill with a few cubes of Camembert, a pinch of salt and grated cheese. Reset the polenta shapes and lay them in a buttered baking dish and bake at 430°F (220°C). Heat the béchamel sauce and prepare 4 plates. On each, place a bed of sauce and 2 polenta bites. Serve immediately, sprinkled with grated cheese and accompanied with boiled asparagus (sautéed in butter).

MICHELLE ICE

INGREDIENTS ·

APEROL
CAMPARI
PEACH VODKA

A.C.E. (ORANGE/CARROT/
LEMON) ICE CREAM

ORIGINS AND ODDITIES

According to legend, this drink was
created by a bartender in Bremen at the
end of the 1990s, in honor of a customer
who loved the Beatles' song *Michelle*.

PREPARATION

Measure 60 ml (1/4 cup) of Aperol in a graduated
cylinder and pour into a blender. Repeat with
30 ml (2 tbsp) of vodka and 10 ml (2 tsp) of Campari.
Add 2 tbsp of A.C.E. ice cream and 1/2 a tumbler
of crushed ice below. Blend for 15–20 seconds
and pour into a tall tumbler. To serve, garnish
with 1/2 an orange slice and 2 long straws.

SUGGESTED USE

A refreshing drink that is excellent for any happy hour.

Club Sandwich   EASY

ingredients for 4 people
time: 30 minutes

sliced white bread (toast)
12 slices bacon
12 slices turkey
3 tbsp butter
1/3 cup mayonnaise
2 tomatoes
lettuce
salt and pepper

Brown the turkey slices in a pan with a knob of butter and set aside. In
the same butter, fry the bacon but make sure it does not get crispy.
Meanwhile, wash, clean and slice the tomatoes thinly and wash and
dry 4 large leaves of lettuce. Remove the crust from the sliced bread
and butter. Lay it on the grill of the oven, preheated to 248°F (120°C),
for about 5 minutes, until the slices begin to brown, being careful
that the bread does not dry out too much. Spread the mayonnaise
on the first slice of bread. Place, in order, 1 leaf of lettuce, slices of
turkey, slices of tomato and bacon. Close with a slice of toast. Follow
the same order to construct the second layer of the sandwich and
then repeat for each portion. Gently split in half with a sharp knife
and pierce with a long skewer. Serve the club sandwich, accompanied with potato chips.

PUFFO ICE

INGREDIENTS

MILK
BLUE FOOD COLORING*
"FIORDILATTE" (WHOLE DAIRY MILK) ICE CREAM

ORIGINS AND ODDITIES

This drink seems to have been created in Rome in the 1980s in an ice cream and pastry shop. At the time the Smurfs were a popular cartoon (they are called "Puffi" in Italian), and the creator loved the show. He decided to create a non-alcoholic, beautifully colored cocktail suitable for all the young fans of the animated series.

PREPARATION

Measure 1/3 cup + 1 tbsp (90 ml) of milk in a graduated cylinder and pour into a blender. Repeat with 2 tsp (10 ml) of blue dye. Add 2 tbsp of "fiordilatte" ice cream and 1/2 a low tumbler of crushed ice. Blend for 15 seconds and pour into a tall tumbler up. To serve, garnish with 2 long straws.

SUGGESTED USE

A cute soft drink that can quench your children's thirst.

* EASILY AVAILABLE IN THE BAKERY SECTION OF MOST SUPERMARKETS

Fruit Palette

EASY

ingredients for 4 people
time: 30 minutes

4 peaches in syrup
8 slices pineapple in syrup
1 banana
8 strawberries
2 kiwis
1 bunch grapes
2 baskets berries
"fiordilatte" (whole dairy milk) ice cream
2 lemons
sugar
ice cream waffles

Drain the peaches and slice them, not too thinly. Drain the pineapple slices and cut in half. Peel the banana and kiwis and cut into thick slices. Wash the grapes and remove the seeds. Wash and clean the strawberries, then cut them in half. Gently wash the berries. In a bowl combine the lemon juice and 2 tbsp of sugar, stirring the sauce well, so that the ingredients blend well. Place the fruit on 4 dessert plates, alternating colors and shapes as desired. Just before serving, pour the lemon-based sauce over everything. Serve with a generous scoop of plain ice cream and some ice cream waffles.

SABBIA
D'ORIENTE

INGREDIENTS

COFFEE LIQUEUR
WHISKY CREAM
"FIORDILATTE" (WHOLE DAIRY MILK)
ICE CREAM OR PLAIN ICE CREAM

ORIGINS AND ODDITIES

This drink was first presented in 2000 at the "Bar
Festival", an Italian bartending competition held
in Milan, by barman Gianfranco Di Niso.

PREPARATION

Measure 70 ml (4 tbsp + 2 tsp) of whisky cream
in a graduated cylinder and pour into a blender.
Repeat with 30 ml (2 tbsp) of coffee liqueur.
Add 2 tbsp of ice cream and 1/2 a low tumbler
of crushed ice. Blend for 15–20 seconds and pour
into a tall tumbler. To serve, garnish with 2 long
straws and a dusting of cocoa.

SUGGESTED USE

A delightful dinner drink.

Dark Chocolate Dates

EASY

ingredients for 4 people
time: 45 minutes

0.55 lbs (8.8 oz) extra-dark chocolate
20 dates
almonds
candied orange zest
powdered cinnamon
walnut kernels
whipped cream

Gently pit the dates and cut them lengthwise. Fill with 1 almond and
some candied orange zests, and close them well. Melt the chocolate
in a bain-marie, along with 1 tsp of cinnamon powder. With the help
of a long toothpick or kebab stick, thoroughly soak the dates one at a
time in the chocolate, letting any excess drip off into the pot. Put the
dates on a tray covered with baking paper and allow to solidify. Serve in
a bowl, garnished with a sprinkle of cinnamon-flavored whipped cream
and a few walnut kernels.

STINGER ICE

INGREDIENTS

BRANDY
CRÈME DE MENTHE BLANCHE
(WHITE MINT)
LEMON ICE CREAM

ORIGINS AND ODDITIES

The origins of this drink, apparently, start around the
turn of the millenium with a lady in Berlin.
Tired of drinking the Stinger that her husband
usually prepared for her (she considered it overly
alcoholic), she proposed this drink, which she started
serving at gatherings.

PREPARATION

Measure 50 ml (3 1/3 tbsp) of brandy in a graduated
cylinder and pour into a blender. Repeat with 50 ml
(3 1/3 tbsp) of crème de menthe blanche. Add 2 tbsp
of lemon ice cream and 1/2 a low tumbler of crushed
ice. Blend for 15–20 seconds and pour into a tall
tumbler. Serve, garnished with a slice of lemon,
1 sprig of fresh mint and 2 long straws.

SUGGESTED USE

A drink with great digestive properties, it can be
enjoyed throughout the evening.

Port Fruit Salad

EASY

ingredients for 4 people
time: 1 hour

0.44 lbs (7 oz, about 1 1/3 cups)
strawberries
1/4 melon
4 apricots
4 peaches
0.22 lbs (3.5 oz) blackberries
wild berry ice cream
4 tbsp white port
4 tbsp sugar
juice of 2 pink grapefruits

Clean and wash the strawberries, then cut them into 4 wedges. Peel
the melon and cut into cubes (not too small). Wash the peaches and
apricots, removing their pits and cutting into slices of the same size.
Wash the berries and put them in a glass bowl. Add the rest of the
fruit, drowning everything with the Port and the pink grapefruit juice.
Add the sugar and give a gentle stir. Let stand in the refrigerator for
30 minutes. Just before serving, arrange the Port fruit salad in 4 low
cups (including the juice), accompanied with a generous scoop of wild
berry ice cream.

STRAWBERRY DAIQUIRI ICE

INGREDIENTS

LIGHT RUM   LEMON JUICE
LEMON ICE CREAM
LIQUID SUGAR
STRAWBERRIES

ORIGINS AND ODDITIES

It seems it was bartenders in Stuttgart who first added ice cream to the famous Daiquiri, creating, in the process, one of the most delicious drinks in the "Ice" family.

PREPARATION

Measure 60 ml (1/4 cup) of rum in a graduated cylinder and pour into a blender. Repeat with 30 ml (2 tbsp) of liquid sugar and 10 ml (2 tsp) of lemon juice. Add 2 tbsp of lemon ice cream, 5–6 fresh strawberries and 1/2 a low tumbler of crushed ice. Blend for 15–20 seconds and pour into a tall tumbler. Serve, garnished with 2 strawberries and 2 long straws.

SUGGESTED USE

An excellent digestive, recommended throughout the day.

Sweet Cakes

ingredients for 4 people
time: 1 hour and 30 minutes

4 cups flour
0.53 lbs (8.5 oz) sweet potatoes
0.88 oz (2 tbsp + 2 tsp) fresh yeast
2 tbsp sugar
1 1/4 cups milk
1 egg
4 tbsp extra virgin olive oil
butter
salt

In a bowl of tepid water, dissolve the yeast and let stand for 15 minutes. Finely grate the potatoes in a bowl. In a large bowl, work the egg and sugar with a whisk until creamy and frothy. Add the extra virgin olive oil and 1 tsp of salt, stirring constantly. Gradually combine the potatoes, flour and softened yeast. Add the warm milk, mixing all the ingredients until the desired consistency is achieved. Divide the dough into rectangular cakes about 10 cm long and, after covering with a wet cloth, let rest in refrigerator for 30 minutes. Grease and flour a baking sheet and gently place the sweet cakes. Bake at 356°F (180°C) and, just before they are ready, brush the surface with the beaten egg yolk. Sprinkle with sugar and serve, either hot or cold.

TESTAROSSA ICE

INGREDIENTS

DRY VODKA

CAMPARI

STRAWBERRY ICE CREAM

ORIGINS AND ODDITIES

A drink created in 2007 by a bartender who was particularly fond of Formula 1. It was named in honor of the last world championship won by the Ferrari team.

PREPARATION

Measure 50 ml (3 1/3 tbsp) of vodka in a graduated cylinder and pour into a blender. Repeat with 50 ml (3 1/3 tbsp) of Campari. Add 2 tbsp of strawberry ice cream and 1/2 a low tumbler of crushed ice. Blend for 15–20 seconds and pour into a tall tumbler. To serve, garnish with 2 strawberries and 2 long straws.

SUGGESTED USE

An excellent aperitif.

 Four-Cheese Farfalle   EASY

ingredients for 4 people
time: 45 minutes

0.80 lbs (12.6 oz) farfalle pasta

0.33 lbs (5.3 oz, about 2 1/2 cups) sautéed mushrooms

0.11 lbs (1.76 oz, about 12) walnut kernels

0.13 lbs (2.1 oz) sweet gorgonzola

0.13 lbs (2.1 oz) brie cheese

0.13 lbs (2.1 oz) formai de mut (literally "mountain cheese"), from lombardy, or a similar cheese

0.13 lbs (2.1 oz) pecorino cheese

4 tbsp béchamel

parsley, butter, salt and pepper

Cook the pasta in abundant salted water. Meanwhile, melt a knob of butter in a large saucepan. Add the Formai de Mut, Gorgonzola and Brie (cut into small pieces). Cook everything, stirring continuously, until the cheese is completely melted, creating a flowing cream. Add the pecorino, the béchamel sauce, the nuts (chopped coarsely), sautéed mushrooms, salt and pepper to taste. Mix well for a few minutes over low heat. Drain the farfalle "al dente" (slightly underdone) and pour them directly into the saucepan. Just before serving, add a generous sprinkling of chopped parsley.

TIRAMISÙ ICE

INGREDIENTS

COFFEE LIQUEUR
EGGNOG OR EGG LIQUEUR
DARK RUM

"FIORDILATTE" (WHOLE
DAIRY MILK) ICE CREAM
OR PLAIN ICE CREAM
POWDERED COCOA

ORIGINS AND ODDITIES

According to legend, the creator of this drink
was a housewife from Basel, who, in the late 1990s,
grew tired of serving the typical tiramisù. She came
up with the idea of creating an alcoholic version
of the cake that everyone loved.

PREPARATION

Measure 40 ml (2 3/4 tbsp) of egg liqueur in a
graduated cylinder and pour into a blender. Repeat
with 30 ml (2 tbsp) of rum and 30 ml (2 tbsp) of
coffee liqueur. Add 2 tbsp of ice cream and 1/2
a low tumbler of crushed ice. Blend for 15–20 seconds
and pour into a tall tumbler. Serve, garnished with
a dusting of cocoa and 2 long straws.

SUGGESTED USE

A gourmet dinner drink, it is good as a digestive.

Small Croissants   MEDIUM

ingredients for 4 people
time: 1 hour

1 roll of ready-made puff pastry
creamy hazelnut spread
icing sugar

Flour the work surface and rolling pin, stretching out the dough until
it reaches a thickness of 1 cm. Cut into numerous 2 cm thick slices. Roll
the strips into a spiral to shape the croissants, making sure to overlap
the edges. Gently place the croissants on a baking sheet, covered with
baking paper, spaced at least 7–8 cm apart. Bake at 400°F (200°C) for
about 15 minutes, until the dough is puffy and golden. Remove from
the oven and let cool. Remove the croissants and, with the help of a
small pastry syringe, stuff them with hazelnut spread. Dust with icing
sugar and serve.

TROPICAL ICE

INGREDIENTS

MINT SYRUP
ORGEAT SYRUP
MILK

"FIORDILATTE"
(WHOLE DAIRY MILK)
ICE CREAM

ORIGINS AND ODDITIES

It's been said that this cocktail was served for the
first time in 1992 in an ice cream shop in Stuttgart.
It was created to meet the unique demands
of a French nun who wanted an alcoholic long drink,
but not something fruit-based.

PREPARATION

Measure 60 ml (1/4 cup) of milk in a graduated
cylinder and pour into a blender. Repeat with 20 ml
(4 tsp) of mint syrup and 20 ml (4 tsp) of orgeat
syrup. Add 2 tbsp of "fiordilatte" ice cream and
1/2 a low tumbler of crushed ice. Blend for 15–20
seconds and pour into a tall tumbler. To serve, garnish
with 1 nice sprig of fresh mint and 2 long straws.

SUGGESTED USE

A greatly refreshing drink, it is also suitable for
children.

 Candy Apples   MEDIUM

ingredients for 4 people
time: 1 hour

4 yellow apples (average size)
1 1/4 cups sugar
0.06 lbs (1 oz) honey
1/2 a vanilla sachet
3 1/3 tbsp water
2 cloves
red food coloring (easily available
in the bakery section of most
supermarkets)

Wash apples and remove the cores. Skewer from above with a thick
wooden stick (like big amusement park lollipops). In a saucepan pour
the warm water, sugar and honey and cook over medium heat, stirring
continuously. Just before it boils, add the cloves, cinnamon and 1 tbsp
of red food coloring. Continue to cook over medium heat until boiling is no longer evident (maximum attention is needed at this stage of
preparation, given the very high temperatures reached by the sugar).
Dip the apples completely in caramel foam, turning them several times
and draining the excess before gently placing them on a tray covered
with baking paper. Allow to cool completely before serving apples.

FANCY APERITIFS

Aperitivs are beverages that have a special function: they prepare the body for a meal. These drinks are aqueous, hydroalcoholic or vinous, with aromatic and bitter substances. The bitter aspects make the taste buds more sensitive by increasing the stimulation and by creating the conditions for a more abundant gastric secretion. The physiological action of aperitifs are not only linked to bitters, however, but also to other substances, including alcohol and carbon dioxide, which act directly on the mucous membranes of the stomach.

Since ancient times, Greeks, Etruscans and Romans had the custom of starting their banquets with drinks based on wine, honey and spices, which were said to open the stomach. In fact, the term aperitif derives from the Latin verb *aperio* which means "to open".

In the fifth century BC, the greek doctor Hippocrates prescribed an appetite-stimulating drug of his own invention: the *Hippocratic vinum*, which was like a sweet white wine, with macerated dittany flowers, wormwood and rue. The Romans called it *vinum absinthiatum* (absinthe, with wormwood), and to improve the decidedly bitter flavor, added rosemary and sage.

This tradition was also found in the Renaissance, and Catherine de' Medici, bringing these drinks to the court of France, gave the word "aperitif" its "before the meal" meaning.

Geographical discoveries and the opening of trade with the East made new and expensive spices known in Europe, all of which seemed made specifically to improve the flavor of the "aperitif": nutmeg, cloves, cinnamon, rhubarb, China, myrrh, pepper, etc.

The aperitif as a consumer product (intended as a food product and not a medical remedy) was created in Turin in 1796 in a small liquor and wine shop run by Antonio Benedetto Carpano, who had the brilliant idea of selling, in an elegant liter bottle, a wine flavored with herbs and spices. He called this concoction Vermouth, from the German *wermut*, "wormwood".

Many years later he sent vermouth, as an homage, to King Victor Emmanuel II, who

was said to appreciate it for its *punt e mes* ("one and a half" in the Turin dialect) of bitterness that gave the drink a better balance (compared to similar drinks). The Carpano vermouth (immediately renamed Punt e Mes) became an official court aperitif.

The drink's success was enormous; Cavour, Verdi and Giacosa went crazy for it and the Carpano shop, from 1840 to 1844, stay opened 24 hours a day to meet the demand.

Meanwhile, in 1815, Ausano Ramazzotti of Milan had created a non-vinous aperitif, created with an infusion of as many as 33 herbs and roots from around the world: South American cinchona, Chinese rhubarb, bitter orange from Curaçao, sweet orange from Sicily, gentian from Val d'Aosta, etc.

Following these successes, Turin-based winemaker Alessandro Martini entered into a partnership with the Commendator Luigi Rossi, putting a different kind of cocktail, of his own invention, on the market: a Moscato di Canelli in which they had soaked melissa, sandalwood, cinnamon, artemisia, violet, china, thistle, rose and oregano. The Martini White, which was sweet, quickly won over female drinkers. To appeal to male palates, Martini and Rossi replaced the Moscato with very dry wines, thus creating the Martini Dry.

Not to be outdone, in 1862, Gaspare Campari, the owner of a popular cafe in the Galleria Vittorio Emanuele in Milan, launched a new aperitif and – to distinguish it from the vermouth – called it by another name of Germanic origin: Bitter.

Among these drinks it is also important to mention other popular drinks, such as pastis and French Picon, greek ouzo and arak from the Eastern Mediterranean.

During the twentieth century, the taste of the aperitif has evolved, becoming more refined and sophisticated, with the gradual emergence of a sort of drinking fashion scene, with trends coming and going. In the mid-'80s, for example, we drank cocktails like Long Island Ice Tea, Whisky on the Rocks, Campari and White, and the Bloody Mary, now the most widely consumed are the Negroni, Americano, Pirlo, Spritz, Campari and cocktails from Central and South America, like the Daiquiri and Margarita, the Vodka Martini and long cocktails made with fruit juices. All of these have helped us enjoy our dinners (and maybe a few "happy hours").

AMERICANO

INGREDIENTS

CAMPARI
RED VERMOUTH

SODA WATER
OR SPARKLING WATER

ORIGINS AND ODDITIES

Legend has it that this drink was created in Italy during the fascist regime in the 1930s, the intent of this drink was to distribute and promote a cocktail made solely from Italian products (Martini was from Turin and Campari was produced in Milan). Legend has it that the name of this cocktail was chosen to honor the achievements of the boxer Primo Carnera, who in 1933, became world heavyweight champion by winning a bout at Madison Square Garden in New York.

PREPARATION

Measure 30 ml (2 tbsp) of Campari in a graduated cylinder and pour in a low tumbler filled with ice. Repeat the process with 30 ml (2 tbsp) of red vermouth. Fill almost to the brim with soda water or sparkling water. Gently stir everything with a long-handled spoon and serve, garnished with 1/2 a slice of orange and lemon peel.

SUGGESTED USE

Excellent as an aperitif.

 Beef Tartare

MEDIUM

ingredients for 4 people
time: 45 minutes

1.1 lbs (17.6 oz) fillet of beef
1 shallot
juice of 1 lemon
2 tbsp Worcestershire sauce
2 tbsp extra virgin olive oil
salt and pepper
parsley
4 chopped capers
mustard
4 egg yolks

With a sharp knife, cut the fillet into very thin strips. Then cut the strips into even smaller pieces. Put the meat in a glass bowl. Finely chop the parsley, shallots and capers. Combine with the meat and add a bit of mustard, extra virgin olive oil, lemon juice, salt, pepper and Worcester sauce. Mix all the ingredients with your bare hands so that they are evenly distributed. Divide the mixture into 4 large spherical meatballs. Place them directly on appetizer plates, and with the help of a small bowl, create a cavity in the tartare, so you can lay a whole raw egg yolk in the center. Serve immediately.

APEROL BIT ORANGE

INGREDIENTS

APEROL

CAMPARI

ORANGE JUICE

MANDARINETTO ISOLABELLA

ORIGINS AND ODDITIES

This tasty aperitif was presented for the first time in 2006 at the "Bar Festival" competition held in Milan.

PREPARATION

Measure 40 ml (2 3/4 tbsp) of Aperol in a graduated cylinder and pour in a shaker. Repeat with 80 ml (1/3 cup) of orange juice, 10 ml (2 tsp) of Campari and 30 ml (2 tbsp) of Mandarinetto Isolabella. Shake vigorously for a few seconds, then pour everything into a tall tumbler filled with ice. To serve, garnish with 1/2 an orange slice, 1/2 a slice of grapefruit, 1/2 a slice of lime and 2 long straws.

SUGGESTED USE

An excellent aperitif, it can be enjoyed at all hours of the day.

Caesar Salad

EASY

ingredients for 4 people
time: 30 minutes

4 slices bread
1 clove garlic
1 egg
4 chicken breasts
1 head of escarole
vinegar
juice of 1 lemon
salt and pepper
olive oil
Worcestershire sauce

Cut the slices of bread into cubes and toast them in a pan with 1 tbsp of extra virgin olive oil and 1 peeled and crushed clove of garlic. Salt and pepper the chicken breasts and put them on the grill. Wash and dry the salad, slicing them roughly. In a bowl, prepare the sauce for the Caesar Salad, combining 1 tbsp of Worcestershire sauce, 1 egg, 2 tbsp of extra virgin olive oil, the juice of 1 lemon and a few drops of vinegar. Mix the ingredients well with a small whisk, until you get a smooth sauce. In a dish, arrange a generous bed of lightly salted escarole and serve with a drizzle of extra virgin olive oil. Lay the chicken, cut into fairly thick slices, on top and finish with a layer of croutons. Serve at room temperature, accompanied by the sauce.

APEROL CRODO

INGREDIENTS

APEROL

PEACH VODKA

CAMPARI

CRODINO

ORIGINS AND ODDITIES

This drink was first presented in Rimini in 2005 at an international bartending competition organized by the Italian magazine *Bargiornale*, whose theme was the preparation of unpublished aperitif cocktails.

PREPARATION

Measure 30 ml (2 tbsp) of Aperol in a graduated cylinder and pour into a shaker. Repeat with 20 ml (4 tsp) of peach vodka and 10 ml (2 tsp) of Campari. Stir gently for a few seconds and pour into a tall tumbler full of ice. Mix lightly and serve, garnished with 1/2 a slice of orange, 3 cubes of lime, 2 cherries and 2 straws long.

SUGGESTED USE

Excellent as an aperitif, it can be enjoyed at all hours of the day.

 Quiche Lorraine

MEDIUM

ingredients for 6/8 people
time: 1 hour and 15 minutes

0.83 lbs (13.4 oz) shortcrust pastry
0.39 lbs (6.35 oz) diced pork guanciale (lard from the pig's cheek) or pancetta (pork underbelly)
1 1/4 cup cooking cream
0.33 lbs (5.3 oz) grated gruyère cheese
salt and pepper
nutmeg
4 egg yolks
chopped parsley

Flour the work surface and rolling pin and roll out the dough. Line a round baking tin. Curl the edges and prick the bottom with a fork. Fill the pan with beans and bake for 15 minutes at 400°F (200°C). Remove from the oven and replace the beans with the grated cheese. Blanch the guanciale in water for 10 minutes and drain, placing it in order, after the Gruyère. Beat the eggs in a bowl and add salt, pepper and a good sprinkling of nutmeg. Add the cream and mix everything vigorously, until you have a smooth cream. Pour into a baking pan to completely cover the cheese and guanciale. Bake again at 356°F (180°C) for about 25 minutes, before the surface of the Quiche Lorraine becomes solid and golden. Remove from the oven and let cool for 10 minutes. Serve, garnished with chopped parsley.

BEETHOVEN

INGREDIENTS

PUREE OF BERRIES
BRUT SPARKLING WINE OR CHAMPAGNE

ORIGINS AND ODDITIES

This drink was successfully presented in Rimini
in 2005 at an international bartending competition
organized by the Italian magazine *Bargiornale*: the
theme was the conception of innovative aperitifs.

PREPARATION

Measure 30 ml (2 tbsp) of berry puree in a graduated
cylinder and pour into a pre-chilled cup in the freezer.
Fill almost to the brim with fresh sparkling wine or
champagne. Stir gently with a long-handled spoon
and serve.

SUGGESTED USE

An excellent aperitif that can be enjoyed at all hours
of the day.

Red Currant Prawns and Saffron   EASY

ingredients for 4 people
time: 45 minutes

0.35 lbs (5.6 oz) prawns
flour
1 sachet saffron
salt and pepper
brandy
6 tbsp cream
1 clove garlic
chopped parsley
1 basket fresh red currants
extra virgin olive oil
mashed potatoes

Shell the prawns, leaving only the tail and head and removing the black
thread that runs along the back. Add salt and flour them lightly. In a
large saucepan, heat 2 tbsp of extra virgin olive oil and fry the finely
chopped garlic. Add the prawns and cook on high heat for 5 minutes.
Soak with brandy and let it flame. When the flame has diminished, lower
the heat and add the cream and saffron (previously dissolved in a cup
of water). Complete the cooking of the prawns, sprinkling with pepper
and chopped parsley. Put a good portion of soft mashed potatoes in
the center of 4 plates. Place the prawns on top, covering everything
with saffron sauce. Serve, garnished with a handful of fresh currants.

BELLINI

INGREDIENTS

PEACH PUREE
BRUT SPARKLING WINE OR CHAMPAGNE

ORIGINS AND ODDITIES

This famous cocktail was created in 1948 by a
bartender at Harry's Bar in Venice. The occasion was
an exhibition of paintings of Giambellino (real name:
Giovanni Bellini).

PREPARATION

Measure 30 ml (2 tbsp) of the peach puree in a
graduated cylinder and pour into a cup pre-chilled in
the freezer. Fill almost to the brim with fresh
or sparkling brut champagne. Stir gently with
a long-handled spoon and serve.

SUGGESTED USE

An aperitif par excellence.

 Delicious Zucchini Flowers   EASY

ingredients for 4 people
time: 30 minutes

16 zucchini flowers
0.22 lbs (3.5 oz) cooked ham
1 egg
milk
0.13 lbs (2.1 oz) smoked scamorza
cheese
flour
breadcrumbs
sunflower seed oil
salt and pepper

Carefully clean the zucchini flowers, removing the stamen. Fill with
small pieces of ham and a few cubes of smoked scamorza. Prepare
3 bowls. In the first, beat the egg, adding a dash of milk. In the second, sift the flour and pour the breadcrumbs in the third. Working in order, dip the flowers in the flour, the egg and finally the
breadcrumbs. Fry everything in plenty of boiling sunflower seed oil,
stirring gently from time to time. Lay the flowers on two sheets of
absorbent paper and serve with salt and pepper to taste.

GARIBALDI

INGREDIENTS

CAMPARI
ORANGE JUICE (PREFERABLY RED)

ORIGINS AND ODDITIES

Created in the 1960s, it is also called "Orange Campari" by the group that seems to love it most: Germans. Its name in Italy, however, is inspired by the famous head scarf worn by Giuseppe Garibaldi.

PREPARATION

Measure 70 ml (4 tbsp + 2 tsp) of Campari in a graduated cylinder and pour into a tall tumbler filled with ice. Repeat with 90 ml (6 tbsp) of orange juice. Stir for a few seconds with a long-handled spoon and serve, garnished with 1 orange slice and 2 long straws.

SUGGESTED USE

Excellent as an aperitif, it can be enjoyed at all hours of the day.

Artichoke Hearts Risotto

EASY

ingredients for 4 people
time: 1 hour

scant 2 cups carnaroli rice
4 artichokes
4 tbsp extra virgin olive oil
4 1/4 cups boiling broth
2 finely chopped shallots
fresh marjoram
1 glass white wine
salt and pepper
grated Parmigiano Reggiano cheese
2 knobs butter
chopped parsley

Clean the artichokes, removing the top and tough outer leaves. Divide in half and remove the fuzz inside. Slice the artichoke hearts and soak them in water made slightly acidic with lemon juice. Heat the oil in a saucepan and let the chopped shallots cook on low heat. When the shallot has become transparent, add the drained artichokes and a few leaves of marjoram. Season with salt and pepper, and cook, stirring continuously. Add the rice, letting it toast for a couple of minutes. Add the wine and let it evaporate, then add hot broth. Stir constantly and continue to add broth every time the last ladleful has been absorbed. After about 20 minutes, remove the risotto from the heat and stir in the butter and grated Parmigiano Reggiano before serving. Garnish with chopped parsley.

GAS-BAG

INGREDIENTS

DRY VODKA
STRAWBERRY PUREE

CAMPARI
BRUT SPARKLING WINE

ORIGINS AND ODDITIES

This drink was the winner of the city of Bergamo's
(Italy) Cocktail Competition in 1993.

PREPARATION

Measure 20 ml (4 tsp) of vodka in a graduated
cylinder and pour in a shaker. Repeat with 30 ml
(2 tbsp) of strawberry puree and 10 ml (2 tsp) of
Campari. Add a few ice cubes and shake vigorously
for a few seconds, then pour it into a pre-chilled
cup. Fill almost to the brim with brut sparkling wine
fresh. Stir gently with a long-handled spoon and serve.

SUGGESTED USE

An excellent aperitif, it can be enjoyed at all hours of
the day.

 Tuna Pepper Baskets   EASY

ingredients for 4 people
time: 1 hour and 15 minutes

0.66 lbs (10.5 oz, about 2 small or
about 1 1/2 medium) boiled potatoes
4 peppers
4 anchovy fillets
chopped parsley
chives
0.44 lbs (7 oz) tuna in brine
breadcrumbs
salt and pepper
extra virgin olive oil
8 black olives
1 egg

Pit the olives, and coarsely chop and mince the chives. Chop the
anchovies and mix the tuna in a mixer. Peel the potatoes. Reduce
them to a puree and place them in a large bowl. Combine the egg,
tuna, parsley, chives, black olives, anchovies and 2 tbsp breadcrumbs.
Season with salt and pepper, mixing all the ingredients vigorously until you have a smooth, creamy filling. Wash the peppers and remove
the top of each. Remove the seeds and fill to the brim with the tuna
filling, closing them with their tops. Put the pepper baskets in a baking dish greased with extra virgin olive oil and bake at 356°F (180°C)
for 40 minutes. Serve piping hot.

ITALIAN BITTER

INGREDIENTS

APEROL

CAMPARI

PEACH VODKA

SANBITTÈR

ORIGINS AND ODDITIES

This drink was also presented for the first time in Rimini in 2005 at the international bartending competition whose theme was the conception of innovative aperitif cocktails.

PREPARATION

Measure 30 ml (2 tbsp) of Aperol in a graduated cylinder and pour into a shaker. Repeat with 20 ml (4 tsp) of vodka and 10 ml (2 tsp) of Campari. Stir for a few seconds and pour into a tall tumbler filled with ice, then fill almost to the brim with Sanbittèr. Stir gently with long-handled spoon and serve, garnished with 1/2 a slice of orange, 2 cherries and 2 long straws.

SUGGESTED USE

Excellent as an aperitif.

Clam Stew   EASY

ingredients for 4 people
time: 2 hour and 30 minutes

2.2 lbs (35.2 oz) clams
0.44 lbs (7 oz) natural bean sprouts
extra virgin olive oil
salt and pepper
garlic
white wine
chopped parsley
2 tomatoes (not too ripe)
8 roasted croutons

Soak clams for 2 hours in boiling salted water, so that most of the sand is eliminated. Filter 2 tbsp water and set aside. Rinse clams thoroughly under running water, then place them in a large pot with 1 tbsp of extra virgin olive oil. Cook over medium heat until all the valves are open. Finely chop 2 cloves of garlic and fry in a saucepan with 4 tbsp of extra virgin olive oil. Combine the clams and cook on high heat for 3 minutes. Drench with 1 glass white wine and cook for other 3 minutes, letting everything thicken with some ladlefuls of filtered water. Just before serving, add the bean sprouts (drained earlier), a generous sprinkling of chopped parsley and tomatoes (previously washed and cut into cubes). Give a final mix at high heat and serve in 4 terracotta bowls, accompanied with croutons (previously roasted in the oven) and a clove of raw garlic.

LORY

INGREDIENTS

APEROL

CAMPARI

PEACH VODKA

ORANGE BITTER

ORIGINS AND ODDITIES

This lively cocktail was presented by barman
Gianfranco Di Niso in 2005 in Bordeaux, at an
international competition between 80 bartenders
from around the world. It finished among the top
ranking.

PREPARATION

Measure 50 ml (3 1/3 tbsp) of Aperol in a graduated
cylinder and pour into a shaker. Repeat with 30 ml
(2 tbsp) of peach vodka and 10 ml (2 tsp) of Campari.
Shake vigorously for a few seconds and pour into
a tall tumbler filled with ice. Mix delicately and serve,
garnished with 1 orange slice, 1 slice of grapefruit,
2 cherries and 2 long straws.

SUGGESTED USE

Perfect as an aperitif.

 Deviled Mussels   EASY

ingredients for 4 people
time: 45 minutes

2.2 lbs (35.2 oz) fresh mussels
8 slices bread
0.66 lbs (10.5 oz) tomato sauce
2 big tomatoes
chopped parsley
paprika powder
3 cloves of garlic
oregano
salt and pepper
extra virgin olive oil
white wine

Wash the mussels under running water, carefully scraping the shell of
all impurities. Open the mussels by cooking them in a high sided pot
with 2 peeled and crushed cloves of garlic, a handful of parsley and 1
tbsp extra virgin olive oil. When the mussels begin to open, sprinkle
with 1/2 glass of wine. Once opened, allow to cool, filtering the cooking liquid and carefully removing the empty shells. In a large pot sauté
1 finely chopped clove of garlic along with 2 tbsp of extra virgin olive
oil. Add the tomato sauce and cook for 5 minutes. Add the mussels
and the sauce and cook for another 3 minutes. Just before serving,
sprinkle with plenty of paprika and oregano to taste. Give a final stir
and serve in an elegant bowl, accompanied with slices of toast.

KIR ROYAL

INGREDIENTS

CREAM OF CASSIS
CHAMPAGNE OR SPARKLING BRUT (CLASSIC METHOD)

ORIGINS AND ODDITIES

An evolution from the classic Kir, it was created in Paris in the Belle Époque, when champagne replaced the still white wine.

PREPARATION

Measure 20 ml (4 tsp) of cream of cassis in a graduated cylinder and pour into a cup (pre-chilled in the freezer). Fill almost to the brim with champagne or sparkling brut. Stir gently with a long-handled spoon and serve.

SUGGESTED USE

An elegant aperitif that can be served throughout the day.

Black Truffle Sirloin   EASY

ingredients for 4 people
time: 2 hour and 30 minutes

4 beef fillets
flour
2 tbsp extra virgin olive oil
juice of 1 lemon
1 small black truffle
grated Parmigiano Reggiano cheese
salt and pepper
green beans sautéed in butter

Flour the fillets and lay them gently in a pan with the lemon juice, extra virgin olive oil, salt and pepper. Let it all marinate for 90 minutes. Heat the grill and cook the meat 5 minutes per side. Halfway through cooking, add salt and pepper and lay a slice of truffle on each fillet. Sprinkle with grated Parmigiano Reggiano and continue cooking for 3 minutes. Serve, accompanied with a side of green beans sautéed in butter.

MICHELLE FOREVER

INGREDIENTS

APEROL

CAMPARI

WHITE VERMOUTH

ORANGE JUICE

ORIGINS AND ODDITIES

A particularly summery drink presented for the first time in 2005 at the "Bar Festival" competition held in Milan.

PREPARATION

Measure 30 ml (2 tbsp) of Aperol in a graduated cylinder and pour 3 in a shaker. Repeat with 30 ml (2 tbsp) of white vermouth, 10 ml (2 tsp) of Campari and 90 ml (6 tbsp) of orange juice. Shake vigorously for a few seconds and pour into a tall tumbler filled with ice. To serve, garnish with 1/2 an orange slice, 1/2 a slice of lemon, 2 cherries and 2 long straws.

SUGGESTED USE

An excellent aperitif, it can be enjoyed at all hours of the day.

Octopus and Spinach

EASY

ingredients for 4 people
time: 2 hours + cooling time
(30 minutes)

1.3 lbs (20.8 oz) octopus
0.33 lbs (5.3 oz, about 4 medium stalks) celery
2 boiled potatoes
1.1 lbs (17.6 oz) boiled and squeeze dried spinach
1 big carrot
1 onion
cloves
chives
extra virgin olive oil
salt and pepper

Clean the octopus and cook in salted water for about 50 minutes, adding the onion with cloves and carrots cut into large pieces. Clean the celery and cut into very thin slices. Let the octopus cool in its broth and drain, then cut it into 1 cm thick slices. Pour into a bowl and add the potatoes (previously cut into cubes) and chopped spinach. Stir and sprinkle with 2 tbsp of extra virgin olive oil, salt, pepper and chopped chives. Give a final mix and let stand in refrigerator for 30 minutes. Serve, garnished with the sliced celery.

MIMOSA

INGREDIENTS

ORANGE JUICE
SPARKLING WINE OR CHAMPAGNE BRUT

ORIGINS AND ODDITIES

Created in London in 1921, this drink was conceived by the imagination of Mr. Harry, the bartender at Buck's Club, one of the most important establishments at the time in the English capital. The original name of this cocktail was Buck's Fizz.

PREPARATION

Measure 30 ml (2 tbsp) of orange juice in a graduated cylinder and pour into a pre-chilled cup in the freezer. Fill almost to the brim with fresh sparkling wine or champagne. Stir gently with a long-handled spoon and serve.

SUGGESTED USE

An excellent aperitif that can be enjoyed at all hours of the day.

Sashimi

MEDIUM

ingredients for 4 people
time: 45 minutes

0.26 lbs (4.2 oz) fresh tuna steak
0.17 lbs (2.8 oz) fresh salmon fillet
0.13 lbs (2.1 oz) fresh squid
0.13 lbs (2.1 oz) fresh turbot fillet
horseradish
2 radishes
2 carrots
soy sauce
lime

Cut the tuna vertically into 5 mm thick slices. Repeat with the salmon fillet. Cut the tuna into 1 cm wide slices and then cut them down into small cubes. Slice the squid into 3 mm thick sticks. Thinly cut the fillet of turbot crosswise. Peel the radish and cut into thin matchsticks. On a large cutting board, lay out the fish fillets and horseradish in a decorative fashion, garnished with slices of lime, radishes and carrots and accompanied with the soy sauce.

NEGRONI SBAGLIATO

INGREDIENTS

CAMPARI
RED VERMOUTH
SPARKLING BRUT WINE

ORIGINS AND ODDITIES

The origins of this famous drink are quite unique, as they stem from a bartender's mistake at the Bar Basso in Milan in the 1960s. Trying to make a Negroni, he accidentally substituted the classic gin with sparkling wine. This "Negroni sbagliato" ("wrong Negroni") was so well-liked it quickly spread around the world.

PREPARATION

Measure in a graduated cylinder and pour 30 ml (2 tbsp) of Campari in a low tumbler filled with ice and repeat the process with 30 ml (2 tbsp) of red vermouth. Extend almost to the brim with fresh sparkling brut and stir gently with a spoon around in a long handle. To serve, garnish with 1 orange slice.

SUGGESTED USE

An aperitif par excellence.

Grandma Nina's Casonsei

MEDIUM

ingredients for 4 people
time: 3 hours

3 1/5 cups white flour
1/3 cup durum wheat semolina flour
5 eggs
about 1 cup breadcrumbs
0.44 lbs (7 oz) minced beef
1 cup (16 tbsp) grated Parmigiano Reggiano cheese
beef broth
salt and pepper – nutmeg
4 amaretti biscuit
chopped parsley – sage
0.33 lbs (5.3 oz) thick pancetta or bacon slices
butter

Arrange the sifted white flour like a fountain and place the bran at the center with a pinch of salt, a dash of water and 3 eggs. Mix everything with your hands until the dough is smooth and homogeneous. Form a ball and let it rest in the refrigerator for 1 hour, covered with a damp cloth. Saute the meat for a few minutes in a pan with a knob of butter. Pour into a large bowl. Add 2 eggs, breadcrumbs, Parmigiano Reggiano, salt, pepper, grated nutmeg, and ground amaretti, then add chopped parsley to taste. Work all the ingredients until you have a smooth, homogeneous filling. Season with 1 tbsp of warm broth and give a final mix. Flour the work surface and rolling pin, then roll out the dough into a thickness of about 0.5 mm. With a glass, cut the disks to a diameter of about 7 cm. Distribute a knob of the filling in the center and brush the edges with water. Close to form half moons ravioli and gently press the center. Cook in salted water. Meanwhile, heat up 4 knobs of butter in a pan: when it is dark and frothy, fry pancetta (or bacon) cut into strips. Add a few sage leaves and cook over high heat for 1 minute. Drain the ravioli and pour into a baking dish, topped with butter and hot bacon. Sprinkle with Parmigiano Reggiano.

NEW LULÙ

INGREDIENTS

APEROL	PEACH VODKA
CAMPARI	ORANGE JUICE

ORIGINS AND ODDITIES

This drink was first presented in Bordeaux in 2005 at an international competition among 80 bartenders from around the world. It finished among the top.

PREPARATION

Measure 40 ml (2 3/4 tbsp) of Aperol in a graduated cylinder and pour in a shaker. Repeat with 20 ml (4 tsp) of vodka 10 ml (2 tsp) of Campari and 90 ml (6 tbsp) of orange juice. Shake vigorously for a few seconds and pour into a tall tumbler filled with ice. Serve, garnished with 1/2 a slice of orange, 2 cherries and 2 long straws.

SUGGESTED USE

Excellent as an aperitif, it can be enjoyed at all hours of the day.

Mug of Chicken Salad

EASY

ingredients for 4 people
time: 1 hour + cooling time
(1 hour)

4 chicken breasts
4/5 cup mayonnaise
0.33 lbs (5.3 oz) celeriac
to the natural
8 lettuce leaves
salt and pepper
extra virgin olive oil
lemon juice
1 big potato
chopped parsley

Wash and dry the lettuce, thinly slice and drain the celeriac. Salt and pepper the chicken, then roast the breasts on the grill. Let cool and cut into strips. Lay the chicken in a bowl and add the celery and mayonnaise, mixing everything gently. Season with 1 tsp of extra virgin olive oil, a few drops of lemon juice, and salt and pepper to taste. Give a final mix and let stand for 1 hour in the refrigerator. Put a bed of lettuce at the bottom of 4 transparent mugs, then fill almost to the brim with the cold chicken salad. Garnish with potato cubes, previously boiled in salted water, drained and cooled.

PUCCINI

INGREDIENTS

TANGERINE JUICE
SPARKLING WINE OR CHAMPAGNE BRUT

ORIGINS AND ODDITIES

According to legend, this cocktail was created in
1948 by Renato Hausmann, a bartender at the Hotel
Posta in Cortina d'Ampezzo, Italy. One evening three
ladies sitting at the bar asked what the name was
of the delicious drink they were drinking. "Puccini,"
Hausmann said, as the composer's work was just
then being transmitted on the radio.

PREPARATION

Measure 30 ml (2 tbsp) of tangerine juice in a
graduated cylinder and pour into a cup (pre-chilled
in the freezer). Fill almost to the brim with fresh
sparkling brut or champagne. Stir gently with
a long-handled spoon and serve.

SUGGESTED USE

An elegant aperitif that can be served throughout
the day.

 Light Vitello Tonnato   EASY

ingredients for 4 people
time: 4 hours

2.2 lbs (35.2 oz) eye round
(or round steak)
1 onion
1 stalk of celery
1 carrot
parsley and bay leaves
cloves
0.33 lbs (5.3 oz) tuna in oil
2 anchovies
salted capers
juice of 1 lemon
salt and pepper – extra virgin olive oil
3/4 cup + 1 tbsp low-fat yogurt

Put the meat in a saucepan and cover with water. Add the carrot, celery
and chopped onion. Add cloves, bay leaves, salt and pepper. Place the
beef on the stove and cook over medium heat for about 90 minutes.
When the meat is cooked, remove it from the stove and allow to cool
in its broth. Prepare the light tuna sauce, whisking tuna with yogurt,
anchovies, capers, salt, pepper and the juice of 1 lemon. Drain the meat
and cut into thin slices (preferably with a slicer). Arrange the slices on the
plate and cover them with plenty of sauce. Let stand in refrigerator for at
least 1 hour and serve, garnished with slices of lemon, some capers and
a sprinkling of whole parsley.

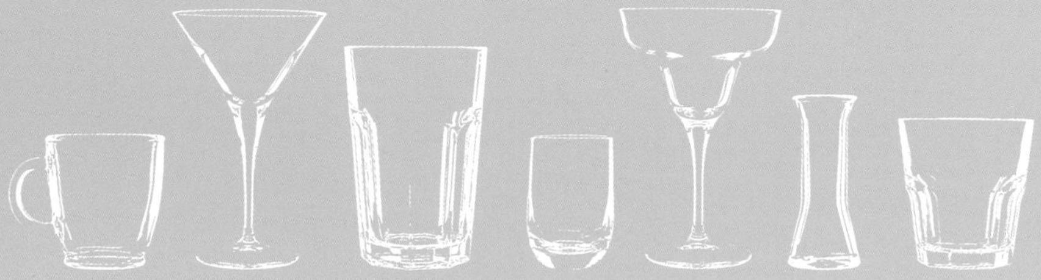

ALPHABETICAL INDEX – COCKTAILS

ALPHABETICAL INDEX – FOOD

NOTE

To my wife Barbara.
Your immense love, tenderness and patience light up my days.

Gianfranco Di Niso

AUTHORS

GIANFRANCO DI NISO, a professional bartender and winner of national and international competitions, is a lecturer at various training courses for bartenders. Since 1986, he has worked at several establishments in Bergamo and the surrounding areas.

DAVIDE MANZONI is a graduate from the Institute of Tourism and Hospitality in San Pellegrino Terme (BG). He also holds a degree in Cinema from the Catholic University of Brescia. Manzoni alternates a passion for cooking with one for film and writing.

FABIO PETRONI was born in Corinaldo (AN) in 1964. He currently lives and works in Milan. After studying photography, he has collaborated with the most talented professionals in the industry. His line of work led him to specialize in portraits and still life, areas in which he has shown an intuitive and rigorous style. Over the years he has portrayed prominent figures of culture, medicine and the Italian economical and political world. Working with major advertising agencies, he has participated in numerous campaigns for prestigious companies known worldwide.

ACKNOWLEDGEMENT

Gianfranco Di Niso and Davide Manzoni wish to thank:

White Star Publishers, Valeria Manferto de Fabianis and Laura Accomazzo for having believed in their project.

Gabriel Aresi and Rossana Cortinovis of 30 & Lode Cafè in Bergamo for their trust and willingness to help; *L'Eco di Bergamo*, *Il Giornale di Bergamo*, *Affari di gola*, *Lombardia a tavola* and *Bargiornale* for their collaboration.

Demis Vescovi, a graduate of viticulture and enology at the University of Milan, for participating in the project and all the people who have contributed to this volume.

Gianfranco Di Niso would also like to thank: ASCOM and Planet One for giving him inspiration; Luca Castelletti, AIS National Councillor, and Nives Cesari, Regional Vice President of AIS, for the enlightening lessons that guided his writing. Ezio Falconi, a bartending professor and author of numerous books on cocktails. He is a model of professionalism, who permitted the representation of some of his creations. A heartfelt thanks to Pierluigi Cucchi, bartender, ASCOM teacher and member of the National Council FIPE, and to R.O.S. hotel suppliers and Segafredo.

A final thank you to all the bartenders, baristas, students and employers who have worked with him, giving him inspiration and knowledge.

Gianfranco Di Niso and David Manzoni apologize in advance for the possible (and inevitable) presence of inaccuracies in this collection. These are related to the ongoing evolution of the sector around the world. If you use material from this volume, the authors kindly ask to be cited as sources.

The publisher would like to thank **ALESSI** for providing images of cocktail equipment published on pages 12-13. Alessi, an Italian company founded in 1921, designs and manufactures home accessories known worldwide for their quality design, creativity, and functionality, the result of a collaborative process with leading international designers. **www.alessi.it**

WHITE STAR PUBLISHERS

WS White Star Publishers® is a registered trademark
property of De Agostini Libri S.p.A.

© 2012, 2014 De Agostini Libri S.p.A.
Via G. da Verrazano, 15
28100 Novara, Italy
www.whitestar.it - www.deagostini.it

Revised edition

Translation: Salvatore Ciolfi
Editing and Layout: www.bookgenie.in

ISBN 978-88-544-0810-4
1 2 3 4 5 6   18 17 16 15 14

Printed in China